DONALD B. MILLER

Personal Vitality

▲▼ **ADDISON-WESLEY PUBLISHING COMPANY**
Reading, Massachusetts • Menlo Park, California
London • Amsterdam • Don Mills, Ontario • Sydney

The quote on page 90 was reprinted by permission of *Psychology Today* magazine. Copyright © 1974 Ziff-Davis Publishing Company.

ISBN 0-201-04739-X
BCDEFGHIJ-MA-7987

To: Avis, my mother;
Alice, my wife;
and Chris and James, our sons

Preface

Introduction

This book is about human resources. It is about changes in goals, about managing careers, about work. Most of all it is about personal vitality, about what George Bernard Shaw called the "life force."

Vitality is the opposite of dying on the vine. It is growing physically, mentally, psychologically, spiritually. It is the ability to adapt to new conditions, new information, new outlooks. It is growth in awareness, understanding, forgiveness. It is the transcendent, evident quality of an alive and growing organism. The thesis of the book is that personal vitality is an integrating life purpose, an emerging work ethic, a viable personal, managerial, and governmental strategy for survival, improved meaningfulness, and quality of life.*

We are living in exciting times of rapid change. Change puts a high priority on continued learning, adaptation, and growth for each of us if we are to gain satisfactions from using our capabilities and contribute to improved life quality. Adult change is part of life management. Adult change includes shifts of values both in response to our inner needs and in response to the world around us. Adult change may mean change in life-style, change in career or job, change in the purpose and central theme. Change is necessary for enhancement and extension of personal vitality, and so this book is about managing change.

Both as individuals and as a nation we are becoming increasingly aware of the price we must pay for quality in our lives. Much of our progress has been accomplished without assessing possible

---

*   For a definition and discussion of vitality see Chapter 1.

costs in the loss of quality. Now we are stepping up to tough decisions about air and water quality, about living conditions, about the
balance between individual rights and the necessity for government. In a way this book is about "human ecology" ways of
assessing the price we are paying to live our lives as we are living
them. It is about making improved choices and thus emphasizes
another aspect of quality. This quality should be an output from all
our activities, our work, our families, our special interests, and even
our private or unshared time. This quality is directly related to
human development.

Human development takes place in several areas. It takes
place in the context of the community. Here we learn what it means
to be a citizen, to gain from our membership and to contribute to
the whole. It takes place in a private or individual sense. It is here
we learn of our strengths and weaknesses, how to grow our skills
and knowledge, and gain a sense of who we are and what we are
worth. It takes place in the context of the organization of which we
are part. In our work or employment, for example, we learn the
rules of the game, the values and goals of the organization, and
what is success in that special world. Human development also
takes place in the context of the group. It is here we learn the meaning of team, of loyalty, of support, and of the fact that a group in
synchronism is more than the sum of its parts. This book is about
human development and is designed to provide the reader with
ways to improve personal growth and development.

My awareness of these issues facing adults and my sense of
need for this book comes from several sources. First, it comes from
my own life. I have learned that a life strategy is essential and that
the pursuit of vitality should be part of it. Second, it comes from my
experiences in trying to help organizations build environments
which capture the interest and commitment of their members and
contribute positively to the growth and development of their members. Third, it comes from my attempts to counsel and help others
improve their lives, make tough value choices, decide what to study
and how to enrich their careers and their work experiences. Fourth,
it comes from my experiences as a manager where I have discovered the need to try to match individual needs and capabilities with
organizational needs and capabilities. I've seen the improvement in
productivity for the company and satisfaction for the individual
when there is a good match. And lastly, it comes from my experi-

ence in design of continuing education and in teaching about the issues in this book in an industrial and work environment. These teaching experiences have both shaped the content and convinced me of the desire people have for the suggestions and ideas expressed here.

Acknowledgments

Certainly many of the thoughts expressed in this book have grown in the positive work environment of IBM. I owe much to my experience at IBM for it has shown me the value of respect for the individual in the organization and high humanistic goals. The views expressed are my own, however, and should in no way be construed as representing IBM policy or position. I take full responsibility for the book as a personal statement. The statements and thoughts—both good and bad—are my statements. If there are flaws in the logic, errors of commission or omission, they are my errors.

I'm deeply indebted to many who have shared research, experimentation, dreams, and thoughts with me. Some have done this through their writings or speeches and some have exchanged ideas with me face to face. The list is long, but a few include James Kip Finch, my boss at Columbia and former Dean of Engineering; H. Tyler Marcy, Assistant Secretary of the Navy for Research, who taught me many things as my manager at IBM; Albert B. Cherns, a leading British social scientist, friend and searcher for improved quality of work life; Alan Watts, philosopher; Carl Rogers, psychologist; Arthur G. Anderson, one of my IBM managers, executive and philosopher; Lou Mischkind, IBM San Jose psychologist and coworker; W.A. Goddard, IBM engineer, friend and coworker; Jack Downing, M.D., friend and searcher; Sidney M. Jourard, psychologist; Richard W. Schmelzer, retired, formerly of Rensselaer Polytechnic Institute, teacher and writer; and Peter Drucker, management author.

Several people have read the manuscript and made detailed comments and suggestions. They are William A. Weimer of IBM, Albert B. Cherns, and Richard Schmelzer. Lou Mischkind and Bill Goddard, both of IBM, have read and commented on parts. For their time, interest, and helpful suggestions I'm deeply grateful.

Special thanks go to my wife, Alice, whose love and skills as a wife, critic, editor, and typist have made this book possible. In addition, my secretary, June Fujii, my former secretary, Madeline Pinsent, and the IBM administrative center have all assisted with typing of early drafts and a few of the final chapters. I'm indebted to each of them for their assistance.

Saratoga, California   D.B.M.
January 1977

Contents

Introduction

Vitality and work

Why should I write and why should you read a book on personal vitality? Because the priority for maintaining and enhancing vitality has skyrocketed. Vitality has become critical to both personal and organizational survival. At the same time, however, enhancement of human effectiveness, growth, and a sense of accomplishment, all part of vitality, are becoming more difficult for the individual and the organization. We are caught in a convergence of changes in values, which intensifies our concerns about the purposes and nature of life. A central life purpose is necessary for vitality. A central purpose is necessary for extending and enhancing life. Yet we are at odds with our purposes.

One of these changes in values has to do with work. Alienation from work has become pervasive: the daily news refers to this attitude as the "blue collar blues," caused, in part, by jobs which require individuals to act like machines. Many feel there is a broad general decline in positive attitudes about work. Headlines feature executive dropouts. People are returning to craft activities in which they experience a sense of accomplishment and satisfaction they have lost or are denied in the tasks of the business world. Unions have begun to raise questions about work content and nonfinancial satisfactions as major elements in future planning. Leading business organizations like Mead Paper, General Foods, and Volvo are experimenting with major changes in the nature of work as a way of regaining individual commitment and improving the psychological income from work. It is *absolutely necessary* for each individual and each organization to reestablish a *sense* of purpose and meaningfulness for life as well as to create new ways to learn and grow. Good work can provide such a purpose.

The impact of changes in cultural values about work is becoming evident in many groups. It first appeared with the phenomenon of "dropouts" in the younger generation. Next there was a significant shift away from career-related studies in the universities. Students failing to see the connection between study and life began turning away from preparation for work. Why indeed should they study engineering and business when the probability of obtaining a job using their training had dropped significantly?*

More recently this trend away from a study/work relationship has been heightened by the economic crunch which made it tough just to find a job. This leads to a lack of fulfillment for the new seriousness expressed on campus. Recent graduates are increasingly demanding that their work be meaningful and fulfilling. This will heighten their problems in relating to work as they fail to find realization of their expectations for utilization of their educational preparation. They are demanding their work have social purpose and provide for their personal growth. This establishes their need for the insights and understandings expressed in this book. Expectations about satisfaction from work grow as our educational level grows. But economic pressure for a job, any job, forces us down the Maslow need hierarchy toward survival need.

Not only is there a shortage of jobs and careers for people trained to be "knowledge workers," but there is concern as well about utilization of those knowledge workers who do have jobs. In the highly developed nations there are questions about the proper utilization of highly talented people. Underutilization means lost vitality and lost potential for growth and development of individuals and the country. With the great increase in the numbers of university graduates there is a real shortage of opportunities for them to apply their training, interests, and talents in ways they believe they should. This problem was highlighted in a United Nations Office of Economic Cooperation and Development Conference in Venice in October 1971.† It is in the most advanced countries that there seems to be the greatest increasing need for challenge. How to

---

*   For further discussion, see James O'Toole, "The Reserve Army of the Underemployed, I—World of Work," *Change Magazine*, May 1975, pp. 26-33, 63.

†   For a more complete discussion, see "Intergovernmental Conference on the Utilization of Highly Qualified Personnel," Education Committee Document #7 OECD, Venice, October 25-27, 1971.

generate new levels of challenging work in fields not previously considered important seems to be a key issue. On a short-term basis, the problem was exemplified in the United States in the early seventies by the layoffs of aerospace engineers. Many attempts to apply the skills of these specialized and highly trained people to urban or environmental problems or other activities of increased social importance have ended in failure or frustration. The unsolved problem seems to lie more in the definition of work assignments and the reassignment of monetary resources and facilities than in any real shortage of work to be done. Lack of challenging activity turns people off in regard to work, careers, and life itself. At the very least, this lack creates conditions which intensify the personal struggle to maintain vitality.

Beginning in the fifties and intensifying in the late sixties, scientific-based industries recognized a problem of technical obsolescense in people. Early solutions focused on the need for continuing education, and many new graduate programs were established. More recently it has become evident that problems of obsolescence are intensifying despite opportunities for continued education. Now the emphasis has shifted to lifelong learning rather than just continuing engineering education. Obsolescence results in part from the continued onrush of technological change. It is complicated by an increase in the average age of practicing engineers and scientists which is the result of a decrease in the rate of growth of numbers of persons being educated in and entering the field. Increased age brings about a shift in the dominant personal motivation pattern, and thus industry faces the prospect of declining professional and technical vitality. Loss of vitality for professionals leads to lessened organizational vitality; for professionals, as the creators of new products and systems, have great leverage on the organization. This loss leads, in turn, to potential loss of work satisfactions for all in the organization, to potential inroads from competition, and perhaps to the death of the enterprise.

While continuing education programs can help maintain personal vitality, problems show up even in organizations where continued study has become a way of life. Knowledge and skill are only part of being vital. Organizations are, therefore, recognizing the need for a better understanding of work and how, through improved design, work can stimulate personal growth and development. Survival of industrial enterprise and continued scientific and technical advance for the world will depend in large part on discovering how to build learning into work. This means learning which contributes to growth in the sense of increased capability, not just growth as represented by promotion. Ways of continued stimulation and introduction of change are necessary to assure the vitality of professional personnel.

This does not mean that vitality is important only for professionals. The vitality of all employees is important. In fact, the vitality of all humans is important—employed or not. "Knowledge workers" (a term coined by Peter Drucker) in all enterprises create concepts and ideas; they must push on the frontiers; they must lead and spawn work for others—so their vitality is most critical. Knowledge workers in this role include legislators, professors, doctors, lawyers, scientists, engineers, programmers, and all those who add to or apply knowledge.

Those commenting on and studying work have talked of the death of the Protestant work ethic.* The thesis of this book is that personal vitality and growth are emerging as the new work ethic. This is happening not so much because of a growth of new humanitarian values but, instead, from a recognition that finding a new ethic is the only way to attract and motivate people to work and the only way to continue progress toward a better life. Of course, this is not just a managerial problem. Each of us as an individual is facing increasing questions about the importance of work, its value to us, and how we can gain more satisfaction from it. Questions about work are part of our quest for meaning in life.

Whatever your perspective—professional or nonprofessional, manager or employee, government leader or citizen—and regardless of which of these issues about work excites your interest, the concept of vitality is intended to excite you, to stimulate questioning and personal experiment. It should help you arrive at answers which lead to the ability to manage an improved life. A primary aim is to see if together we can find a way to improve the relationship between the job and personal growth and satisfactions. This means we must design work which does not turn us off but, rather, turns us on. The job, if properly designed, can provide a focus for interest and a stimulus for activities which contribute to our vitality. This does not mean we should live for the job alone but, neither, by

---

* This is discussed in detail in Jerome M. Rosow, ed., *The Worker and the Job: Coping with Change* (The American Assembly, Englewood Cliffs, N.J.: Prentice-Hall, Spectrum Books, 1974).

contrast, should the job be just a means to support a separate out-side life.

There is no one right work/life balance. Each of us must find our own particular balance; it is personal and changing. This book is intended to help you find out what you need from work and how to achieve it. Regardless of our separate priorities and needs, I believe personal vitality is a deep, pervasive, and useful rallying theme.

Vitality and life

While work is a central theme of life and a prime vehicle for growth, we do not gain vitality and growth from work alone. Early growth occurs in the context of the family. The newborn infant grows in muscle control and ability to communicate. Vitality is evidenced by learning and growth. The adolescent does a lot of growing at school and through social contacts with contemporaries. The adult grows through social contacts, hobbies, work, family responsibil-ities, and continued learning. Growth can result from any experi-ence which the individual integrates and makes a part of his or her knowledge or skills in a way which makes it usable. If in the process of using capabilities the individual gains satisfactions, it is probable that this reinforcement adds to the motivation for more doing, learning, and growth. The sequence of experience leading to learn-ing, which leads to use, which leads to payoff, which contributes to desire, is the central process for maintaining and extending vitality. This cycle should be a product of all our activities.

Being able to utilize experience and manage change and growth while maintaining some sense of personal centrality and sta-bility are primary life challenges. One of the factors that makes this difficult today is rapid and pervasive change. Our "future shock" experiences make managing change a necessary skill. Failure to manage change successfully leads to withdrawal, reduced open-ness, and a loss of vitality and potential for growth. Finding out how to make growth and change less threatening, and more pleasantly stimulating, is necessary for vitality.

Another way of looking at vitality is in terms of maintenance of health. Vitality may be the theme which finally brings together all of the preventive and curative arts for the "well person." If we can find techniques for maintaining psychological and physical health it is possible we will be establishing the precondition for learning and growth. At the very least, good health will ensure that we have energy available to spend on positive pursuits rather than trying to overcome illness. The balance, or homeostasis, good mental and physical health, is probably an element of the security and safety one needs to take on the risks of personal growth and change.

Coming to the fore in Western culture at this time are the teachings of the East as represented in Chinese and Indian philosophies or practices. These philosophies and teachings, exemplified by meditation and exercises such as Tai Chi, emphasize the need to find the "natural way" as a key to succeeding in life. They teach the importance of finding and transcending self and of learning to become at once more conscious, more awake, and more relaxed as keys to growth. The search for the meaning of these trends, new to Western culture, is part of the challenge of finding the inner self and the internal controls or programs which extend and enhance personal growth and vitality.

Also emerging as applicable techniques are the outputs of the growth movement and scientific advances. These take the forms, for example, of encounter, organization development, team building, and biofeedback; and all highlight the importance of experiential learning as opposed to book or cognitive learning. Biofeedback, for example, holds the promise of extending personal learning by providing a mirror for feedback, permitting correction and control of aspects of our lives we did not previously control. While not endorsing all these activities, this book will attempt to help you analyze their meaning. This should set the stage for you to draw from them anything which appears to help in the maintenance and extension of your vitality.

Decision points and change

One of the requirements for vitality is understanding careers, career planning, and career management. There was a time when a career was believed to be lifelong. For some years we've recognized that life is increasingly made up of a sequence of careers. The first view was that there were definite breaks between careers. We thought that career change meant dramatic shifts. Now it is becoming evident that most careers overlap and that one carries skills and interests from one to another. Each career is built on new knowledge and skills, but also utilizes some skills and knowledge from prior careers. Historically, career counsel was designed to help

high-school and college students make their lifelong career decision. With this new understanding of careers, it is obvious career
management is a continuing process. We are just beginning to
develop concepts and ideas about career counsel for the mature
adult. These are explored in this book.

An important part of navigating through life is learning how to
deal with the explosion of opportunity. Career decisions and
counsel are difficult because we are no longer able to stereotype
relative to existent models. Talking about an engineer, a lawyer, or
a doctor will not reveal the fact that each of these professionals may
participate in activities with similar skill needs and personal payouts.
Learning how to communicate about the "multiplexity" of opportunities is necessary to extend our ability to manage our careers.

One of the decision points in life is the so-called mid-career
crisis. It occurs not at any specific age, but rather at that point where
the life perspective of the individual undergoes a major shift. This
change in perspective results from reassessment of goals, the recognition that retirement is real or within your planning cycle, and with
the early signs of declining physical health and energy level. Knowing how to negotiate this fork in the road of life is important in
extending growth and insuring a continuing productive life.

Developing a holistic view of life at work and outside of work
and establishing the proper dynamic balance between the two is
also a challenge to our vitality. Throughout the course of life the
desirable balance changes. The balancing process depends on
learning ways of managing success by finding satisfactions in one
part of life when another part fails to provide satisfactions. Also
central to achieving balance is the need for achieving the right personal balance between "living for today" and "living for tomorrow"!
The chapter on life balance discusses these issues.

Two decision points particularly concern women. Today's
women can now more freely decide between a career outside the
home and homemaking and decide whether or not to embark on
other activities once their children are grown. Late entry or re-entry
into the working world means that one has missed the period when
reputations are established and that one has to maintain vitality
through a period of nonuse of special capabilities. These adjustments probably call for special kinds of life-management techniques, transition training, and re-education.

Retirement as a concept is firmly embedded in our culture. The
social-security system and most retirement plans set arbitrary ages,
like 62 or 65. It is probable that the radical change from being

needed daily at work to having no work or purpose at all actually shortens life and, because of increased potential longevity, is wasteful of human capability. Replacing automatic retirement with the option of a new career and finding activities of importance for senior citizens are critical needs as our nation manages the demographic shift to higher percentages of older people. This understanding is particularly important for those considering early retirement. Designing activities and ways of maintaining vitality for the increased older population is part of what is necessary to manage the transition from a growth economy to an economy built on improvement in the quality of life. Vitality as a goal leads to improved quality of life.

Navigating the decision points of life requires understanding and managing change. How the individual decides that change is desirable, what kinds of activities he or she can use to prepare for and create appropriate change, and how to make the decision about what change will improve life are all important questions in the pursuit of vitality.

Sources of solution

This book is interdisciplinary. I have brought together many ideas not previously associated. The discussion draws some ideas from recent progress in the behavioral and social sciences. The book also presents ideas which come from business experiences, personal search, philosophy, and science. The philosophical inputs are existential or Eastern. The special training and growth-enhancing techniques were developed from industrial activities normally called organization development. Vitality concepts came from my own work and industrial experience in combating obsolescence. Some ideas came from educational activities or management consultants. I can no longer identify the source of many of the ideas. The theme and the connective tissue provided by vitality come from my own experiences.

Because my experiences have been primarily in a company whose business is highly technical and performed by professionals, many of the examples will be drawn from this environment. This may mean that those who will find the language of the book most familiar will themselves be professionals, engineers, or managers of knowledge work. Still, the message is broader. If the book meets its objectives, it should lead readers in all walks of life, regardless of their role, to make their personal lives and work more stimulating and growth-producing, and to help others to do so, too.

The ways to change organizations and to redesign jobs for increased satisfaction and stimulation of learning are new. The ideas presented here have been related to social-science research where possible, but I have tried to present practical ideas in a way you can put them to use.

The success of the book will be measured by its ability to stimulate new thinking, encourage redesign of jobs by individuals and managers, and extend one's contributing, meaningful life. This direction implies new policy and strategy on personal, organizational, and governmental levels. How to fit the goal of vitality into the myriad of goals which form the central fabric of our world today will be primarily up to you, the reader, and others who are traveling routes similar to the ones suggested.

Organization of the book

The book is divided into two main parts. Part I, Vitality in our Lives, is divided into two sections. The first section describes The Challenge. It presents the concepts of vitality and individual growth and discusses some factors which make vitality important and difficult to achieve. Vitality is defined and the elements that make it up are reviewed. What growth is, the challenge of continued growth, and how individuals grow are covered next. Individual change and growth are then related to the environment and society. The pressures of technological change and social change and their effect on each of us through creating a "future shock" environment are highlighted. The conflicts between work and other interests are reviewed in an attempt to look at the work/life balance.

The second section presents Sources of Solution to the challenge. Personal-growth concepts, how one learns, and how to bring about the conditions for learning throughout life are examined in detail. Pieces and parts of the solution are drawn from many areas. The solutions are presented with an experimental perspective designed to encourage redesign of the environment to create motivation and facilities for improved vitality. Solutions are suggested for individual application. These should be what you can do on your own to improve your life. Tools, techniques, and devices are suggested. You are encouraged to experiment and pick those which work for you. Some of the devices discussed are included in the companion volume, *Personal Vitality Workbook*, which is designed to help you assess where you stand, increase understanding of the issues, and chart a personal course for change. The workbook is based on the concepts examined in this book.

The second part, Putting It All Together, brings this material into focus in terms of the individual, the organization, and the nation. Here techniques are offered for setting and achieving personal goals, for implementing personal change, and for redesigning your job. A strategy is proposed for the individual, for the business manager or leader, and for the congressman or legislator formulating policies and establishing national priorities.

Each chapter is designed so that it stands alone. Although the sequence of chapters seems logical to me, you should not be bound to that sequence. Each chapter has its own introduction, body, and summary.

Personal experiments

Throughout the book there are suggestions of ways in which you, the reader, can test the concept being discussed or experience the feeling described. The intent of these experiments is to make it possible to participate instead of just passively accepting what is read with little residual effect from the reading. Some of these experiments are easy to perform and some require personal creativity, time, and energy. Some action proposals will require enlisting the help of others. Some of the experiments should appeal to you but certainly not all of them will. As in anything we do, what we get out of an experiment is related to what we put in. Try several of these experiments and make your own judgment about whether participation of this type enriches your experience.

Suggested readings

At the end of each chapter are some books and articles that present ideas related to the chapter from another author's perspective. Some of these books present directly related material which can enhance your understanding; others are only tangentially related.

One reference has been singled out with a brief description. This is the reading which I recommend most strongly because it had a great impact on me. As with personal experiments, reading one of these referenced books or articles is a way for you to participate and enhance your experience and your vitality.

Summary

This is a book about how people grow and change. It is designed to stimulate your interest in the process of growth and to increase your growth consciousness. It presents the premise that increased vitality is a desirable and achievable goal for the individual, for business, and for government. It provides a basis for analysis of how people grow and change, discusses the values and functions of work, and provides techniques for choosing the satisfactions you want from work and life. You are introduced to techniques which you can apply in maintaining and extending your vitality and growth. These ideas are also discussed as ways you can influence and change an organization and even a nation. In suggesting how to put it all together I have tried to integrate the many suggestions into a strategy. The strategy is to experiment, to take responsibility for change, to pick vitality as a goal for all your activities, and to increase the positive payout and satisfaction from life. Although work is presented as a primary source of vitality, growth and vitality in all aspects of life are not ignored. Vitality as a necessary, useful, and desirable output of all your activities is the primary message of this book.

—

Vitality in our lives

THE CHALLENGE

1 Vitality
2 Work and growth
3 Changing career concepts and the opportunity explosion
4 Obsolescence and aging
5 Life balance

SOURCES OF SOLUTION

6 Personal-growth concepts
7 Learning to learn
8 Unlearning
9 Continued learning
10 Job and organization design
11 Career management
12 Personal assessment

The
challenge

1

Vitality

Introduction

What is vitality? It is the essence of an alive, growing organism. In this chapter, we will explore its meaning and discuss ways of achieving it. Here we will set forth the goal, establish the challenge. Personal vitality is a necessary component of a good life and seeking it is the proper strategy for improving success, productivity, and satisfaction in life. This is true for the individual, the organization, and the nation. Building and extending vitality requires a willingness to experiment and to take personal responsibility for managing the course of one's life. This chapter and this book will present techniques which can help us improve vitality.

Vitality is a meaningful life goal. We should deliberately improve vitality as a strategy for enhancing the lives of individuals and organizations. For a variety of reasons, however, achieving and maintaining vitality is difficult.

This whole book is based on the thesis that personal and organizational, and even national, vitality are necessary, interdependent, and achievable. It is suggested that vitality improvement be studied and systematically developed as a promising new work ethic. It is increasingly evident that the goal of materialistic growth and expansion, which has been the foundation of Western capitalism, is inadequate today. As our values undergo profound reevaluation, I suggest here that we consider the enhancement of personal vitality as a fundamental goal of all our activities and as the appropriate reward for achievement.

What is vitality?

When we meet two new people on the street and one is active, animated, and radiating interest through listening and responding, and the other is nonresponsive, dull, and nonparticipative, we feel we know which one is vital. We are responding to surface indications which may or may not reflect the truth. These surface indications most often project energy, interest, and purpose. By contrast, when we are visiting someone in a hospital who is in a coma and we get a report that the vital signs of life are declining, we can sense the absence of vitality. Vitality is most easily identifiable in its extremes through observation of the behavior of an organism, organization, or individual. It is closely related to being alive, but it's more than that. It is a life of growth in skills and capabilities; it is life with a purpose and direction; it is a life of accomplishment. Vitality is being awake and interested in life, motivated to get the most out of life; it is growing and achieving successes in life. Vitality is the product of any activity when there is improvement, gain, or amplification of output in relation to the energy we exert. In the vernacular of the day, it is being "turned on" and "tuned in" to life. Let us start off our personal and organizational search for vitality with a definition.

Personal vitality is the desire and the ability, capacity, or power to perform effectively and vigorously in life and at work. The vital person gains personal growth and satisfactions from life and work. Vitality is growing in the game of life and doing it in the context of work as well as in all other aspects of life. It is being up-to-date. It is being motivated to engage in activities which meaningfully exercise one's abilities. It is getting the satisfactions which motivate further growth. It is being open and receptive to new experience. Although these descriptions are stated in terms applicable to the individual, many also apply to the organization. A vital organization is one which aggressively designs and sells its service or product and gains profit and growth from the activity.

It is important to think through the several elements of the definition. First you and I must have the knowledge, the skill, and the ability. This means knowing what is to be done and having the information and skill at our disposal to do it. Aptitude without capability is not enough. Having the information or knowledge without the skill to apply it is not enough. Even having the aptitude, the knowledge, and the skill is still not enough. Vitality results from the *use* of these combined abilities. The individual must be motivated to use the capabilities.

The definition also suggests that vitality will not ensue from applying these capabilities unless we receive some payout, some reward. This payout relates to the gain in the process. Payout which is reinforcing must be compatible with your values, needs, and goals. If the payout is in alignment with your needs, then the process is reinforcing and the receipt of the payout leads you to do more and gain in ability. If, on the other hand, the payout doesn't meet your criteria, you can become "turned off." In a turned-off condition, you or I can have the aptitude, knowledge, and ability and still not be vital.

Vitality has not usually been considered as a possible, expected, or required product of work because the image of work is that of an activity using something up rather than adding to it. Many people see work as tiring, taxing, and energy depleting. We understand conceptually that using our muscles is necessary for their health and that using our brain is necessary for its maintenance. But most people think of the work activity as a discharge rather than a recharge. Yet in *Work In America* there are two statements which demonstrate the negative effects of poor work and indicate that life itself may be dependent on positive psychological income from work.

> *Moreover a growing body of research indicates that, as work problems increase, there may be consequent decline in physical and mental health, family stability, community participation and cohesiveness, and "balanced" socio-political attitudes, while there is an increase in drug and alcohol addiction, aggression and delinquency.*
>
> *Satisfaction with work appears to be the best predictor of longevity — better than known medical or genetic factors — and various aspects of work account for much, if not most, of the factors associated with heart disease.* *

A German psychiatrist believes he has seen a direct relationship between work and life expectancy. Curt Donig, head of a Berlin psychiatric clinic, says one year of unemployment can reduce life expectancy for the job-loser by five years. "We have observed over 300 men and women with nervous disorders," explains Donig. "These people have been out of work for lengthy periods of time. The processed data on these people leads to the conclusion that unemployment and its attendant anxieties can reduce a person's life expectancy by as much as five years, especially if they have been job-seeking for more than a year."†

Certainly vitality and longevity are related, since satisfaction with work is the best single predictor of longevity. What you get out of work is directly related to your aliveness and vitality; the right work has a profound effect on your well-being. Work in this context is a central purpose for life; as Hans Selye, a biologist, states it,

---

*   *Work in America*, A Report of a Special Task Force to the Secretary of Health, Education, and Welfare, U.S. Dept. of Health, Education, and Welfare (Cambridge, M.I.T. Press, 1973), p. xvi and xvii. Reprinted with permission.

†   Lloyd Shearer, "Intelligence Report," *Parade Magazine*, October 5, 1975. Reprinted with permission.

"work is a biological necessity!"* Therefore, we conclude, vitality can be enhanced by the right work and such enhancement is a necessary part of staying alive. Vitality is a necessary ingredient you bring to work, and the right work is a source of growth and thus vitality.

These twin concepts of growth and vitality are, therefore, primary needs for the individual, and work should contribute to them. Our proposed strategy is to focus on these as a central purpose of work. This contrasts with past strategies where the central purpose was product output, profit, or trying to create employee happiness. By seeking vitality the individual and the organization can gain improved work motivations, productivity, more valuable individual and organizational payouts, and improved quality of working life. Vitality in a business environment can result from both the business and the individual working to achieve it. Vitality is building for tomorrow by putting first priority on enhancing human capabilities.

Vitality was identified by Frederick R. Kappel of AT&T as a prime component of business and personal success in his 1960 McKinsey lectures at Columbia University. From the business leader's view, he says, "Vitality is the power a business generates today that will assure its success and progress tomorrow."† In taking the concept to the human level, he says

> What makes a vital business? Vital people make it. . . . Vitality is something people demonstrate through sustained competence; through creative venturesome drive; and through a strong feeling of ethical responsibility, which means an inner need to do what's right and not just what one is required to do.‡

He suggests that a business can operate in ways that will enhance its vitality by contributing to the growth and vitality of the people who work for it. His suggestions are as follows:

Elements of a vital business

■ *It can provide opportunities and incentives for work that is meaningful to the man who does it.*

---

* From *Stress Without Distress* by Hans Selye, p. 84. Copyright © 1974 by Hans Selye, M. D. Reprinted by permission of J. B. Lippincott Company.

† Frederick R. Kappel, *Vitality in a Business Enterprise* (New York: McGraw-Hill, 1960), p. 3. Reprinted with permission.

‡ Ibid., p. 5.

- *It can set demanding and exciting goals.*
- *It can encourage relationships that are constructive and stimulating.*
- *It can support attitudes of independence and self-reliance.*
- *It can identify the individual with the kind of business character and ethics that will help maintain his standing as a valuable and respected member of his community.*
- *It can demand his best at all times.* *

With these statements Kappel sets forth the proposition that vitality is a mutual goal. He points out that it is not sufficient to expect the individual to be vital but that the business must set up conditions which both demand and support growth and vitality.

As viewed by the individual, the components of vitality are several characteristics of "being." Being vital includes aspects of energy, "aliveness," growth, and learning. The following list of some aspects should bound the concept in a way which we can use to understand it and to manage our own lives. All of these elements together form a belief and value structure necessary for vitality.

Elements of personal vitality

1. A good usable energy level and good health.
2. The capacity to encompass new experience.
3. The ability to use new learning.
4. Openness to and respect for others.
5. The understanding of self, the ability to be at home with oneself, and the ability to transcend self.
6. The capacity to draw positive reinforcement from living.
7. The ability to set and achieve goals.
8. The ability to achieve congruence between one's goals and the goals of the organizations of which one is part.
9. Personal competence and the motivation to experiment, to grow, and to try.

Energy level

If I were to identify the one factor which most often in my experience differentiates the successful from the unsuccessful, it would be energy level. This does not mean that high energy level is alone

---

*   Ibid., p. 9.

sufficient. One's energy level relates to the amount of power one has to apply to a task or to living. Applying energy is as necessary to succeed as having it. Energy level is higher when health, both mental and physical, is good. Energy is both psychological and physical. Concepts of energy are found in almost all historic philosophies and systems. The concept of energy is inherent in the oriental *Tao*, in the flow through the meridians in acupuncture, and in the human aura now controversially revealed or not revealed by Kirlian photography.* Achieving your potential through the application of your energy is the result of knowing what you want and taking responsibility for your life. Put another way, it is knowing your strengths and weaknesses and effectively directing your energy toward a desired goal.

Some who have handicaps that others would consider defeating have achieved vitality in spite of or because of those limits. One of my early teachers had had polio, which caused one hand and one arm to be weak and deformed. In his life he chose to do things which required manual dexterity. In his retired years, he rebuilt historic homes in Nantucket, achieving a reputation for meticulous detail and outstanding craftsmanship. Somewhere he found the energy, applied it, and achieved the skill despite his handicap. Having high energy and vitality is not just being granted it, but being motivated to develop it, to use it, and to achieve.

High energy level might be interpreted by some to mean spending long hours or expending large amounts of physical energy. The concept of energy as used here is broader than endurance. One can demonstrate high energy without running a mile or lifting great weights. The concept of energy is not just physical but also psychological. It is interest- aptitude- task- and skill-related.

One can demonstrate high energy through strong commitment, quick response, highly analytical capability, or unusual skill. Where it comes from and why some people are judged to have it and others not to have it are intriguing questions. The main point is, however, can we increase it in ourselves? It is probable that energy level is as much an attitude as a state of being. Since it is generally accepted that human beings apply only a part of their capability, it is highly probable that energy increase can result primarily from stopping self-defeating and energy-wasting processes or habits.

---

*   Thelma Moss, in *The Probability of the Impossible: Scientific discoveries and explorations in the psychic world* (Los Angeles: Tarcher, 1974) provides one of the most complete discussions of aura and Kirlian photography.

PERSONAL EXPERIMENT 1

Select some near-term task you have set for yourself, preferably one which is of limited length—hours or days, not months. Next establish goals and schedules which really require a burst of extra energy but which you have some reasonable chance of achieving. Put out all you can and test your ability to raise your energy output to achieve a higher level of performance and create a burst of activity. Vital people have the capacity to do this. Vital people usually achieve exhilaration and a sense of satisfaction from such an experience. How did you feel? What did you learn about yourself? How do you rate your vitality on the basis of this experiment?

There are two other aspects of energy level to discuss. The first is the relationship of health to energy level. A healthy person, one who has a well-functioning body, is in a better condition to produce energy than one who is not well. This is in part because the creative process takes energy. The second is the role of anxiety. Anxiety is an aspect of lack of psychological health. Anxiety, like physical illness, is energy using. When we are spending energies worrying we are diverting them from positive purposes and subtracting from our capabilities to apply energy to positive ends. The production and use of energy is therefore highly dependent on both physical and psychological health. Health is thus a prerequisite for vitality enhancement. As you pursue your reading of this book, think both of how you may be inhibiting the positive use of energy and of the choice of activities which can produce energy.

Encompassing new experience

The capacity to encompass new experience is related to one's feeling of security and safety as well as to the desire to learn the new. Being secure in oneself is a necessary prerequisite for taking the risk of openness and exposing oneself to something that may not be publicly acceptable, may not work, or may even be uncomfortable.

In part, taking in the new relates to what one already knows—new learning is generally built on previous learning. (For example, some aspects of physics require the ability to use and understand calculus.) On the other hand, the capability to encompass the new is also built on the willingness to set aside or overcome consequences of previous learning which may be incompatible with the new experience. (If, for example, an experiment yields results which do not fit the previous "law" or hypothesis, it is necessary to have the ability to set aside the previous concept and build with the new.)

Being able to use previous experience or to set it aside might be thought of as unlocking energy. In fact, "unlearning" (covered in Chapter 8) is an important life-management technique necessary for staying vital and alive. Setting aside previous learning may require special capabilities of functioning at an emotional as well as at an intellectual level. Much of what we do is emotionally based, not logical, not intellectually established. To do any of these things that are necessary to take account of new experience, the individual must feel secure, able to withstand the threat to position and self-worth inherent in giving up a previous position or postulate.

One challenge of encompassing the new, then, is finding the way to make change more comfortable to us. This does not mean it is ever easy to change. We can, however, change the threshold at which we can bring about change. Both individuals and organizations have many different thresholds dependent on timing and conditions. Each of us as individuals and every organization must learn techniques which minimize and manage the fears of change to create the climate for acceptance. Since we live as part of groups or organizations, the relationship between the individual and the organization is an important part of this climate. This is what we mean by changing the threshold for change. Changing the threshold is part of making it OK to change. The need for this technique stems from the fact the new data or a new role may not fit, may literally upset our position. It may even mean the loss of some of the underpinning for our personal feeling of security in the organization. Failing to find or devise techniques for acceptance of change means being stuck where we are. Being stuck leads to obsolescence and to being out-paced by someone who does change. Out-pacing can happen to both individuals and organizations. Taking in and being able to use new learning and data is, therefore, key to vitality, productivity, and staying in the game of work, of life, and of achieving in the enterprise with which we are associated.

Using new experience

Closely related to encompassing new learning is using it. Both learning and using new learning are components of sustained personal competence or sustained success for an enterprise. Using it effectively requires not just adding it to the store of information but also integrating it. For example, in the early days of transistors there were many who were mentally able to substitute the transistor for the tube. They were the ones who started using the transistor. They used transistors as if using tubes. This type of acceptance of the new is better than nonacceptance, but it is a substitution which does not achieve the added capability which is part of the new. It is forcing the new into the old framework. Real acceptance of the transistor came when a few found out how to use the transistor in new ways. Integration in the electronics industry, putting many devices on a small chip, was the real beginning of matching the new technology to new concepts.

On a more personal level, the importance of using the new to create vitality can also be demonstrated. For example, suppose you read or learn something about the concepts of "transactional analysis."* With this exposure you learn about a technique to analyze and improve interpersonal communication. Accepting the knowledge but not using it will not improve communication. You have to ask yourself what roles you are playing, what roles your partner is playing, and whether these are compatible or in conflict. By understanding the roles, you can attempt to acknowledge these roles and change your approach for more effective communications.

Openness to and respect for others

Openness is a necessary prerequisite to growth. If we are closed, we live in our own world and what goes on around us has little effect. If we're open, we expose ourselves to input from and reactions of others and the possibility that these contacts may lead to our having to change. Openness does not require that we neces-

---

*   See Muriel James and Dorothy Jongeward, *Born to Win; Transactional Analysis with Gestalt Experiments* (Reading, Mass.: Addison-Wesley, 1971) for a discussion of the concepts of "transactional analysis."

sarily accept and integrate others' views, but it does require that we be open to listening, to exchange, to seeing, and to contact. Openness requires self-understanding, self-respect, and respect for others. Openness in relating to others is similar to encompassing new experience. There are parallel risks. Contact with another may supply new data when two people come together at an interface. Communication requires negotiation at that interface and exchange of views about reality. In fact, reality is that which we can agree to and use as a common base for communication, learning, and further experience.

The process of negotiation requires a statement from one of the parties which transmits perception, feeling, and data about an experience. The other party to the transaction then puts forward the comparable perception. Each individual then tries to relate the other's view into his or her own. This open meeting and discussion of views requires mutual respect. Arriving at agreement may take time, patience, energy, and certainly openness to change of view. Data received from another person is different from firsthand experience but it can be integrated into personal experience. I believe an example will help.

If a friend says, "You look as though you are coming down with a cold," this does not mean that you actually are coming down with a cold or that you are experiencing such feelings. Upon receipt of the data it is normal to check its validity. You ask yourself whether you have any other data to confirm or deny this new information. In the absence of corroboration you will probably decide on nonacceptance. What you must then do is explain to yourself how your friend's perception can fit with your interpretation that you do not have a cold. If you cannot do this, then you will seek more input from the friend and attempt to negotiate the view. You might, for example, agree upon a third interpretation such as lack of sleep or indoor pallor or an allergic reaction. Openness requires that you reach a shared view or negotiated reality to which you both agree. If by chance you find corroboration of your friend's view, you engage in whatever activity you believe will avert or cure the cold.

Openness is two-way. Self-disclosure is a necessary part of a healthy personality. Openness then requires both telling and listening. By these processes of letting yourself be yourself, you gain new insight—a necessary part of growth, change, and vitality. Accepting and using the new insights are separate processes. Both are necessary. Openness is an aspect of direct personal confrontation with life, necessary for growth.

Understanding, being at home with, and transcending self

Being vital requires understanding who you are—your beliefs, your strengths, your weaknesses, and your goals. Vitality also requires developing a positive image of self—self-respect. These understandings are necessary because vitality requires growth, change, and accomplishment. To change, one must start somewhere—a base. Accepting yourself for what you are provides that base. Success is dependent on building congruence between one's ideal image of self and the real self. Surprisingly, one of the ways to understand oneself and to find the base for change is to tell someone else about yourself. Another is to learn to listen to oneself. Carl Rogers puts it this way in "This is Me":

> *A second learning might be stated as follows—I find I am more effective when I can listen acceptantly to myself. I feel that over the years I have learned to become more adequate in listening to myself; so that I know, somewhat more adequately than I used to, what I am feeling at any given moment—to be able to realize I am angry; or that I do feel rejecting toward this person; or that I feel very full of warmth and affection for this individual; or that I am bored and uninterested in what is going on; or that I am eager to understand this individual or that I am anxious and fearful in my relationship to this person. All of these diverse attitudes are feelings which I think I can listen to in myself. One way of putting this is that I feel I have become more adequate in letting myself be what I am. It becomes easier for me to accept myself as a decidedly imperfect person, who by no means functions at all times in the way in which I would like to function.*

> *This must seem to some like a very strange direction in which to move. It seems to me to have value because the curious paradox is that when I accept myself as I am, then I can change. I believe that I have learned this from my clients as well as within my own experience—that we cannot change, we cannot move away from what we are, until we thoroughly accept what we are. Then change seems to come about almost unnoticed. **

Understanding yourself, accepting and respecting yourself, is a prerequisite to all the activities necessary for maintenance of vital-

---

*   Carl R. Rogers, *On Becoming a Real Person* (Boston, Mass.: Houghton Mifflin, 1961), p. 17. Reprinted with permission.

ity. For example, if you are to redesign work to increase its payout and your satisfactions, you must understand your personal priorities and needs for various satisfactions. If you are to improve your ability to communicate with others, it is necessary to know what you know and feel, as well as to understand how you relate to others. If you are to increase your learning you must know first what conditions support your best learning and what techniques work for you. If you are to redirect your life or change careers, you need to know how your current goals and career are working for you. Self-knowledge is equivalent to the ship-captain's need for position and bearing before giving the command for right or left rudder and a change in power to the propeller.

The capacity to gain positive reinforcement from living

For life to have meaning and purpose we must feel we're gaining or getting some positive payout. This is both an internal process of providing ourselves with positive reinforcement and an external process of recognizing and receiving reinforcement from the environment. Individuals have different capacities and an individual's ability to gain satisfactions varies with time, conditions, and attitude. For example, if I approach playing bridge with the expectation that it will be fun and I feel I am a reasonably good player, I can influence the outcome positively. If, on the other hand, I carry negative experiences and a negative outlook to the bridge table, I will influence the experience negatively. Actual conditions will also affect outcomes. For example, it will make a difference if I sit down at bridge with experts or amateurs. One reason for variation has to do with self-image. Another seems to be based on expectations. If we expect positive reinforcement and get none, then we are disappointed. If we expect positive payouts and they come in proportions roughly equivalent to our expectations, that is better. Sometimes we set up negative expectations to protect ourselves from disappointment. However, getting positive results and accepting them are two different aspects of the process. It is the acceptance which is necessary as part of vitality. A further example may clarify this.

Sometimes when we do something which pleases someone else he or she says "thank you." A simple "thank you" which is perceived as spontaneous and sincere is usually acceptable. Accepting it provides positive reinforcement. Suppose, however, you know this person is overly profuse in positive statements but has the reputation of making negative remarks behind one's back which seem to reflect more nearly his or her real opinion. If this is true you may not accept this apparently positive result from your actions. Hearing it does little for your vitality. Acceptance requires respect for the other person.

The capacity to see, to accept, and to use positive reinforcement depends on openness and self-understanding, which have already been discussed. Your ability to identify positive outcomes can be shaped by previous experience, as well as by your expectations, by what you look for. If you look for an outcome which is improbable, such as income from arts or crafts on first starting, you set up the conditions for probable negative reinforcement. If, on the other hand, you start artistic endeavor with the attitude "I'll take what I get—anything is OK," then the activity will be more likely to provide positive reinforcement and improve vitality.

Goal
congruence

When my goals and your goals are the same, compatible, or additive in the same direction, we have congruence. When the individual feels that personal goals can be achieved within the context of the goals of the organization, there is congruence of goals. Congruence creates the potential for greater application and commitment and leads to improved outputs or satisfactions. Lack of congruence tends to cause the motivated individual to search for other goals and associations which are more congruent. Lack of congruence causes low motivation.

Achieving congruence with an organization requires that the individual understand the organization's objectives and that the organization understand the individual's desires. Both the individual and the organization have needs and capabilities to align. Communication of goals (needs) and capabilities in open exchange is necessary to achieve this understanding. Communication does not assure that the two sets of goals will move toward each other, but without communication little chance exists. Gaining congruence requires negotiation and adaptation on both sides. Congruence leads to improved productivity and increased payout for both the organization and the individual. Chapter 17 will cover this concept in greater detail.

> **PERSONAL EXPERIMENT 2**
>
> **In contrast to Personal Experiment 1, another action suggestion is to test your ability to "cool it." Vital people are able to relax, to do nothing, just as they are able to turn on extra power. Locate a quiet place where you will not be disturbed and try taking a few moments out of a busy time to do *nothing*. Don't go to sleep; just assume a relaxing position and let your mind drift, not struggling to stop mental activity but not completing every thought sequence; just let what happens happen. How did you feel? Were you successful or were you still racing? Vital people have the power to make a pause a rejuvenating experience. Are you vital, based on this experiment?**

Maintaining vitality requires that one's energies be expended in positive directions. Positive directional movement provides positive feedback. Not having to fight a conflict in goals, which saps strength, contributes to your available energy for positive ends.

Competence, experimentation, and growth motivation

To do things we must have skills and abilities. To do things well we must be competent. Vitality is represented both in the application of our competencies and in the outcomes which flow from being competent. Competence matched to the task is, therefore, a sign of vitality and contributes to increasing our vitality.

Through both the personal experiments included in this book and the messages of this book I am trying to encourage you to experiment. An experimental outlook or approach to life is an important contributor to increased vitality. Experimentation, trying the new, is the opposite of being stuck or being obsolete. Experimentation requires thrusting yourself into contact with the world. Experimentation is part of learning and growth.

Wanting to grow and to be vital are important parts of the challenge of being vital. This means making growth in skills and knowledge personal goals. Growth and vitality use energy to create more. In order to expand energy the individual must put a value on growth which establishes a priority for growth activities that is high enough to beat out alternative activities that are not growth-oriented. A simple example is the choice between going to class in the evening or going bowling. Although both activities may contribute to growth, the class probably has the higher long-run payout. How strongly you feel the need for growth will contribute to your decision as to which you do.

How does growth become important for the individual? If the individual belongs to and lives with a group for which growth is important, then it is probable the individual will put a high value on growth. Our values tend to reflect the values of the culture and the groups in which we live and work. In IBM the development of Technical Vitality* programs has depended on this concept. The programs are designed to raise the value of maintaining vitality for the organization as a whole and thus influence values held by the individual.

Another reason why an individual may choose to assign growth a high priority is self-insight, which could start with a crisis or a failure. This could lead to the decision to change. It can be internal or personal or it can flow from the environment or be some combination. The main factor in maintaining vitality is the individual's belief that being vital is necessary and important.

Organizational vitality

As I have indicated, vital people are necessary for a vital organization. In this section the organization will be discussed as if it were a separate entity, and some of the things contributing to its vitality will be suggested.

There is no simple formula for achieving organizational vitality, but there are four levels of activity to be considered. The first is communication of the necessity to maintain personal and organizational vitality and the necessity of management support through environmental signals. This includes policy statements and actions which place a priority on vitality. Second, is the provision of facilities for personal vitality through opportunities for study, growth,

---

* Donald B. Miller, "Technical Vitality—Key to Extending Engineers' Productivity," Dallas, Texas, August 1974, Workshop on Continuing Education for Engineers at Mid-Career.

and new experience. Third, is management commitment and understanding which leads to the redefinition and redesign of work to enhance human growth and work quality. Fourth, is providing the space for individuals to express themselves and to grow through the use of their capabilities into fuller, more successful people. Vitality infusion happens, therefore, at four levels: environmental (including organizational change), facilities, management, and personal.

How can you spot a vital organization? First, it reaches out and demonstrates leadership. It is not afraid to part with the past, does not rest on past achievements, and is not satisfied with past successes. A vital organization sets goals for which there is some risk of nonachievement along with a reasonable probability of achievement. Vital organizations have mechanisms for effective communication of goals with the result that the members of the organization commit themselves to and pursue the goals with vigor and understanding. A vital organization also provides for employee participation in goal setting.

We associate vitality with growth and change; and in organizational terms this means reorganization, reassignment, and realignment of function and adaptation to changing business conditions. Organizational change can include growth in numbers, profit,or output. As for the individual, however, corporate growth in capability and improvement in quality are at least as important as growth in numbers or size.

An organization, by the way it organizes, can dull or enhance the vitality of the individuals who work in it and dull or enhance its own response mechanisms. If, for example, the individual perceives that the expectation of the organization is for him or her to follow the rules without thinking, then the individual turns off and stops trying to reach out for the new. If the organization is perceived as expecting adaptation, new answers, and challenge of the status quo, then this will tend to support vitality in its members. In other words, the philosophies, policies, and expectations transmitted by those who lead the organization through their words and deeds establish a culture which reinforces or inhibits organizational vitality, growth, and responsiveness.

The following example of the effect of organizational policy on the environment and values may demonstrate this concept.

Currency of knowledge is one aspect of vitality, especially in an organization based on rapidly changing technology. Keeping abreast of current knowledge requires continual study. In the fifties many people entered the work force with the idea that their education had prepared them for their entire working life. The organizational belief, by contrast, was that continuing education would be essential. By publicly acknowledging and rewarding those who continued learning, the organization endeavored to change their attitudes. Another force for change was the establishment of educational programs which were easy to use. Another was making specific knowledge and experience a requirement for advancement or a desirable job assignment. Still another was making success at continuing education a part of the annual performance appraisal. In all these ways and more, management of high-technology companies affected the values of those who worked and lived in their organizations.

Another evaluation of organizational vitality can be made by assessing the power, frequency, and compatibility of making organizational change. This was brought home to me once when I was lecturing on managing change. The audience consisted of managers from the steel industry and associated industries. My perspective was that of a high-technology organization where change is the only constant and where reorganization is continual. I expressed this outlook, saying I expected change. In one statement in the speech it was suggested that the adaptive organization creates rumors in anticipation of change when the time since the last change is perceived as longer than normal. After the speech some of the audience commented that they did not understand what was being said because generally they came from an environment where the rate of change was slow and the expectation of change was unusual. Thus, change begets change and sets up expectations of change. An unchanging organization tends, by contrast, neither to change nor to expect change.

Vitality as a challenge

Maintaining vitality has always been a challenge for the individual, the organization, and the nation. It is, however, becoming harder to maintain vitality at all levels because of several changes in our world. Let us look at some of the events or trends which are making achievement of vitality difficult for the individual. By describing those difficulties in personal terms we establish the challenge both for ourselves as individuals and for the organization.

First, we live in an era of pervasive and rapid change. Since change contributes to vitality, one's first reaction would be that this should make being vital easier. Actually, it probably works against individual vitality by causing the individual to seek stability—to seek benchmarks or anchor points for security. In maintaining personal balance, we attempt to compensate for what is going on around us. Therefore, the greater the changes around us the greater our tendency to hold on and to resist. By contrast, in more stable times the individual is free to seek change which will contribute to vitality. In *Future Shock*, Toffler suggests that perhaps we should design special environments which provide protection from change in the short run where the individual can recover and rejuvenate.

A second reason that vitality is difficult to maintain is the result of changes in values about work. Like stability of environment, which makes personal change possible, stability of values makes life-management easier. Work values are in transition: we are in the process of discarding or changing the "Protestant work ethic"; we have discovered that one does not have to work to live (possibly an anomaly); we are not sure what we should expect out of work, and the variety of work alternatives is greatly expanded. When we are not sure why we should work, developing a personal work philosophy becomes extremely difficult.

A third trend increasing personal difficulty also has to do with values—those that provide direction for enterprise and government. These values affect our motivation and our sense of the meaningfulness of our lives. Our recent disenchantment with technological progress and its costs, for example, raises questions for those inclined and interested in science and engineering. Since work is a way of gaining meaning and a feeling of self-worth, the worker is surely affected if there is public debate about the value of cars, nuclear power, insecticides, medicines, and other products of technical endeavor. Or if one is interested and skilled at social service and there is great debate over the value of aid versus the requirement for self-help, this can affect one's motivation and enthusiasm for that field. With the current distrust of government, one may, even though so inclined, be discouraged from working for government. We need to feel that what we do has value, and changing cultural values can leave us out on a limb and questioning whether what we want to do is of value.

A fourth trend is closely related, and that is the change in our level of trust or faith in institutions. We need to relate closely to a business, an organization, a church, or a government to make our own contribution. If, as in current times, we have lost faith in these institutions then we feel frustrated in our attempts to do anything. Lack of employee trust in the institution, for example, raises doubts about personal commitment and reduces productivity. Making any relationship contribute to vitality requires trust. We must trust the leadership of the organization for which we work. Management must also trust us.

Vitality improvement as a strategy

For years the proper outcome of the activity we call work has been fair pay for the employee, profit for the employer, and service to or an improvement in living for society. Now, with the growing understanding that many people want more than pay from work and that society wants careful use of resources and improvements which do not lead to environmental deterioration, we are searching for new values. Our challenge is to find a new rallying theme to replace growth in numbers and size and improvement in such material aspects of life as larger, faster autos. Vitality improvement, which includes growth in capability and increased satisfactions from life, is offered as this rallying theme.

Vitality as a necessary output from activity is a concept that can be shared by individuals, business, and society alike. This is so because vitality means qualitative improvement. Policies, programs, and activities which contribute to vitality tend to benefit all three elements. A vitality improvement strategy provides a basis for making necessary value tradeoff decisions. It also fits with our search for greater meaning in life. The challenge is to find those policies, programs, and activities that will help us achieve increased vitality.

Summary

Personal vitality is the desire and the ability, capacity, or power to perform effectively and vigorously in life and at work. The vital person gains personal growth and satisfactions from life and work. This is the definition described in this chapter and the basis for the theme of this book. Vitality improvement was presented as a necessary and valuable output from all activity. It was presented as a concept applicable to individuals, organizations, and countries. The elements of personal vitality, which include high energy, the capacity to encompass new experience, the ability to use new learning, openness and respect for others, understanding of self, the ability to draw positive reinforcement from living, the ability to set and achieve goals, the ability to achieve congruence of goals with organizations of which we are part, and personal competence, experimentation, and motivation for growth, were presented and discussed. Some trends of our times which make achieving vitality more difficult were cited as part of the challenge. Choosing vitality as a strategy to substitute for growth in materialistic ways commits us to the building of harmonious relationships which lead to increased quality of life.

Suggested readings

Berkowitz, Bernard, and Newman, Mildred. *How To Be Your Own Best Friend*. New York: Random House, 1971.

Gardner, John W. *Self Renewal*. New York: Harper & Row, 1974.

James, Muriel, and Jongeward, Dorothy. *Born To Win; Transactional Analysis with Gestalt Experiments*. Reading, Mass.: Addison-Wesley, 1971.

Jourard, Sidney M. *Healthy Personality; An Approach from the Viewpoint of Humanistic Psychology*. New York: MacMillan, 1974.

> *This book is about human vitality. It is well organized and easy to read. Dr. Jourard views psychological health from many different perspectives. He covers such diverse aspects of a healthy personality as consciousness, reality contact, the body, defense versus growth, social roles, work, and religion. He suggests ways you can improve your satisfactions from and sense of success in life. Each chapter has a clear introduction, a good summary, and notes and references which can lead you to further exploration and experiment.*

Kappel, F.R. *Vitality in a Business Enterprise*. New York: McGraw-Hill, 1960.

Olson, Kenneth. *The Art of Hanging Loose in an Uptight World*. Greenwich, Conn.: Fawcett, 1974.

Rogers, Carl R. *On Becoming A Person*. Boston: Houghton Mifflin, 1961.

2

Work and growth

Introduction

Why work? What do you want to get out of work? Have you grown as a result of your work? These are some of the questions addressed in this chapter. Changing values and changing expectations from work are presented in the context of work as a central purpose for life. Some of the causes of alienation from work and how the individual can decide what is important are presented with the thought that work can be designed to contribute significantly to added skills, knowledge, and vitality. Congruence between personal goals and organization goals is seen as a prime factor in motivation for commitment and productivity. The need to develop an improved personal understanding of work, redesigning work for increased payout, and gaining growth and vitality through work are challenges for us all.

Work

Work is what we believe it should be. That is, our expectations about work are formed during our education and our experiences which build from our belief and value structures. How we feel about work is affected, too, by our roles. That is, it is probable that doctors as a group will look at work differently than coal miners do. What work means to us goes a long way toward shaping our lives, affecting our goals, and setting the framework for our satisfaction or lack of satisfaction with our lot in life. We spend a major portion of our time and energy at work. Work is central to our lives and the satisfactions we gain from it are the best predictors of how long we will live.

One purpose of this chapter is to help you confront your personal feelings about work, to assist you in getting past the surface feelings to reach a point of real understanding. Once your beliefs are understood you have the opportunity to choose to keep those feelings and beliefs if they are working for you or change them if they are not. Once you know where you stand concerning work you can start redesigning your work to improve the payout for you. If you manage other people, you need to understand their views of work and know how to develop jobs to improve growth, vitality, and satisfactions for others. If you set policy, you need to understand work concepts in order to establish meaningful organization goals. Understanding work and how it affects your life is a necessary part of improving your life.

Our culture carries a set of beliefs about work. These beliefs may coincide with or influence an individual's beliefs. They come from a long history of attitudes, starting with work as punishment or slavery in Roman times, to work as a way of achieving nearness to God in the Reformation, and to work as a means of gaining a livelihood in modern times. There is a good description of the development of our cultural heritage about work contained in *Work In America** and in *The Worker and the Job.*† It is not my intention to recount this history other than to establish the fact that what the individual believes, or what a company expounds as a set of values about work, is to some extent shaped by our cultural heritage. The important point of this chapter is not so much what these cultural trends are but what you, the reader, feel about work and how these feelings affect your ability to achieve vitality. Your beliefs and their compatibility with those of the organizations of which you are a part establish your challenge.

Let's start our personal confrontation of our work values by revealing our sterotypes. Certain clues are built into physical stance, dress, and surface attitudes. For example, a man leaning on a shovel among a group of persons all shoveling is "goofing off," resting, or tired—but he's not working. I remember an incident early in my working career when a supervisor beckoned me to join him standing outside his office observing employees at a sea of desks. When I joined him he commented on the fact that a group in one area was not working. His clue had been that they were talking and laughing, which he saw as incompatible with work. Another time a top executive toured our facility and commented late in the day that he didn't think much of our management. Why? He'd seen some thirteen people with their feet up on the desk and to him this meant they couldn't be working. We usually react to a work scene where dress is unique partly because of the uniform, as in the case of nurses, mechanics, or officers of the law. We react in other cases to facial expressions, the worried or frustrated look of someone at work. Our first level of work attitudes is therefore near the surface. These attitudes often provide a filter through which we see our work.

Another attitude about work has to do with the belief that work uses energy, and that in the process of working we discharge or use

---

*   Introduction to *Work in America* (Cambridge: MIT Press, 1973).

†   Jerome M. Rosow, ed. *The Worker and the Job* (The American Assembly, Englewood Cliffs, N.J.: Prentice-Hall, Spectrum Books, 1974).

up something. This probably comes from the historic picture of work as physical labor. Despite this negative feeling, we know that failure to use our muscles means that eventually we won't be able to. We have here a conflict between our feelings and our intellectual understanding: work seems to be a cyclical process which in one sense uses us up and in another sense builds or restores us. We must spend energy to gain more. We must work to grow in our ability to work and live. This regenerative concept is probably as applicable to brain work as to muscle work.

What is work? It is some kind of activity. Doing something, even if it is not physical, is inherent in the meaning of work. Most often work is associated with the idea of earning a livelihood. That is not to say that working in our garden is not work but rather it may not be thought of as work. In other words, the same activity under different conditions may be perceived differently. Phoning a list of people to make business connections is different from phoning them to invite them to a party. Writing poetry for enjoyment is different from writing poetry for publication. One aspect of this difference, therefore, relates to the "why" for the activity. Another aspect has to do with the "initiator" of the activity. If I *choose* to do something, I may not consider it work. If I'm *requested* to do the same thing, I may think of it as work. If I "have to" or feel forced to do it, this will affect my attitude—then it really becomes work.

Eli Ginzberg, Professor of Economics, Columbia University Graduate School of Business, has over the years studied and written about work, careers, and human resources. In his writings about work he suggests that *every* discipline looks at work from its own perspective. That is, theologians look at moral dimensions, political scientists at legal implications, and medical professionals at health ramifications. So another dimension of work has to do with the viewer's training and interests which cause an emphasis on a particular aspect of work.

To round out our description of work, it is necessary to reflect on the effects of social change. In the last twenty years there has been a relaxation of the "social compulsion" to work. Partly as the result of many years of relative prosperity and partly because of increased productivity we have discovered we can survive without everyone working. It's probable that this change increases the opportunity and the need for psychological payouts as a prime part of the reason to work. In other words, it is no longer just the wealthy but even the person on welfare who can and does look at what one gets out of work besides pay. We have, for example, increasing incidence of people choosing to stay on welfare because they see the change in living standard afforded by work as not having sufficient value.

Work is central in life. A longitudinal study of veterans, extending over thirty years, sought physical, psychological, or other predictors of longevity. The factor which was found to provide the best correlation with the expected length of life is whether or not the individual is gaining satisfaction from work. From your own experiences you can probably verify this need. Have you known someone who lost a job or retired and then seemed to come apart physically and psychologically? This is often attributed to the loss of central purpose—the reason to live. The problems of adjustment to retirement are cited by Morton Puner in *To the Good Long Life* when he says:

> There are at least three good reasons why those who retire often seem to be victims as well as beneficiaries of the pension system. One is the matter of reduced income; a second is the tradition of the work ethic and the loss of role in society; and a third is lack of preparation for retirement and simply not knowing how to use leisure time. *

The loss of role mentioned by Puner is loss of purpose. Hans Selye, biologist, says:

> Man must work. I think we have to begin by clearly realizing that work is a biological necessity. Just as our muscles become flabby and degenerate if not used, so our brain slips into chaos and confusion unless we constantly use it for some work that seems worthwhile to us. The average person thinks he works for economic security or social status, but when at the end of a most successful business career, he has finally achieved this, there remains nothing to fight for—no hope for progress, only the boredom of assured monotony. †

Such a definition of work as a "biological necessity" means broadening our concept of work to include all meaningful and purposeful activity.

---

*   Morton Puner, *To the Good Long Life* (New York: Universe Books, 1974), p. 166. Reprinted with permission.

†   From *Stress Without Distress* by Hans Selye, p. 84. Copyright © 1974 by Hans Selye, M. D. Reprinted by permission of J. B. Lippincott Company.

Some of the many ways of defining or describing work are shown in the following listing. Review of this brings us to a first principle about work. If we are to improve our relationship to it and the outcomes from it, we must know what our perspectives and expectations are for that activity at a specific time and under defined conditions. The specification of time and condition is important because our personal perspective about work is a variable, not a constant.

What is work?

- The activity at which we earn our living.
- The activity which builds self-esteem.
- An opportunity to interact with other people.
- An opportunity to utilize and develop abilities.
- A central theme for life.
- A break between weekends—support for the "real" life.
- A way of finding ourselves.
- A way to gain a sense of worth in the world—status.
- A requirement to live.

There are several ways the individual can bring beliefs to the surface and identify feelings and expectations about work. One way is by means of an exercise of writing completions to phrases. Personal Experiment 3 is this type of self-revelation. It is important in any such self-questioning to delay judging and analysing your answers. Thinking too long about the questions may lead you to list the rational, acceptable, expected answers rather than your real feelings.

A higher level of confrontation can be created by a more extensive set of questions and by applying more energy and time to self-analysis. Questions of this type are included in the companion volume, *Personal Vitality Workbook*. If you are motivated now to dig deeper you may wish to look at Section 4 of the Workbook, Questionnaires 1, 2, and 3. These questions help you to see more sharply "who" it is you take to work, what you bring to work (capabilities, interests), what you find when you get there (environment), and what you take home (outputs). This relationship is shown pictorially in Fig. 2.1, The Work Process, described later in this chapter. As this chapter develops, therefore, you will learn

PERSONAL EXPERIMENT 3

Take a few moments and jot down one or more completions to the following questions. Work rapidly and try not to analyse your answer until you have exhausted your responses. When you have your several answers try to use these answers to describe your outlook toward work.

- Work is_____
- Work should _____
- Work can _____
- Hard work is _____
- My work is _____

more about some of these other aspects of work. So far we have been talking about the beliefs and expectations we take to work.

A still higher level of confrontation of our outlook toward work, leading to deeper understanding, comes from still broader-ranging questions about our values, our goals, and our lives included in the Personal Growth and Vitality Inventory, Section 5 in the companion volume. This inventory helps the individual to assess not only work values but other life values. Sharing these views with others, rapping about them, and seeing how our views stack up with those of others can also deepen understanding and sharpen our perspective. How we confront our work values is up to us but doing so is absolutely necessary in improving our personal vitality. The first principle in understanding work is, therefore: It is necessary to understand our work attitudes, what we bring to work and what we want from it.

The work environment

What we find at work is shaped in part by our perspective and expectations and in part by the values of the organization where we work and its culture. Our far-ranging expectations were addressed in the previous section. In this section we will discuss the work environment and our relationship to work as if the environment can be defined as consisting of a social system and a technical system. Extensive discussion of the social system which transmits values, includes reward and punishment techniques, role assignment, and interpersonal relationships can be found in Katz and Kahn.* Some of the suggested readings also discuss the technical system which includes the process determinants, the work assignments, the equipment and facilities, and the characteristics of the materials. For our purposes now, it's only necessary to presuppose that we are talking about work as represented by an open socio-technical system.

An open system is one which is influenced by outside events and forces. Work conditions are, for example, affected by societal values, laws, and economic conditions. A socio-technical system is one which has both social and technical determinants. As we have seen, work is affected by the relations among people and the values of the working group, and thus has social determinants. The technical processes and the equipment we use in performing work are part of the technical determinants. This perspective will help us share a view of the environment and assure that we communicate clearly about the characteristics of that environment.

There are many work environments and each set of working conditions has several dimensions or aspects which affect those who work in it. Some special characteristics are easily identified but some work cultures and environments are so complex as to require the anthropologist's expertise to unravel. One dimension of work environment is the relative amount of structure, planned control, or programming of individual activity. Each of us can identify work situations which we have classified as highly structured, either because of rules, policies, and practices or because of the technical system. For example, we generally describe bureaucratic governmental work environments as limiting, rule-bound, and highly structured by policies and practices. One has but to contact the Post Office, the IRS, or the auto license bureau to be greeted by books of regulations—rigid structure. At the other extreme, we probably think of the advertising agency work situation as unstructured. This is probably because the Madison Avenue image is one of free-wheeling brainstorming, creativity, and a wide range of individual personalities and styles. For me, the image conjured up is one of a

---

*   Daniel Katz and Robert L. Kahn, *The Social Psychology of Organizations* (New York: Wiley, 1966).

chaotic, unstructured environment. Structure, rules, and limits can also be imposed by the size of the organization, the complexity of the process, or the character of the work. Structure can also be imposed by the technology which is necessary to do the work. The railroad is an example of a highly structured work environment where the rails, the trains, and the signal and control systems set defined limits to individual work variability, creativity, and innovation. Here the technology limits human freedom. By contrast, the technical system can also provide opportunity for unstructured work by building in structure which frees the human being. An example of this is a graphic display terminal tied to a computer with which, by observing a few simple rules and the use of a light pen, myriads of abstract forms and lines can be created with greater ease, freedom, and speed than by hand.

On another dimension, work environments can be described by the clarity of their direction and purpose; that is, defined by the nature of organizational goals and the quality of communications which tell employees what the organization's objectives are. In some organizations these goals are clear and specific and in others vague and remote. Some conglomerates, for example, have had real trouble in spelling out organizational objectives. This is especially true when they are formed by acquisition of unrelated businesses. The process used to define organization goals can create another dimension of the work environment. One organization may be built on extensive individual participation in goal setting while another is characterized by directives from the top. Organizations are big or small, pyramidal or flat, responsive or unresponsive, aggressive or unaggressive, intellectual or anti-intellectual, and on and on. All these are dimensions affecting the work environment. The second principle in understanding work is, therefore: it is necessary to describe and understand the dimensions or characteristics of our work environment, the one we actually find ourselves in and in defining the ideal one that will better suit our needs and enhance our vitality.

An important aspect of work is the need through work and its associations to build identification between the organization and the individual. Environments and particular jobs differ markedly in the ease with which one can build this identification. Each of us needs to belong, needs to feel we are part of something bigger and, hopefully, something we feel is important and worthwhile. When the individual joins an organization, one of the first goals is to gain acceptance, to be seen as an individual who is part of the group. On a person-to-person basis this is considered by those who study work* to be social support. However, here we are putting more stress on organizational identification. One gains organizational identification by accepting the goals and beliefs of the organization at the personal level. One gains organizational identification by receiving feedback from the organization that indicates that what the individual does matters to the organization. This means having an impact on the organization. The individual is, therefore, searching for what it is the organization stands for and testing for a match with personal values. Each person wants to find acceptance and the ability to use personal values in the work environment. The more explicit the organization is about goals and values, the easier it is for the individual to make this match. Written goals and policies and defined management practices make values explicit. Procedural policy manuals and educational programs can also be used to communicate values. Goal-setting and decision-making practices can communicate and create values. An important aspect of an organization's environment is the clarity with which it communicates values. What the values are is also highly important in gaining the commitment of the energies of employees.

The current emphasis on nuclear safety in a time of energy shortages can provide us with an example. Blackouts, brownouts, and electrical power rationing attest to a shortage of generating capacity. Oil shortages tend to force us to look to nuclear power. If we are engaged in the design and manufacture of nuclear power plants our priorities and values with respect to safety will affect the salability of our product and our ability to gain the support and the energies of our employees. In this business, therefore, it is necessary both to state our policies and to demonstrate our support of these policies in our actions. Only if we demonstrate commitment to safety will it be possible for employees who are worried about safety to determine where they stand and if they will work with us. Only if we are open in the creation of policy will professionals feel they have been heard and therefore be committed to achieve the company goals.

---

*   Einar Thorsrud, "Job Design in the Wider Context" in *Design of Jobs*, edited by L. E. Davis and J. C. Taylor (Hammondsworth, Middlesex, England: Penguin, 1972).

The third principle in understanding work is, therefore: organizations differ in their support of the individual's need to build a bond and, therefore, it is necessary to understand the policies and environmental characteristics which affect this if we as individuals are to match our goals and values with the organization.

On a more intimate basis, most of us work as members of work groups. Just as it is necessary to understand the environment of the organization, it is necessary to understand the characteristics of the work group.

Work groups can be supportive or nonsupportive of our individual efforts. If the group is one which accepts each individual and expects performance of each in accordance with ability and need, it is probably supportive. On the other hand, if the group relegates the newcomer automatically to the least desirable activity, this might be nonsupportive for the newcomer. Characteristics which might affect the individual's relationship to the group are numerous; some might include:

- size of the work group
- stability of group work requirements
- range of skills and capabilities within the group
- range of skill requirements in the tasks of the group
- ability of the group to control its inputs and outputs
- ability of the group to monitor its own performance
- freedom of self-determination of schedule and pace
- how much of the process is defined and structured by technology
- reward and pay system
- openness of communication
- method of joining or leaving the group

All these things and more would tend to shape the group work environment and affect the ability of the individual to relate to the group. The fourth principle in understanding work is, therefore: we must understand the character of the specific work group since its characteristics affect our ability to be productive and to gain a sense of satisfaction.

An approach to describing the work environment is presented in Section 4 of the *Personal Vitality Workbook,* Questionnaire 2.

This brief set of questions merely starts the process of personal examination. You are left to find the words and values which seem to you to classify your work environment. As with attitudes about work, the work environment is not constant but ever changing. Sometimes our ineffectiveness at work relates directly to the fact that our perception of the organization's environment is yesterday's and there has been a change. The process of sampling, analyzing, and understanding must be continuous, and the adjustments in our attack must also be continuous as we try to match the changes in the work situation. In other words, understanding the work environment and making it support your goals is a special kind of intelligence.

Two short work examples may help place this need in perspective. Suppose you worked for a manager with dramatic mood swings. You would need to develop a technique for relating to these changes. You might do this by sampling the mood and adjusting your style and activities. For example, when you first engage the manager in conversation you could raise several unimportant issues. By doing this you could test his or her responses, judge the mood, and determine how to bring up the important issue or perhaps decide not to bring it up at all that day. This is sampling and analysis of the social system at a very personal level.

In the late fifties in one of IBM's laboratories we had begun to worry about human obsolescence created by rapid technological changes. After studying the evidence of loss of capability, we decided that massive new educational efforts were necessary. The question was whether to educate those who we thought were already obsolete or those who had yet to become obsolete. Should we try prevention or cure? As we reflected on motivation, we realized no one would be positively motivated by being labeled obsolete and shoved into a class. Instead we established a class in differential equations taught by a dynamic and inspiring teacher and invited the most-recent college graduates to attend. Soon the more senior, potentially more obsolete, employees were demanding to be included. This was an example of environmental design, or the deliberate use of the environment to transmit and change values. The social system was, in this example, modified by the implementation technique and new values were established to which all could respond.

Job descriptions

Many of the problems in finding, defining, or designing the right job result from the inadequacies of our vocabulary and ability to describe jobs. In conversation we tend to use broad terms like doctor or lawyer, but these tell us little about the tasks or the types of satisfactions one can gain. In personnel departments we tend to describe jobs with respect to educational requirements, numbers of people supervised, or financial responsibility.* Such job evaluation helps us set values on jobs and determine proper pay, but it is only marginally useful in matching the individual to the job in the aspects of organizational goals, personal payout, or growth. Some advanced personnel functions have tried skills inventories. In a skill inventory, the individual's capabilities and the job skill and knowledge requirements are all coded. A computer program is used to match individuals to jobs. These systems stress capabilities which are an important part of matching. These systems sometimes fail, however, because of the required, often burdensome information collection and updating.

They also fail because of the inaccuracy of evaluation of an individual's capabilities or because of the inadequacies of the description of the job. In any case, all these systems, other than one-on-one skilled counsel, fail to address the dimensions we are stressing here—the dimensions of goals, psychological needs, payout or satisfactions, and growth and vitality through work.

Thus learning how to describe jobs in new dimensions is part of the challenge of improving the individual's relationship to work. These dimensions must be so constructed that we can teach people how to differentiate and communicate their requirements for these different aspects of work.

Work outputs

Alienation with work makes headlines. When the individual is alienated by work he or she is expressing the fact that the personally desired payouts are not there. What is it we need from work? Do

---

* G. Strauss and L. R. Sayles, *Personnel: The Human Problems of Management* (Englewood Cliffs, N.J.: Prentice-Hall, 1960), Chapter 25.

we all need the same things? Are our needs stable and predictable? Can we design work that fulfills our needs or is there an inherent characteristic of some work that must be done which makes it impossible to provide useful personal outputs? How do our needs change from day to day and throughout life? How do we find out what our needs from work are? Even though there are almost as many lists of needs as there are people studying work, there are still some common elements. The existence of these lists to which most of us can in some way relate our own needs does not mean we value these needs equally. Three aspects are important as we look at work outputs: (1) What is important is the outputs we desire. (2) There is no universal work pattern which will supply all individuals or organizations with the outputs they need. (3) Individual output needs change with time, changing goals, and altered perspective.

The first broad look at outputs can be gained from Fig. 2.1. In this figure the work process is shown as something to which both

---

PERSONAL EXPERIMENT 4

Identify a task which you have to do as part of your work. Pick a relatively simple, short-duration task. Look at the characteristics of that task and see if you can discern any learning which is currently taking place. Place a pad near you on which to take notes while you do the task. Set some arbitrary times for taking stock of what is happening. For example, if it is a one-day task pick several arbitrary clock times (i.e., 8:35, 10:15, 11:00, 2:10, 3:50, 4:30). At those times record *what you are doing, whether you feel stretched or challenged, whether you can learn anything,* and *how you feel* in the process occurring at that time. This type of arbitrary logging of your activity is an easy way to sharpen your attention to your relationship to work. It is not uncommon in this process to find you are not really working; you are bored; you are excited (and skip making any record); you are on some other task; or you are doing something which is not really necessary. What did you find?

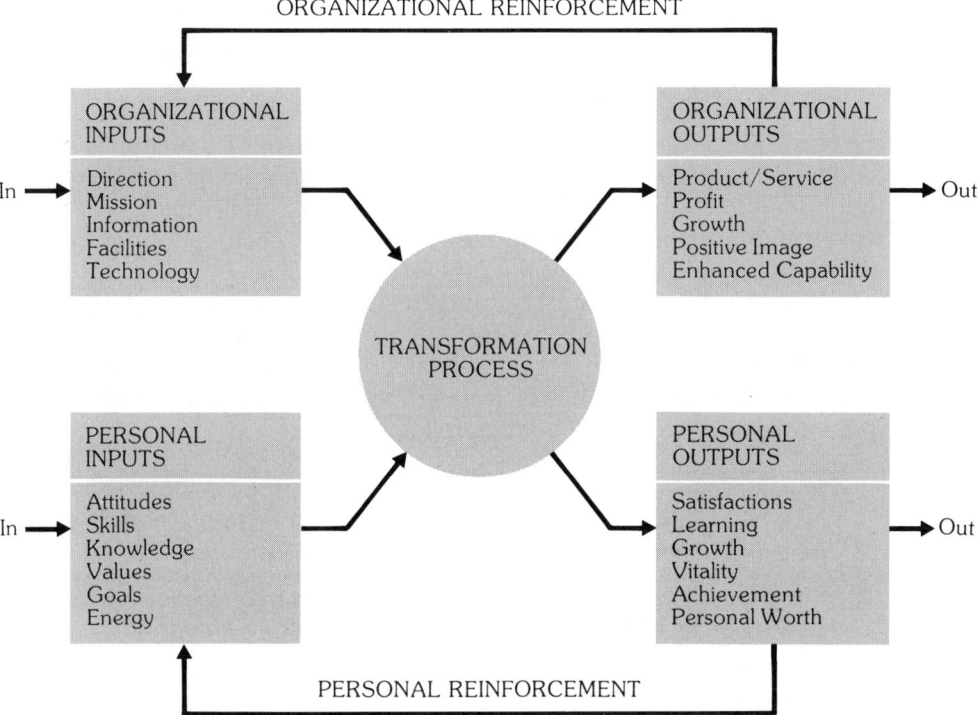

Fig. 2.1 The work process

the individual and the organization bring inputs, combine to do something which we call the transformation process, and take away something which we call outputs. Questionnaire 3 in Section 4, *Personal Vitality Workbook*, asks questions about these outputs. Motivation to work, growth, vitality, and payouts that satisfy are more probable when there is congruence between the goals and objectives for the individual and the organization—if I can gain my desired objectives by pursuing the company's goals, then I will work toward its goals. If the organization as represented by management can understand and agree that pursuing my goals helps them, then they will be influenced to give me some of the freedom I want and need to pursue my goals. The transformation process is the change in the state of material, data, or concepts which is the work to be done. Examples include conversion of raw material into finished product or arranging data so that it has meaning and can affect a decision.

There are direct outputs and there are reinforcements which are reintroduced into the process as inputs. This reintroduction is a feedback loop. An example would be the organization providing the individual with rewards in the form of more challenging work which might in turn cause the individual to increase commitment and apply more capability to the process—work.

Probably the best list of outputs to start with is one developed by Einar Thorsrud at the Work Research Institute in Oslo, Norway. In the Institute's search for industrial democracy and improved quality of working life it has isolated six items as psychological requirements of work. They are as follows:

1. Widened Jobs—*the need for the content of a job to be reasonably demanding of the worker in terms other than sheer endurance, and yet provide a minimum of variety (not necessarily novelty).*

2. Continuous Learning—*the need to be able to learn on the job and to go on learning again is a question of neither too much nor too little.*

3. Decision-making—*the need for some minimal area of decision-making that the individual can call his own.*

4. Social Support—*the need for some minimal degree of social support and recognition in the workplace.*

5. Meaningful relations between the job and the outside world—*the need for the individual to be able to relate what he does and what he produces to his social life.*

6. Desirable Future—*the need to feel that the job leads to some sort of desirable future (not necessarily promotion).* *

There are other outcomes of work which are important depending upon how finely we want to define them. The Thorsrud list does not, for example, mention economic rewards. This is probably good because of our historic tendency to overemphasize this outcome. This particular list of outcomes was chosen to make my point here because it is short and the items relate well to the

---

* Jerome M. Rosow, *The Worker and the Job,* © 1974, by the American Assembly, Columbia University, p. 6. List developed by Emery and Thorsrud. Reprinted by permission of Prentice-Hall, Inc., Englewood Cliffs, N.J.

concept of growth and vitality. There are a few special segments of work which relate even more closely to the vitality goal. Such an expanded list might include the opportunity to teach, the opportunity to communicate beyond the organization in writing and speaking, being on a winning as opposed to a losing program, working with an organization which has high ethical standards, and the chance to have many of the payouts usually associated with being an independent entrepreneur.

Whatever the list, the greatest danger for the individual or the manager is in assuming that because he or she places a high value on one of these outcomes others do also. The goal should be to design a work environment where each person is able to build a good match between his or her desired outcomes and those available within the goals and objectives of the enterprise.

Table 2.1.   Job outlook and job payout

		TYPE OF WORK	
		Repetitive/Boring	Challenging/Growth-Oriented
INDIVIDUAL'S OUTLOOK AND NEED	Work as a vehicle for self-actualization	1 High job frustration Job not delivering what is expected Searching for alternatives—job change (Dissatisfied)	3 High job satisfaction Growing and learning High interest in the job itself (Satisfied)
	Work primarily as means to an end	2 Work provides desired end-income Not too interested in the nature of the work Puts high value on benefits and working conditions (Satisfied)	4 Job fails to deliver what is expected Requires high personal commitment which individual does not want to give Search for job change (Dissatisfied)

Before we start to design outputs which make growth possible, it is important to review the caveat that all people don't want the same outcome. Table 2.1 demonstrates the need for compatibility between job outlook and job payout. Work is divided into two broad categories, simplified for the purpose of highlighting the point. Work that provides little satisfaction (in the forms suggested as necessary by Thorsrud) is shown in squares 1 and 2, labeled repetitive and boring. Work that does provide Thorsrud-type payouts is shown in squares 3 and 4, labeled challenging and growth-oriented. People also are divided into two categories. Those who want work to provide growth, learning, and self-actualization are shown in squares 1 and 3. Those who see work only as a means to an end-life outside work are shown categorized in squares 2 and 4. This latter group subscribes to George Bernard Shaw's aphorism: "Labor is doing what we must; leisure is doing what we like." This table shows that it is just as bad to give a boring job to the person desiring growth as it is to give a challenging, growth-oriented job to the person who works only to support ends which are outside work. Job design, which will be discussed in Chapter 10, should aim at achieving congruence between outlook and payouts. While it is probable that given the opportunity to make work rewarding most of us would want such work, it's also probable that many non-professional employees currently see life as outside of their work. *

Growth through work

One of the identified necessary outputs from work is personal growth. This term can mean a variety of things, and we probably have different images of the way it can happen. Although when we apply the term "growth" to the early stages of life, what we generally mean is physical development, our meaning changes when we are speaking of adults. Then "growth" relates to improved ability to communicate and to acquire skills and knowledge and their use. Growth, then, is being able to do something tomorrow we can't do today. Growth is changing our approach, our perspective, or our values. Growth is gaining in capability.

---

* For those who because of their own liking of work find it hard to take the other view, we suggest a reading of *Working* by Studs Terkel (New York: Avon, 1975). This book consists of interviews with workers about work.

For the individual to grow through work, the activity must stimulate learning by stretching the individual at least slightly beyond his or her capabilities. Work must also provide the information and the opportunity to practice using it which will make adding knowledge or skill possible. Ideally, learning should not be confined to the narrow limits of the specific work but should also provide a vehicle for personal change and expansion of interests and perspective. Referring to the list of psychological requirements, we see that demanding content or challenge are aspects of work which stretch people. A job which leads to something better reflects still another aspect of growth.

Who is responsible?

Responsibility for the process of growing rests with the individual. This is because learning and growth are not things which can be done to people but rather things which result from activity initiated by the individual. Nevertheless, because the activity is the province of the individual does not mean that others have no responsibility.

The organization, through its agents, the managers, has the responsibility to build an environment which encourages growth, to demonstrate that growth is a valid goal, and to provide jobs which stimulate growth. In other words, the internal motivation for growth and the activities of growth in the individual are more likely to appear where the environment provides reinforcements and facilities. An example will bring this point home. Suppose on a job you discover that you lack some information which you learn is available from another employee who is in another part of the organization or is available from a report in a library. You must be free to obtain this information. If your supervisor sets up an environment in which leaving your work place is referred to as "goofing off" or letting the team down, then there is a psychological barrier to your getting the information. Such a barrier, perceived or real, might encourage you to do it the best way you can without the desired information. It would then be discovered later that the information was needed and that the job could have been done better. By contrast, if your manager makes it clear you have the responsibility and the freedom to seek out any information you need, you will be encouraged to grow, to learn, and to do a better job. Responsibility for growth is in this respect mutually shared between the individual and the organization; both must engage in the process.

Summary

The challenge for each individual is to gain self-understanding, which includes knowledge about why we work and what we want from work. By learning about the nature of work and the nature of work organizations we can begin the process of selecting careers and designing jobs and tasks to provide the necessary satisfying outputs. In this chapter some principles necessary in understanding work were described. They are:

- It is necessary to understand our work attitudes—what we bring to work and what we want from work.
- It is necessary to describe and understand the dimensions and characteristics of the work environment.
- Organizations differ in their support of the individual's need to build a bond and, therefore, it is necessary to understand the policies and environmental characteristics which affect this if we as individuals are to match our goals and values with the organization.
- We must understand the character of the specific work group since its characteristics affect the individual's ability to be productive and to feel needed and useful.

When we understand our answers and these principles it is possible to begin learning how to grow through work and how to build a proper work/life balance for the several stages of our lives. Although the chapter discussed work in respect to the individual, this sets up a challenge for the organization which is to learn how to specify, divide, and design tasks, jobs, and work so that work attracts people and provides an environment for growth, personal development, and vitality. In addition, the business must improve and better define and transmit its goals, and its managers must *listen* to the individual's goals.

Only with both the individual and the manager listening and communicating is it possible to negotiate for congruence between individual and organizational goals. This means the organization must find ways for the individual to see that pursuit of organizational goals can lead to reaching personal goals.

For most of us work is a central purpose for life. As such it can contribute to our growth, our sense of success, and our vitality. This will only occur when we as individuals take the time to understand ourselves in the context of work and when we do take the responsibility and initiative for making our work fit our expectations and needs.

Suggested readings

Davis, L.E., and Cherns, A.B., eds. *The Quality of Working Life, Vol. I, Problems, Prospects, and the State of the Art.* New York: Free Press, 1975.

Ford, Robert N. *Motivation Through the Work Itself.* New York: AMACOM, 1969.

Gooding, J. *The Job Revolution.* New York: Walker, 1972.

Hackman, J. R. and Suttle, J. L., eds. *Improving Life at Work: Behavioral Science Approaches to Organizational Change.* Santa Monica, Calif.: Goodyear, 1977.

> *Here is a book which brings together in highly readable form the current thinking about career development, job redesign, rewards, group dynamics, management strategies for improvement, and methods for bringing about organizational change. Quality working life is defined as including fair compensation, safe working environment, opportunity for human development and personal growth, life balance, and social purpose. This book should be a ready reference for anyone interested in improving life at work.*

Herzberg, F. *Work and the Nature of Man.* Cleveland: World, 1966.

Hinrichs, John R. *The Motivation Crisis, Winding Down and Turning Off.* New York: AMACOM, 1974.

Jenkins, David. *Job Power.* New York: Doubleday, 1973.

Katzell, R.A., and Yankelovich, D. "Improving Productivity and Job Satisfaction." In *Organizational Dynamics.* New York: AMACOM, Summer 1975.

Morris, William T. *Work and Your Future: Living Poorer and Working Harder.* Reston, Va.: Reston Publishing Co., 1975.

Posner, B.Z.; Randolph, W.A.; and Wortman, Max S., Jr., "A New Ethic for Work—The Worth Ethic. *Human Resource Management.* Ann Arbor: University of Michigan, Fall 1975.

Sheppard, H.L., and Herrick, N.O. *Where Have All the Robots Gone? Worker Dissatisfaction in the Seventies.* New York: Free Press, 1972.

Work in America, a report of a special task force to the Secretary of Health, Education, and Welfare, U.S. Department of Health, Education, and Welfare. Cambridge: M.I.T. Press, 1973.

3

Changing career concepts and the opportunity explosion

Introduction

Managing life's opportunities is the challenge of this chapter. The changing concept of a career from a single lifelong set of activities to a multiple and changing series is described here as a means for understanding today's career-management challenge. This change in concept and opportunities means we need new ways of describing work, tasks, jobs, and careers. It requires us to build a new vocabulary and new ways to talk about characteristics of work in order to do a better job of matching people and careers throughout life, to take advantage of the myriad of opportunities. A successful career is one which provides the individual with the opportunity to turn his or her self-image into a reality of activities and accomplishments. Career counsel and planning for the adult at the many decision points in life are discussed both as we know them today and as areas needing extensive development.

What is an opportunity for us and how do we recognize it, talk about it, and seize it? This is the challenge. The various elements of the opportunity explosion and our management of it make the process complex. Vocational alternatives have been thought of in terms of classical jobs or careers. But it is now possible to do many new things and invent or design careers or career sequences which can become new central purposes for human activity. Pie Face International, the organization you can hire to throw a pie in someone's face, is a fad-type example of creative invention of a new career. A more fundamental example is a new organization in Palo Alto, California, which will help the individual take advantage of the Freedom of Information Act. This organization will help you search the many records the government keeps about you. Finding new kinds of opportunities is part of this challenge, and this chapter presents suggestions for ways to chart new courses for our lives.

The career

How does a career differ from a job? In the historical sense the distinction was based on the extent of training and the social level of the activity. Working as a shoemaker would have been a job, and working as a doctor a career. Today, although there is some carry-over of this attitude, one's life activity or work most often associated with earning a living has come to be thought of as a career. Thus in today's terms one could call being a stoker on a ship one's career just as appropriately as one could call being a trial lawyer a career. Career now seems more to be characterized by the length of time the activity is pursued and the importance of the activity in the total life of the person. The career thus has become synonomous with one's life work. The career is the pervasive set of activities which distinguishes one person's work from another.

Although in the past careers tended to last a lifetime, people did sometimes change them. But their reasons were different from those we will discuss as representing today's new mobility in career concepts. Formerly reasons for change usually involved lack of the kind of work for which one was trained. Natural disaster such as a long drought might, for example, force a farmer off the farm. Or change came about because of a new opportunity. The advent of a manufacturing plant in a previously rural area is an example of this. Career shifts were often the result of taking a job which seemed to appear by chance. Career changes also resulted from change of locale or travel and exposure to new opportunities. The moving represented by pursuit of the frontier as in Horace Greeley's "Go West, Young Man," was this type of change. The same pressures for career change continue to exist and they have intensified in a future-shock era where change is pervasive. Change is thrust upon us and we can either be buffeted by it or take advantage of it.

A "career" as used in this book will be the individual's pursuit of a series of related activities, built on an educational base and a specific set of skills. This is the central life work for a period of time. Thus an engineer might shortly after graduation be described by his or her education as an electrical engineer. This individual, upon taking a job in an automotive industry, might become an automotive engineer, and later a specialist in ignition systems. In one sense we could say the individual remained an engineer. In another sense we could say that a minimum of two careers have been described here. The first was learning and working at automotive engineering and the second as a specialist in ignition systems. This finer definition of careers is necessary because of the growing complexity and specialization required by work in today's world.

Historically many career choices were made in the family context. The father's activity was often thought to be appropriate for the son, not just because it was the father's but because it was known, could be taught, and was most available. The choice was made early in life and it was considered to be permanent or lifelong.

It was for many a foreordained conclusion rather than a choice. Certainly in the days of slower technological progress, limited geographic mobility, and greater self-sufficiency this career model was workable. Often the son who did not want to follow the family work had to leave home and travel or apprentice himself to another in order to make a different choice. Choosing something different may even have meant defying the family authority and giving up the security and support of the family.

Another form of early career choice also took place in the home. It was somewhat more dependent upon the skills and interests of the child rather than an arbitrary following of the father's footsteps. But it too was a serious lifelong decision. The child who played happily for hours with an Erector set was seen as a prospective mechanical engineer. The child who peered at samples under the microscope was regarded as a budding doctor. The child who was fascinated with collecting bugs and snakes was seen as a potential biologist. It was expected that these early interests somehow signalled what was best for the individual. It was thought that there was one "best" activity or life work and that it related to some aptitude which one was born with.

As education increasingly began to be recognized as providing the possible base for career choice, career counseling was introduced in schools. Exposure to various subjects was used as a way of determining interest and aptitude. It was often perceived, however, that the education merely exposed or opened up something which was already inside the person. The son or daughter who showed prowess in math and science was counseled to become a math teacher or to go into scientific-based work or engineering. The youngster who showed ability in English was counseled to head toward teaching or writing. As education became a developer of careers, the connection between educational ability and work ability became fixed. Prowess shown in good school grades meant the individual should be what society saw as the logical outcome of these courses. Personal choice was not yet a large factor in career selection.

Inherent in this view of careers were three concepts which may not have been valid then and certainly are less valid now. First was the thought that there was *one right career*. Each human being had a set of interests and skills which, if properly matched with activity, led to the best career. The second concept was that, whatever the career, *it would last for life*. This led to the familiar pattern of joining a company upon graduation, working for many years, receiving the gold watch, and retiring at age sixty-five. The engineer went to college for four or six years and then built a forty-year professional life on that education. The doctor entered long formal education, followed by internship for several years, eventually to embark on a lifelong career of medicine. Even the liberal arts university graduate, although not seen as prepared for a specific career because of the generality of his or her education, was expected after one or two early trials to find a niche and pursue one activity for life. The third concept was that *the career must provide the main income or support*. Careers were seen almost totally in terms of earning a living.

This pattern of early and fixed choice of careers was also a part of the stereotyping of roles for females. Certain play patterns for girls were acceptable in the culture. The girl who played with the Erector set was unusual. The girl who excelled in science and math was facing an uphill battle with parents and school authorities if she wanted to study engineering. Even if she somehow got specific college training, getting married and raising a family was the culturally expected career. Today's pressures for change in the woman's role and acceptance of more open career choice for women have combined to lead to multiple careers. Expanded opportunities exist in part because of the changing concept of careers, and in part because of new freedoms for women.

The new career concepts

In the last twenty years, primarily as the result of rapid changes in technology, the concept of professional life consisting of several careers has begun to emerge. This is a cultural change. A second change, which will be discussed more thoroughly later, has also worked to create the practicality of more than one career. This change is the opportunity explosion. These are associated changes. Technical progress creates change in life modes and increases opportunities for new kinds of activity. Increased opportunities through new activities can in turn also spawn technological, cultural, social, and life-style changes.

There has been, and continues to be, a tremendous growth in the numbers and kinds of activities available for people who seek them out, are interested and motivated to try them, and are persistent in developing the necessary skills. In many cases they must even define or invent the activity. A third change influencing career concepts has been the tendency of the college student to disconnect education from life work and career. It is difficult to separate cause and effect. Thirty years of general availability of jobs and general prosperity helped to create this separation. So too did the fact of not having to work to live. When we do not have to work all day to provide the necessities, we open the opportunity for choice. As a result, students tend to see college as a part of the life experience. Historically we saw it as preparation for life. They see life as a continuation of experiences. Formal education is but one set of experiences.

A fourth change affecting careers and work has been the emerging possibility of separating the job-centered career from the necessity of earning money. An example is a career of prime interest which does not bring in money, although it may have the potential, but provides personal psychological satisfactions. Often "a job" is taken to support the career. An example is the person who drives a taxi to live but whose career, actualization of self-image, is as a writer. One could say there are two simultaneous careers. The same might be true of some artists, philosophers, ski-bums, travelers, and on and on. The rising importance of personal satisfactions and psychological payouts has many far-reaching impacts on career concepts, job design, and maintaining and extending vitality. The chance for satisfaction to become an element of career choice is a benefit of our technological progress and relative affluence.

The early discussions of multiple careers and much of the study of the topic were based on the feeling that it involved dramatic shifts. The engineer who became a doctor or the executive who became a potter or the housewife who became a writer are the images brought to mind. The currently emerging understanding is that for many, probably most, the shifts from career to career are more subtle and often not even recognized or consciously recorded.

Career-mobility models, dramatic shift and subtle change, all require the creation of new career-counseling techniques and the design of personal career-management and migration processes for the adult. Since career counsel was seen as an activity for the young, the need for a whole new kind of planning process and thinking about careers has been recognized and has begun to

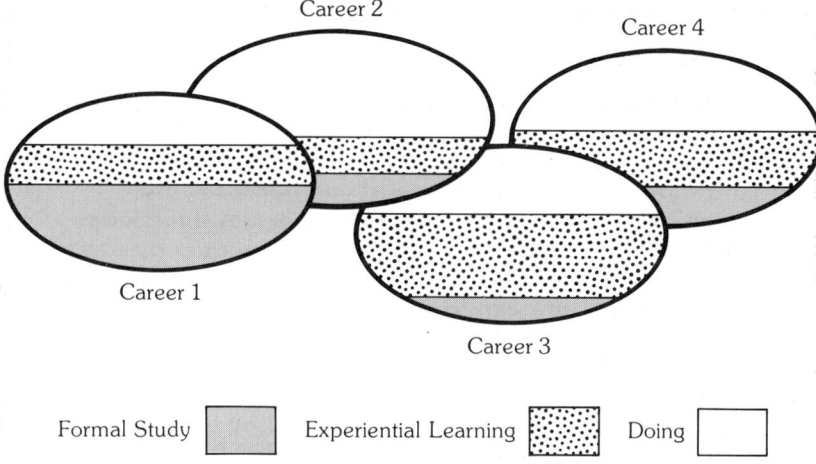

Formal Study [ ]   Experiential Learning [:::]   Doing [ ]

Fig. 3.1 Career transition in today's world

evolve in the last ten years. Except for the counsel of the executive-search outfit, "head hunter," or placement service, the evolution of career-counseling knowledge applied to adults has primarily occurred among a few consultants interested in life planning, those interested in family and social counsel, and personnel professionals generally internal to large organizations. Before further discussion we should understand the career sequence model as shown in Fig. 3.1.

The pictorial representation shows several features of the career sequence which are important. First, each career is made up of at least three elements. A necessary prerequisite for each is a skill and knowledge normally acquired in formal learning. For the first career, building this base, usually in college-level education, is a large element of the activity. Subsequent careers require varying amounts of preparation dependent in part on how much can be carried over and how much is new. The activity proportions are also dependent on the availability in the work situation of formal study as compared with experiential learning, or learning by doing. For adults, generally learning by doing becomes an increasingly important part of building the capability base. In fact, there are studies of adult learning which emphasize the necessity for new learning to be tied into a work need and the opportunity to use the information

PERSONAL EXPERIMENT 5

Describe your current career in a few words on a piece of paper. Next ask yourself some questions about that career. Is it your first, second, or third? Place it in your career sequence. How did you get into this career? List three or four skills or areas of knowledge which are necessary for this career. How did you attain these capabilities? Did you prepare by formal training or gain most from experience? How long have you been in this career? How long do you think this career will last? What might bring it to an end? Can you define a possible next career? Would this career utilize capabilities you now have? Are you doing anything to gain the new skills or knowledge needed for the next career?

or skill.* Each career also contains an element of execution—doing or applying the skills and knowledge. A career is not whole without this application of capability and receipt of feedback from accomplishment including the reinforcement of satisfactions or payout. A career is not whole unless it has the elements of learning, application of capability, and psychological income from doing in the form of satisfactions.

How one manages the transition from one career to another and the timing of the change is important in life management. Little is known about this and what information does exist as knowledge to be passed on seems to be more an art than a science. This subject will be discussed under the matching process.

Another element of career management is the process of making a choice as to what the next career should be. This decision-making requires the self-sufficiency and inner security necessary to take the risk of change. In addition the individual needs understanding about his or her own interests and capabilities, and must make an assessment of the potential payoff of a new career.

---

*   Eunice Belbin, "Activity Learning and the Older Worker," *Ergonomics*, October 1964.

The individual must determine whether the change is worth the price.

An example of the type of career change represented by the diagram should bring home the point. Historically a typical entry career for the electrical engineer joining the computer industry was as a circuit designer. A next career was often as designer of a product or system. This change required increased knowledge of system function and the customer's needs. Some of the computer knowledge gained as a circuit designer could be carried over. However, working on a product or system required a deeper and broader understanding of how computers process data and new knowledge about alternative ways of handling data processing functions. New skills were required which go far beyond the layout of a circuit.

The matching process

It would be good if matching careers and people or people and careers were as simple as finding the right piece for a jigsaw puzzle. The problem is in part that the jigsaw puzzle piece which is the individual keeps changing, being molded by both outside and internal forces. Some shapes simply feel better to an individual than others. In addition, individuals are different in their consciousness of their own shape and their desired shape. From time to time the person-piece is subjected to pressures in the puzzle which create great urges to pop out. So even putting the piece (individual) in place is not a process which is easily accomplished.

The puzzle—the life, career, and work—into which the piece or individual is to be fitted is itself also constantly changing. All of the parts in the puzzle which are already in place are changing shape too, however slightly. Some pieces of the puzzle are popping out seemingly at random, thus creating new openings. At the outer edges the puzzle is still being built and some parts of the puzzle occasionally fall off the table and are destroyed. It is a wonder that we ever fit people and puzzle together, however crudely, even for a short period.

To complicate the picture further, there is probably no great jigsaw-puzzle player in the sky sitting above it all, able to view the whole process and place the right piece. The pieces of the puzzle are expected to play themselves! The individuals must understand their shape, how and how much they can change in shape. Individuals must also assess the openings in the puzzle and how these can be varied. Individuals must also sense the potential of new space at the edges as well as the potential for a part or section of the puzzle falling off the table. Isn't it a wonder any of us ever find a meaningful career even for a short while? Yet viewed from another perspective, what a wonderful place to play with all those career opportunities and all those chances to grow and change.

Matching, therefore, requires self-understanding in the sense of who we are and who we want to become. It also requires some view of the opportunities or the extent of the playing table. Matching is a sequential or iterative process. Successful matching requires trial-and-error testing, feedback, and change of direction. It is as if we don't know how the hole in the puzzle will feel until we attempt to fill it. But there are clues. A clue would be that we've previously gotten a "kick" or positive feedback from a particular kind of activity. If we perceive that this positive feedback is part of the expectation from the new career, we get a positive input for matching and a suggestion of a way to manage transition. Sometimes we can create opportunities to try the new. A temporary assignment is an example. Sometimes a course of study or a training program provides a simulation or trial. Matching thus merges into managing transition.

Other aspects of managing transition include those activities which make it possible to leave the old. For example, arranging to reduce your load by shifting responsibilities to another can create the time and energy available to try something new. This process is both physical in the sense of displacing work, and psychological in the sense of preparing yourself to let go.

This is enough discussion to establish the challenge. "How to" techniques will be presented later. The changing concept and reality of a career today creates needs for new kinds of skills, knowledge, and activities. Even learning and practicing the art of career transition could be a new career.

Describing activities

One of the challenges of managing careers is sensitizing oneself to opportunity and a second is sensitizing oneself to self. This means learning to describe what one wants to do and the needs one has. When a manager needs another employee the tendency is to describe the function with one of the job classifications in common usage. The manager says he or she needs a records clerk, a circuit designer, an applications programmer, a first-grade teacher, or a psychiatric nurse. These examples communicate an image of function and a concept of the training and skills necessary. They are an effective shorthand. But the magnitude of differences in first-grade teaching assignments and the range of functions possible within the job classification of applications programmer are legion. So therefore a manager needs a better vocabulary and needs to get deeper into the activities and characteristics of the job.

In matching people and their desires to a career, job classifications don't help very much. For example, they don't provide a technique for evaluating such factors as the amount of decision making, or the amount and kind of fixed or programmed activities, or the feedback one gets for completion, or the social support from fellow workers. In other words, job classifications are not sufficient to define the design characteristics of the activity and thus don't help in matching people and activities except at a very gross level. If, for example, an individual requires short-term physical evidence of accomplishment for a sense of worth, we must find a way both to determine that a career provides this and to describe it.

When we look at job classifications as descriptions of job tasks and capability needs, we find they are equally deficient. What does the classification of systems programmer tell us about what the person does or what skills the person must have, or how much experience is needed? Is the function primarily one of writing lines of code or is it one of devising systems within which someone else will write the code? Is it a job which uses the language of the computer or a job which uses the language of the user? The questions could go on and on.

These examples have been intended primarily to demonstrate that for career choice and career management we need an improved language or system of description. This descriptive system must provide the capability of describing jobs at the task level and also the availability and kinds of psychological payouts from the activity.

A major challenge, therefore, flowing from the multiplicity of activities which make up our complex world is the need to find ways to communicate and negotiate. Proper career matching is not finding the perfect fit, but rather being able to describe a job well enough to attain a partial fit. It is also possible that being able to describe the tasks is prerequisite to changing or modifying the tasks. For example, we must be able to communicate about a task before we can determine whether it is best done by a human or a machine. We must be able to discuss a job characteristic such as the need for support from fellow workers before we can judge whether the applicant is compatible with that work style. We must be able to describe the types of feedback the person can expect from accomplishment before we can determine whether the applicant will be comfortable with that job.

Opportunities

When we had an agrarian economy and grew up on the farm, our career opportunities were limited. The career was farming. The jobs within that career ranged from milking cows, to planting corn, to cultivating and harvesting. Dependent on whether the farm specialized or was essentially self-sufficient, some marketing and distribution skills were necessary. Today by contrast we live in an environment where the opportunities are so vast no one knows all of them and a prime problem is finding techniques and systems that expose us to opportunities. This has been called an opportunity glut. Within it there are two broad categories of opportunity. First are those opportunities which are defined and described, and second are those that are currently indeterminate and awaiting creative description or design.

Opportunities which are already designed and described are seen in an organization as openings or potential openings. If someone has occupied the position, then what that person did is used to describe the opening. If no one has occupied the position, then the person defining the need tries to describe it sufficiently to communicate the need and attract someone to the activity. Opportunities which are already described show up in the outside world as employment advertisements or openings described by an employment service. Some new services exist which offer you, for a fee, those opportunities that appear to match your skills or knowledge. The major problems in matching with these kinds of opportunities are sheer quantity, the difficulty of categorizing yourself, geographic remoteness, lack of clarity of career and job descriptions, and inaccuracy or lack of timeliness of data.

Far more challenging, more necessary, and yet elusive is the matching of people to potential activities—careers and jobs as yet undescribed. A couple of unique examples will show what is meant.

Our recent heightened interest in air pollution and smog has created new jobs. We now need people as pollution measurers and monitors. Some of these people work with fixed-base equipment stations that are tied into computers. Other measurers are roving samplers who drive from place to place and sit beside the road in cars where they can use portable equipment. Each position requires people with specific interests, abilities, and training. What kind of people are needed? If one had a potential for this kind of work how would one have known it before the job was described? Until we have some experience, we will probably overspecify the skill and educational needs. As an example, early programmers were drawn exclusively from the ranks of Ph.D.'s in math though such accomplishment is no longer required and may not have been necessary.

The advent of a new piece of equipment often changes the nature of a job, the skills required, and the types of people who can be attracted. For example, computer-supported supermarket checkout stations have now been designed and are being tested. Such equipment will eliminate the need for the checkout clerk to read prices and to punch keys to record prices. Many of the other duties remain essentially the same. How will this change in required skills change the nature of the job? Will the checkout clerk's public-relations and sales functions be enhanced? What new functions might clerks take on? Will this make a demanding and tiring job more attractive and thus open this as a job opportunity for new groups of people? If you were to hire a person for this job today how would you set up the specifications for skills and how would you describe the job?

Another feature of our times that extends the range of opportunities is the possibility of separating one's career of interest and aptitude from the work one performs to earn a living. Some members of the younger generation have done this by working at some job until they save enough to live for a while and do what they want. An example of this is the free-lance or roving programmer who works in short bursts. Many who work for organizations such as Manpower Incorporated or Kelly can work in this pattern. Here the interleaving of the realization of self and the required process of earning a living are sequential. The typical historical situation was that these were simultaneous. Although some may consider these people "drop outs," many of them have found creative and meaningful lives. They have learned to manage the system in order to achieve a better match with their psychological needs. They may, in fact, represent a new breed, a precursor of the "career manager" I am saying we must all become. The executive who leaves a job having reached the point at which the financial build-up made possible doing what he or she has always wanted to do is another example. Still other examples are those who respond to their psychological needs part time. They alternate between "the job" and the "desired job"—one night and one day or some other form of regular alternate scheduling.

Life planning as a basis for career management

If we accept the thesis that the proper basis for planning and choosing a career is the understanding of self, then we need a process for revealing, describing, and communicating relative to self-image and capabilities. Various processes exist. Most of them depend on the individual's being asked a series of questions which reveal beliefs, attitudes, goals, interests, personal characteristics, and other aspects which describe him or her as a unique individual. It is not as easy a process as it sounds, for generally the first responses to such questions tend to be the socially acceptable answers. Often the answers are the ones we think we believe, which we feel are safe, fitting our vision of what society expects. For example, when asked whether we like our job we often test the questioner by seeing how he or she reacts to slightly negative material or very positive material. Seldom will we blurt out our honest feelings. We do not because we do not know what is really behind the question. We do not because we feel it may not be safe. Our additional responses will probably be more dependent on our perception of the questioner's values and interpretation of our answer than our true feeling. It is also possible our true feeling is not acceptable to us and, therefore, has been repressed and covered with the same mask we show the world. Whatever the process, we must get through to the true self in order to do life and career planning and life and career management. For those who really have blocks and have deeply repressed themselves, psychiatric or psychoanalytic help may be a prerequisite.

Since I believe in growth, change, and vitality, I believe the self can change. It is necessary, therefore, in the process of revealing self to have a way to deal with "current self" as opposed to "ideal or goal self." Usually this is achieved by questions which reveal how life is working for us separate from those which ask us what we desire or what we feel would be an improvement.

Life planning, life scripting, exercises in drawing life lines, citing good and bad experiences, listing goals, and responding to questions are all part of the process. They are as good as the individual using them will let them be. They will not reveal secrets but they will help the individual to be more explicit. Use of such questionnaires requires strong motivation to find our true self, and strong motivation for improvement. Many such workbooks fail because the individual is unwilling to invest enough energy or take the risks of revealing self. The challenge is to find the technique which helps each of us get closer to understanding ourselves.

One of the ways to find new opportunities is through self-analysis of interests, strengths, and weaknesses. Such self-analysis sensitizes us to what's important, thereby sharpening our ability to identify potential opportunity when it is seen. It is somewhat like our increased ability to see and identify clouds after studying clouds. We may become sensitive to the fact that one of the attributes which makes for a successful experiencing of ourselves has to do with the characteristics of the challenge. That is, we discover that it makes a difference whether it is the challenge of the search, the challenge associated with physical change, the challenge of reaching into the unknown, or the challenge of reaching some new height of achievement. If we know which of these challenges work for us, then we will be sensitized to see these types of challenge in the new activities we look at. Knowing how life works for us heightens our perception and sharpens the definition of our expectations.

Once you can describe yourself, it is then possible to set goals for change and begin to build a plan which moves in that direction. Matching opportunities to yourself requires this understanding.

Career guidance and counsel

Career guidance and counsel is the process of creating the situation which catalytically helps the individual to engage in self-revelations, to make choices and plans. A good counselor is like a mirror. The presence of the counselor helps the individual to see himself or herself more sharply. A good counselor is also a source of information on techniques of understanding self and a source of information about careers, jobs, and opportunities.

Guidance in this sense is not leading; it is the process of providing maps and references. By providing benchmarks, references, and comparisons, the guidance counselor can help the individual see self movement and change. It is only possible to see change with respect to something. The counselor can help to provide this something.

An important responsibility for the effectiveness of guidance and counsel falls on the user of this service. One who seeks counsel must understand the perspective of the counselor and the responsibility differences between counselor and counselee. The counselee must also know when to break off and manage on his or her own. The responsibility of choice remains with the individual. The responsibility of choice must not be put on the counselor or accepted by the counselor.

Summary

The challenge is to improve our ability to identify opportunities which will provide payout in satisfaction for us. The challenge is also to know ourselves well enough to match ourselves with opportunities. By understanding ourselves, our interests, and our capabilities, and where we get our satisfactions, we sharpen our perceptions of opportunity. Successful careers are those which allow us to realize ourselves, to play our roles and gain satisfactions from the process of living and working. Since the process of living includes change and growth of ourselves, then it follows that the right role or career is a changing, moving target. By becoming more conscious of who we are and how we're changing, and by adding to this some knowledge of how careers are built and how we move from one to another, we are able to take the first steps toward responsible management of our lives. This management responsibility never stops since it includes another sequence of choice about careers in retirement. Here, too, we may grow and be vital. We must not let events or our environment stultify us, put us in a corner to dry up and blow away.

Suggested readings

Becker, H.S., and Stares, A.L. "Careers, Personality and Adult Socialization." In *Vocational Guidance and Career Development: Selected Readings*, by H.J. Peters and J.C. Hansen. New York: MacMillan, 1971.

Haldane, B. *Career Satisfaction and Success, A Guide to Job Freedom*. New York: American Management Association, 1974.

> *Bernard Haldane has spent most of his life helping people to change jobs. In this book, he shows the reader how to change jobs and gain more satisfaction from the new job. He introduces his system for identifying motivated skills. This means he helps you to identify those things you can do well which also provide satisfaction or payout. He also addresses goal setting and how you develop congruence between your goals and the company's or your boss's goals.*

Kellogg, M.S. *Career Management*. New York: American Management Association, 1972.

Schein, E.H., and Van Maanen, S. Massachusetts Institute of Technology. "Career Development." Chapter 2 in *Improving Life at Work: Behavioral Science Approaches to Organizational Change*. J.R. Hackman and J.L. Suttle, eds. Santa Monica, Calif.: Goodyear, 1977.

Super, D.E., and Bohn, M.J., Jr. *Occupational Psychology*. Belmont, Calif.: Wadsworth, 1970.

Super, D.E., and Jordaan, S.M. *Career Development: Self-Concept Theory*. Princeton, College Entrance Examination Board, 1963.

Thompson, Paul H., and Dalton, Gene W. "Are R & D Organizations Obsolete? New research findings indicate it is more the organization, than the individual that becomes outdated," *Harvard Business Review*, November–December 1976, pp. 105-116.

4

Obsolescence
and
aging

Introduction

Human obsolescence and aging are believed to be evidences of the erosion of vitality. Probably the greatest damage to vitality is caused by the *expectation* of decline and reduced capability, which in turn contributes to real decline. Obsolescence in people is perceived as reduced motivation and capability. This loss causes them to be seen by others as nonvital—difficult to fit to jobs and utilize—not able to pull their own weight. If others feel a person cannot do a job, that person doesn't get the opportunity. Not being utilized can, in turn, contribute to more loss of vitality.

There are many kinds of obsolescence. Obsolescence can result from not keeping up-to-date in a rapidly changing field. It can result from a diminishment or total lack of need for your particular specialty. It can result from not managing your life or from a defeating career. These and other kinds of obsolescence are discussed in this chapter.

I believe that it is desirable and possible to avoid obsolescence by changing our life and work styles. In this chapter I will suggest preventive techniques or cures for personal and organizational obsolescence. Obsolescence is a point of view which may thwart the individual's confidence in his or her ability to be productive and successful in life and work. The individual need not succumb to this point of view, however. Instead, he or she can choose not to become obsolete and can do something about it.

Age as a cause of decline and obsolescence is most often only a convenient excuse. Concepts of aging, age and achievement, and ways of creating a positive attitude about aging are presented to heighten our understanding of the challenge of maintaining vitality despite aging. Obsolescence and age are discussed as separate but related elements of decline in capability, for it is possible to be obsolete and young, or old and vital. Age itself does not create vitality nor cause its loss.

The changes in perspective, values, and the nature of life which occur sometime between the ages of thirty-five and fifty-five are presented as the valuable crises of mid-life. While these changes can provide motivation for change, opportunities for new roles, and improved vitality, they can at the same time provide the potential for decline. Which potential is realized is up to each of us. Managing the mid-life transition effectively can open a new range of positive outcomes for the individual.

Mid-life crises are crossroads not only for the individual but for organizations as well. They too can age and become obsolete. The phases of birth, adolescence, mid-life, and decline of an organization probably parallel the life cycle of the individual. Ways of turning these challenges to the organization into improved vitality, productivity, and continued success are suggested here.

This chapter, part of the challenge section of the book, cites the problems and suggests ways people can overcome the negative effects of life which contribute to obsolescence and aging. There are three primary themes which pervade this book. First, that for life to be a growing, expanding, successful venture with continued productivity there must be a central purpose. A second theme is that, to a large degree, one's expectations shape what happens. Third, what happens is the individual's responsibility and it can be managed in a way to improve chances for success and vitality. Changing our concepts and expectations about obsolescence and aging is a primary step in maintaining vitality and managing growth.

Obsolescence

To be obsolete is to have low value because capabilities have declined or are no longer useful. A human being can be obsolete. A machine can be obsolete. A concept can be obsolete. An organization can be obsolete. Some things which are obsolete may take on added value when they become classic and are collected for their uniqueness or historical value. Human beings, however, do not share this increase in value by becoming classic except, rarely, many years after their death.

Obsolescence occurs only with respect to some environment or ground. The figure is the individual and the ground the environment or setting against which you see the person. Obsolescence implies that the individual, object, or organization is out of context with its environment. A green eye-shaded clerk on a high stool would be seen as obsolete in a computer-oriented environment. But put this same individual on stage in a production of Dickens' *A Christmas Carol* and the clerk fits. Thus the environment or background changes our perception of the eye-shaded clerk's applicability. So it is in life. Obsolescence is a perception and may or may not be a reality.

Obsolescence is perceived when an individual, object, or concept fails to change in an environment which has changed.

Countering obsolescence, therefore, requires growth—change and adaptation—to match the change in environment. Or it requires a change of environment to one which is compatible with the unchanged element. If we could find an environment which required green eye-shaded clerks and we put the clerk in that environment this would balance the individual with the situation. Life, however, does not provide us with this opportunity. Therefore, the individual must learn to adapt to avoid obsolescence.

Seven kinds of obsolescence are listed here.

Obsolescence — the elements

- Decay of knowledge once learned
- Skill loss through nonuse
- Failure to add new knowledge
- Decline in energy and motivation
- Failure to adapt to change
- Diminished need for functional specialty
- Diminished acceptance by organization

It never occurs as purely one or another of these aspects. And probably the rate of increase in obsolescence or decrease in vitality is neither continuous nor the same for all elements. Just as maturity is not achieved as a monolithic attribute, obsolescence is multi-faceted. Obsolescence in one or more of these aspects probably exists for all people. Obsolescence becomes a problem when it becomes evident, fixed, and a dominant pattern for the individual as perceived by others. It is also a problem if it is perceived only by the individual since this personal perception will lead to changed behavior and probably reduced performance.

A muscle must be used to maintain its health and ability. A piece of knowledge must be used to remain active, viable, and available for use. This is the point behind the first category. An example of decay through nonuse, for the American, is the foreign language studied in school. Decay through nonuse may be all right if there is never to be a need. In this case keeping it active would be wasted energy.

Skills, like knowledge, decay with nonuse, although they are not totally lost especially if they require coordination and muscular control. Once one has learned to ride a bike the skill will remain without use. It can be rejuvenated. One who has once learned to

---

PERSONAL EXPERIMENT 6

**Find an aspect of your work or life which requires
cognitive knowledge for pursuit. An example might be
an activity which requires mathematics and, specifically, certain mathematical calculations. Other examples
might be knowledge of a market, knowledge of English
grammar, or analytical capability tied to a specific
field of knowledge. Make it as simple as you can,
narrowing the example from your work to an area of
information that is fairly easily documented. When you
have picked this piece of work list five types of knowledge you believe are needed to do it. For each of the
five types of knowledge rate yourself as obsolete,
current, or leading. Next test your assessment by
reading the most advanced information you can find in
several of these five areas. The purpose of the exercise
is to test your perception of your own currency. Were
you about right in your assessment?**

---

ski can again ski depending upon motivation and muscular health.
The feel comes back. In both knowledge and skills the rejuvenation
requires a need and the personal motivation and decision to do
something about it.

For the scientist and engineer the failure to keep up with the
onrush of new information has been featured as the main cause of
obsolescence. Certainly it is important in a rapidly changing field,
but stuffing oneself with new facts does not guarantee vitality.

Energy level is related to physical and psychological health and
to motivation. To the extent our health declines, and this is something to which we contribute as much as it befalls us, our energy
declines. Such a decline often contributes to our lack of commitment and thus our not being as useful or productive as formerly.
The expectation that decline is normal and acceptable can itself
contribute to decline in motivation. It is possible too that this decline
is related as much to lack of desire as it is to lack of energy. Our failure to adjust goals and set new objectives or our failure to perceive
payoff from effort can negatively affect our motivation and our
apparent energy, and thus cause us to be perceived as obsolete.

Failure to adapt to change can result from not seeing the change, from too strong a desire to remain the same for personal safety, from lack of understanding of how to change, or from perceived requirements which are seen as keeping one from changing. These examples demonstrate that for each one of these elements of obsolescence there are multiple perceptions of reasons or rationales. Being a glass blower when glass blowers are no longer needed or a horseshoe maker when cars, rather than horses, are used, are examples of loss of need for functional specialties.

Loss of acceptance by the organization is another way of saying one belongs to the wrong team or political party. For a myriad of reasons one can, as a result of past actions, statements, or contributions, be ruled out of play by others. The several types or elements of obsolescence already mentioned demonstrate the pervasiveness and multiple causes of obsolescence.

Aging

Since human beings have a defined life cycle beginning in birth and ending in death, it follows that there is a process of aging. In the biological sense, despite continual replacement, some of our pieces and parts deteriorate and eventually function declines. Much has been done in the last century to extend the duration of human life, but the process of aging is normal, natural, and carries with it some positive aspects. For example, increasing age often allows us to rid ourselves of some self-limiting anxieties that we had in our younger years and thus serves to improve our actual performance.

Although biological aging can reduce our capabilities, it is probable that the results of biological aging seen in the context of our culture are the real problem. Here again we have a figure and ground contrast creating a perception which affects our behavior. Teenagers visiting a retirement home, or senior and graying employees in an organization where the majority are young, create this contrast. These contrasts make aging a problem more than the actual aging itself. For example, the promotion of a young person as manager of a group of senior people can set up expectations for change and declining responsibility. Our organizations then create expectations of decline which reinforce or accentuate the actual biological process. We seem to have made more progress in slowing biological aging than in cultural change which extends the usefulness of the individual.

This cultural reinforcement of aging occurs not only in the context of the organization itself but also in society. For example, we are all affected by the idea that retirement should occur at a specific age. This was an invention of the 1930s. The creation of Social Security set up a prescribed age for retirement. Thus the law has created behavioral-adjustment requirements before sixty-five (phasing down) and after sixty-five (retirement, or adjusting to not being needed). Despite these creations of our society we know we do not all age at the same rate or arrive at the point of retirement at a fixed age.

Upon retirement, the loss of work, the loss of a life purpose, may do more to contribute to a decline than biological aging. Many older people seem to have less purpose today than similar older people had in the preindustrial era when they remained integral to the family and carried on certain necessary family functions.

In the context of work and careers, we have a cultural bias which ties career selection conceptually to the beginning of the decline. Sarason, Sarason, and Cowden suggest:

> The process of making a career choice is the first significant confrontation with the sense of aging, involving as it does the knowledge or belief that such a decision is fateful because it determines how the rest of one's life will be "filled in."*

That this happens is true. It should not happen. Those selecting engineering as a career know, based on much writing and perhaps the experience of friends, that they are starting out in a profession where one can become obsolete in five to seven years. The concept of "one career" is so ingrained that the inevitability of decline is built in at the time of choice. This can and should be changed. It is another example of how social determinants affect aging.

In some fields experience is expected and believed to make the practitioner better. In other fields, in which the rate of change is great, experience may be perceived as getting in the way of creativity, innovation, and progress. In high-technology industry, for example, the young and freshly educated are generally preferred to the experienced. The young are seen as full of fresh knowledge, full of energy, and willing to take risks—not inhibited by past

---

*   S. B. Sarason, E. K. Sarason, and P. Cowden, "Aging and the Nature of Work," *American Psychologist*, May 1975. Reprinted with permission.

PERSONAL EXPERIMENT 7

**Think of something you would like to do which is
childlike and do it. Examples might be building sand
castles on the beach, skipping or jumping rope,
plucking the petals from a daisy, riding a merry-go-
round, trying mirror writing, or creating a fantasy and
sharing it. These are but a few examples. The point is
to let yourself out of your role and see how it feels.
Don't worry or care about what someone else thinks
or says — just do it. Could you do it? How did it feel?
How do you feel about it now? Vitality is being able to
be childlike, and aging is represented by rigidity and
an inability to do something childlike.**

failures. In still another way, this example demonstrates how our
social expectation of decline establishes the conditions for decline.
We tend to give the frontier challenges to the young in science and
engineering; thus the older engineer, not getting the assignment,
doesn't have the opportunity to learn and grow. When an
individual is not expected to try, he or she becomes less capable.

John Gardner expresses the problem of aging and the cultural
reinforcement for aging in *No Easy Victories:*

> We all know people who retire psychologically when they are in
> their thirties or forties. They may continue working for another two
> or three decades, but psychologically speaking they have turned in
> their uniforms. Perhaps they just grew tired. Perhaps they were
> trapped by circumstance. Or perhaps they were defeated by self-
> doubt or fear or cynicism or self-indulgence.
>
> In contrast, we all know people who at advanced ages retain an
> incredible freshness, curiosity, awareness and enthusiasm.
>
> I do not believe we need to leave that outcome to chance. If we
> want to improve the quality of life for older people, we should do
> everything possible to increase the number of persons with the
> capacity for self-renewal.
>
> Every institution in the society should work to that end. We are
> going to have to design our institutions so that they encourage

continued learning and growth through in-service training, career-development programs, career counseling, systematic reassignment in the interest of growth, and sabbatical periods for study. *

Aging in the individual occurs in three broad categories: biological, psychological, and social. Elements of each of these categories are shown below. Biological decline is built into the structure of the body, yet it does not occur alone or in a vacuum. We as individuals can influence the rate and nature of this decline. We can accelerate it by expecting it and giving in to it. We can decelerate it by exercise, positive self-image, and training. Psychological aging affects biological aging. Probably biological aging in turn affects psychological aging.

Types of aging

Biological
Energy
Health
Reaction times

Psychological
Emotions
Capacities
Perceptions
Learning
Feelings

Social
Social habits
Status
Role fit

Psychological aging results from change or deterioration of self-image. For example, our impression of whether or not we are needed affects our feeling of worth. If we feel we were not asked to participate, not needed or involved, this raises questions about our worth. These questions in turn can cause activity patterns which

---

*   John W. Gardner, *No Easy Victories* (New York: Harper & Row, 1968), p. 154. Reprinted with permission.

increase the probability of our not being asked the next time. Our capacity to do something is at first not limited by true inability but rather by our expectation of not being able to do it. The expectation can lead to a loss of ability. There are many examples of tremendous feats of strength which defy our expectations of human capability. This occurs because so many people undervalue their own abilities. The trigger seems to be strong motivation and failure to accept the idea that it can't be done. Breaking the four-minute mile is a good example. There is also, for instance, reasonably good evidence that our real ability to learn does not fall off significantly until very late in life. We are left then with the fact that any decline in learning must relate to personal expectation, goals, self-image, or motivation. Sometimes aging seems to bring on an increased impact of our self-doubts—feelings of inadequacy. That is, we tend to exaggerate feelings which we managed or repressed earlier in our lives. This willingness to accept our doubts can increase psychological aging.

Social aging has to do with the interaction of the individual and the environment. If, for example, society expects older people to slow down, this will set up conditions which encourage, or make acceptable, slowing down. Once we have played a role, it tends to fit and society tends to set up conditions for maintenance rather than change of role. Role rigidity is an aspect of aging. Role rigidity is partly due to our interaction with those around us and partly to our own internal beliefs, feelings, and attitudes. For a fifty-year old to skip from his car to his office door is not expected or acceptable from the perspective of society. It may also not be acceptable to the individual even if we could remove the pressures and presence of society. Failure to adapt and change is the result of self-limitation, actual social pressures, or perceived social pressures or limits. For mom to buy the children balloons is okay. To buy one for herself is not okay—it doesn't fit the role. Yet being able to be childlike is undoubtedly important in maintaining vitality! The child in us is the manager of our vitality.

Aging of the organization

We've talked mostly of the aging of the individual. The processes are similar for an organization. Most often the birth of an organization stems from an idea, a perceived need, and the energies of a founder or creator. In early life the organization draws heavily on the founder and begins to create beliefs, capabilities, and function. As it grows, it begins to do some things repetitively and to institutionalize these activities—it learns. It adds paper and procedures which substitute for face-to-face and spontaneous activity. As it matures it becomes less dependent on the founder and more dependent on its rules, principles, and procedures. Procedures and paper can be thought of as equivalent to hardening of the arteries in an individual. If the organization sticks to its ways in the face of changing needs, it ages and decline begins. It is obsolete and dies when some new organization absorbs or replaces its function.

Phases of life

Each stage in life contains both opportunities and risks. Many early attempts to define life phases concentrated on youth, partly because of psychologists' interest in learning, formal education, and adolescence. Most classifications lumped all adulthood into one category. More recently a better-balanced perspective has developed and with it the understanding that each phase of life has attributes which should be studied. Recent but separate studies developed by Roger Gould of UCLA, Daniel Levinson of Yale, and George Vaillant of Harvard demonstrate this newer approach. They see the stages as : 16-22, leaving the family; 23-28, reaching out; 29-34, questions and crises; 35-43, mid-life explosion; 44-50, settling down; after 50, mellowing. *

The importance of the several phases is in understanding the separate needs and goals they represent. The techniques for managing life necessitated by these phases are closely related to the new understanding of careers. In other words, the interest in and need to define life phases beyond childhood and adolescence has grown with extension of life, the increase in opportunities, and our understanding of the accelerated rate of change.

Understanding the phase of life you are in does not make it easier to live with the stresses and opportunities. It does, however, let you know that something of what is happening to you is normal and others have experienced it. Whether it is mellowing or creating a new life-style that occurs after fifty, it is reassuring to know that it

---

* *Time*, April 28, 1975, p. 69. (The Havinghurst life cycle referenced in Chapter 5 provides a similar total life perspective.)

is a time of change and opportunity. The challenge lies in learning to adjust our goals and apply our energies as befits our stage of life.

Intellectual ability and learning

The great debate on the decline of IQ and the loss of learning ability with age seems to be waning. As new facts come in, it appears that there are different kinds of intelligence and that some decline and some stabilize or grow with age. Measures of learning ability which demonstrated decline with age are generally being shown to be faulty in method rather than showing real decline.

A quote from Baltes and Schaie will clarify the reasons why intellectual ability and ability to learn are now seen as not declining for a given individual.

> For a long time, the textbook view coincided with the everyday notion that as far as intelligence is concerned, what goes up must come down. The research that supported this view was cross-sectional in nature. The investigator administered intelligence tests to people of various ages at a given point in time, and compared the performance levels of the different age groups. Numerous studies of this type conducted during the 1930's, 1940's and 1950's led researchers to believe that intelligence increases up to early adulthood, reaches a plateau that lasts for about 10 years, and begins to decline in a regular fashion around the fourth decade of life.
>
> The first doubts arose when the results of longitudinal studies began to be available. In this type of study, the researcher observes a single group of subjects for a period of time, often extending over many years, and examines their performance at different ages. Early longitudinal studies suggested that intelligence during maturity and old age did not decline as soon as people had originally assumed.
>
> As better intelligence tests became available, researchers began to realize that different intellectual measures might show different rates of decline. On measures of vocabulary and other skills reflecting educational experience, individuals seemed to maintain their adult level of functioning into the sixth, and even the seventh decade. *

---

*   "Aging and IQ: The Myth of the Twilight Years," in *Psychology Today*, March 1974, p. 35. Reprinted with permission.

Work and aging

One of the ways the individual realizes personal potential and becomes an identifiable self is through work. To the extent that specific work is seen as the role of youth or role of the aged, work contributes to the sense of aging. Work can either contribute to the feeling of aging or delay aging depending on what it asks of the individual. If there is a decline in challenge presented to the individual, this will tend to reduce stimulation and thus probably contribute to aging and obsolescence. By contrast, continued challenge could cause striving and thus maintenance of ability. But too much challenge, which frustrates and increases anxiety, could literally cause one to give up and increase the feeling of aging and limitation. Balance between one's abilities and one's job and life demands, therefore, is necessary to maintaining ability and slowing aging.

The absence of work, or some central purpose, can contribute to a loss of the sense of being needed. This loss in turn affects one's feeling of self-worth and capability and thus could accelerate decline at any age. For example, young people laid off because of economic problems have shown a loss of self-worth and decline in motivation which looks very much like one aspect of aging. If they are out of work for extended periods they have to learn to work all over again. Retirement, like a layoff, by depriving the individual of a purpose can contribute to aging. In fact, the concept of retirement, the very thought that it is desirable to give up and do nothing at some point in life, may itself affect aging.

Mid-life or career crises

No one knows where the middle of career or life is. Mid-career does not occur at a fixed age. It results from a combination of factors. It is not the feature of any single profession. To a greater or less extent, mid-career and mid-life can present a problem and a challenge for all people. A mid-life or career crisis is not new to our times but it is probably accentuated by rapid change. It is not fatal. It can be a useful motivator for reexamination, new goal setting, and an opening up and expansion of life quality and potential.

The mid-career challenge

- Boredom—Loss of zest for life and work
- Aging—Biological, psychological, and social
- Obsolescence
- Questioning of values—Goal changes
- Changing work motivations
- Apparent reduction of career potential
- Feeling of increased potential for loss of position or job
- Changing home life
- Onset of apprehension about retirement and death

The central elements or aspects of the mid-life or mid-career challenge are shown above. Because aging and obsolescence have already been discussed nothing further will be said here except that the crisis exists because the individual accepts the reality of aging and obsolescence. It is as if the decline occurs from birth on but somewhere between the ages of 33 and 55 all of a sudden we notice it. At that point we become self-conscious about it, and begin to worry about what it can do to us, worry that we have lost opportunities, and are impacted by a perception of reduced potential.

Questioning of values leads to changing our values and goals. Partly as a result of change in our culture, partly as a result of the phase of life and perceived success or failure, and partly as a result of changing needs for income, one of the values which is questioned is the reason for work. It is normal for such questioning to heighten the interest in and value of psychological outcomes from work as compared to financial and promotional reward. If one can't realistically expect a salary increase, then, for example, the sense of the worth of one's work should and probably does become more important to self-respect. Real change in work motivations may be discovered or created. Certainly, ladder-climbing becomes less probable for most people at mid-career. Accepting this, the individual may realize new freedoms of expression and action. Because of the apprehension about life ending, there is a heightened search for life's value, for an answer to the question, "For what will I be known?"

For some the onset of the crisis will first be perceived as a loss of zest for life and an overwhelming sense of boredom. It may come as a feeling of being "ripped off" by life; that is, "If this is all I get why did I try so hard?" It may come from a feeling of being trapped. At mid-life it is normal for the family provider to find an enhanced feeling of the need to support all his or her dependents, to feel the yearnings for escape, and to blame the lack of risk taking and change on these responsibilities. It may be the result of the way life has been lived with ever-narrowing interests and the turning off of awareness; that is, the very process of living may have reduced the capability to undertake alternatives. It may result from the simple feeling that one's ideas have been exhausted and since the problems remain the same, nothing can be done.

For those to whom life has brought financial success and position, the worry can take on another dimension. The question is usually, "Am I really worth what I'm being paid?" Comparison of self with the new crop, casual or pointed comments about being highly paid by superiors, and a budget "crunch" can bring on this anxiety. Or it can be heightened by seeing someone else get the promotion one had sought.

At home real changes in family structure can cause questions. With the children growing up and leaving home the financial and psychological drains of parenthood are reduced. This may bring on the feeling: Now I can do what I've always really wanted to do. This is an aspect of the freeing up or opening up of potential which is part of the change. On the issue of life planning and setting of objectives, retirement begins to move into the normal planning cycle. When one is twenty-five, retirement is not real. When one is fifty, it is a very real prospect. With this passage of time come new opportunities and new anxieties.

Few of us face all these aspects of the mid-life reassessment at the same time and probably we don't all experience all of them. Identified or not, conscious or not, however, the reassessment goes on and a crisis of sorts develops. Surviving it necessitates taking personal responsibility for managing the transition. While survival requires change, radical and precipitous change should probably be avoided. Instead one should try changes and build in new directions only after payoff from a trial or small change builds self-assurance and security for further change. Opposed to the danger of precipitous change is the problem of becoming mired in constant analysis. Thus the crisis and sense of problem may become circular and self-reinforcing. Such a stewing and failure to make some decisions and changes heightens the crisis. More of how to manage change will be discussed in Sources of Solution and Putting It All Together.

Hobbies and other interests

Breadth of interest is both a characteristic of a vital person and a measure of vitality. A characteristic of aging is a narrowing and a reduction of interests. It follows, therefore, that an individual who can remain open to new ideas and experiences has a better probability of a long and productive life. As individuals we need to search for ways of maintaining openness and expanding our interests. For expansion of interests we should look beyond the central elements of work, family, and self. The challenge is to understand where interests come from and how to cultivate them.

Reading, hobbies, contacts with new people, and associations with groups are all sources of expanded interests. Reading exposes us to the thoughts of others and increases the probability of excitement with new data. Just any reading, however, does not meet the test. Books and articles should be selected which go beyond our normal tracks.

Hobbies are a major source of new interests. This is especially true if they support the development of skills and knowledge not currently needed in the major activities of our lives. New skills build competence for alternative activities. Having alternatives on the back burner, so to speak, provides the individual with flexibility to manage change and ways to develop new and different life patterns, roles, and balance. When the major purpose of life is lost, as in a layoff or retirement, the presence of an alternative interest provides the clues both as to how to change and for direction of change. Such is true when a hobby substitutes for the work that is lost. This is also true when the alternative interest provides entry into new organizational relationships or the base for an entrepreneurial venture. Richness of alternative interests represents vitality, strength, and a way to reduce aging and obsolescence. Cultivation of new interests and finding ways to enhance one's alternatives are challenges of life management.

Contacts with new people provide opportunities for expansion of interest. Because in a new relationship we are not forced to defend our role and the new acquaintance has no detailed knowledge of what to expect from us, a new contact allows us to be more open. This is also true for the other person. A combination of this freedom and openness with the probability that the experiences of the two people are complementary and supplemental thereby opens new interests and ideas for both. To expand your interests, to offset aging—meet new people.

When you or I contact a new group, as in meeting a new person, we open the channel for expansion of interests and ideas. Groups come together for the purpose of sharing and pursuing shared interests and objectives. In joining a group, you or I make a commitment to accept and support some of the group's ideas and objectives. Joining, therefore, is an act of expansion provided we're not just finding compatibility and safety for our current beliefs. Sociability and changing group memberships are also techniques for expansion of interests and extending and enhancing vitality.

Extensions of life

There is exciting work going on in the introduction of people over seventy to some of the growth-movement activities. Known as the SAGE* project, the group has shown that it is possible to take people who were in the process of winding down and turning off and give them new interests, new motivations, new purposes for life and enrich the quality of their lives. Actually these over-seventy participants do it to themselves. Generally all the professionals do is to introduce the techniques and demonstrate that they care. As a result of their successes these senior citizens are extending this activity to other senior citizens. This is an example of new life purpose. Some of these techniques and processes hold real promise for extending useful meaningful life.

Studies of longevity have come up with some findings which we can use in our own lives. For example, the more successful you are the longer you will live. Studies do show that those in any field who distinguish themselves seem to average longer lives. Like many of the things we talk about in this book, this reinforces the need for understanding your work as a major life purpose and designing it so it provides satisfaction, growth, and vitality. For when these are the rewards, you will tend to be more successful and productive. This leads to the finding that those who have a positive outlook toward life, those who enjoy living, live the longest.

---

*   Senior Actualization and Growth Experience, Berkeley, California

Being young and feeling young are different. It is the sense of youth that appears more important than actual age. Feeling young or vital comes from a life that is working, that you feel positively about. Such a feeling is most probably based on a sense of achievement, a feeling that what one is doing will make an impact. This is being productive. One might conclude, therefore, that finding and maintaining a purpose for life which uses your capabilities and leads to a sense of accomplishment is the fountain of youth. Doing these things to extend your life, however, must take place in groups and with others. The ability to relate to others, to transcend self, to communicate, and to serve is closely related to the need for a productive purpose. To find your purpose and perform it in a vacuum will not suffice. We humans are social beings and those who master and maintain their ability to relate to others tend to live longer.

Summary

Aging happens to individuals, concepts, things, and organizations. Sometimes by losing contact with necessary activity, people become obsolete. This chapter discussed the nature of obsolescence, pointing out that obsolescence is not just failing to keep up-to-date in knowledge but rather a multifaceted, multicausal change. Aging and the phases of life with their problems and challenges were also reviewed. The mid-life, or mid-career crises were described as normal changes in the perspective and goals of the individual. The relationship and function of work to the process of aging was described. Positive work was seen as delaying obsolescence and aging. Negative or unchallenging work was seen as contributing to aging. Hobbies and other ways of expanding interests were discussed as sources of delaying decline. The challenge is to maintain vitality and personal growth in a world which can be corrosive and contribute to decline of capability, interest, and productivity. Our future-shock times have increased the forces which contribute to a sense of obsolescence. Our social expectations have conditioned us to accept the debilities of aging. Our institutions tend to support role rigidity, social aging, and psychological aging, even in a time when medical science can delay biological aging. Vitality requires that we find ways to combat these pressures for accepting aging and obsolescence before we really have to.

Suggested readings

Baltes, P. B., and Schaie, K. W. "Aging and IQ; the Myth of the Twilight Years," *Psychology Today,* March 1974.

Birren, J. E. *Handbook of Aging and the Individual.* Chicago: University of Chicago Press, 1960.

Birren, J. E. *The Psychology of Aging.* Chicago: University of Chicago Press, 1964.

Dalton, G. W., and Thompson, P. H. "Accelerating Obsolescence of Older Engineers," *Harvard Business Review,* Sept.-Oct. 1971, pp. 51-67

Kaufman, H. G. *Obsolescence and Professional Career Development.* New York: AMACOM, 1974.

Lehman, H.C. *Age and Achievement.* Princeton: Princeton University Press, 1953.

Leshan, E. *Wonderful Crisis of Middle Age.* New York: McKay, 1973.

Mandelbaum, B. *Add Years to Your Life.* New York: Grosset and Dunlap, 1973.

Puner, Morton. *To The Good Long Life.* New York: Universe Books, 1974.
> *Here is a book all about growing older. It explodes such myths about aging as the supposed decline in intelligence which we now know doesn't really occur. Author Puner discusses nutrition, the role of the older person, the biology of aging, the relationship between the age and achievement, and the challenges and needs of retirement. In the final chapter he discusses the characteristics of those who live a "good long life," including those you can do something about and those you can't.*

Sarason, S. B.; Sarason, E.K.; and Cowden, P. "Aging and the Nature of Work," *American Psychologist,* May 1975.

Zelikoff, S. B. "The Obsolescing Engineer," *Science and Technology,* April 1969, pp. 46-51.

5

Life balance

Introduction

*Among the challenges to success and happiness in the business
world, none — none — is so overwhelmingly difficult and so potentially pervasive in its effects as the challenge of maintaining a
proper balance between home life and business life.* *

This statement by Dr. Barrie Grieff, a psychiatrist at the Harvard Business School, sets the stage for our look at life balance.

Discussing the issue of work/life balance is necessary in part
because in Western culture we have developed a separation of
work from life. Work has taken on separate meaning and separate
values. This separation probably started in early Roman and Greek
times when work was considered punishment and was, therefore,
bad. It was assigned to slaves and was not part of the good life!
Later, work became a way to serve God and, still later, working
became goodness in itself. Even without the separation of work
from life, balance among all possible activities or places to spend
our energies is a necessary goal. Our culture carries with it expectations that certain phases of life will cause us to give priority to specific activities. Balancing our goals and our interests with the expectations of society is a challenge. Schooling, for example, has been
considered the right activity between the ages of five and at least
eighteen. Managing our life balance requires more active personal
management as the alternative life activities increase and multiple
careers become possible. For example, to make education a major
activity past sixty-five years of age is a way of finding purpose in retirement. The freedom from toil, the expansion of opportunity, and
the chance to make personal decisions and take personal charge of
what happens in our lives has created the necessity for increasing
our ability to manage life balance.

"To live to work or work to live, that is the question." This play
on Shakespeare's words is a second part of our challenge. How one
apportions energy and interest to gain the most satisfaction from life
is a question of life balance. We shall consider how the individual
assigns and modifies personal priorities, ways of adjusting to the
various conflicting needs for energies and interests, and the ways
these change, from day to day and life phase to life phase. The process of balancing the three main elements which make up
life—work, family, and private personal activity—are reviewed by

---

*   James Morgan, "The Executive Family," *TWA Ambassador*, Nov. 1975,
p. 16. Reprinted with permission.

using the concept of personal space. Each element is discussed in terms of its potential effects on vitality and growth. A suggestion is made for improving the vitality by changing the design or nature of the element, as well as one's relationship to it. The individual's responsibility for life balance is seen as central to making life a satisfying, vitalizing growth-oriented experience.

Personal space

Learning to use the concept of personal space provides a means for increasing personal understanding of our life balance, and increases one's ability to manage it. Our personal space is that piece of the world which contains all of our relationships, our desires, our goals, and our understanding of our place and role. How we picture this space and how we fit into it is an important part of our self-concept. Every individual needs and develops a self-concept as a means of managing relationships with the world. Life is to a great extent the process of attaining this self-concept. It is not something we're given; rather, it grows through experience. Realization of a healthy self-image requires growth, periodic modification, and satisfaction from the process.

We can think of personal space first as a segment of physical space. We develop a sense of physical space around us which is ours. This can be demonstrated in part by recognizing that each of us has a comfortable physical distance between ourselves and others for various activities. When talking with someone face-to-face, what is your most comfortable distance? Or, for example, if you want to be alone, where would you position yourself on a park bench if others are also present? Where would you sit at a cafeteria table if you wanted someone to sit down with you? Personal space in this physical sense has been well documented by Robert Sommer in *Personal Space*. In this book, primarily for designers, he looks at understanding personal space as a necessary input to the design of cities, buildings, and products.

To work as a guide in achieving life balance, the concept of personal space should be taken beyond physical space. When we are concentrating on some individual activity such as reading, writing, or watching TV and someone speaks to us attempting to get our attention, this may be an intrusion into our personal space. An example is the case of the regular commuter by train who plans on using the time for reading but is invaded by a friend who sits down nearby and wants to talk. When someone interrupts us in the middle of a conversation, this can also be an intrusion into our personal space. Personal space as a concept, therefore, can be seen as including all of our activities—thinking, writing, talking, and relating—anything of which we are part is part of our life space.

In a still broader sense, personal space is represented by our contacts with other people, knowledge we've encompassed, and information about ourselves and our lives. Our beliefs, attitudes, goals, and feelings are all part of ourselves and therefore part of our personal space. Our innermost thoughts and desires are part of private personal space, and those we have shared are part of a revealed space which is public. In this sense, there are layers which represent how far we've gone to make our relationships and perspectives explicit. Private or unshared and shared or public are two different layers. By revealing some aspect of ourselves, we don't lose it; it's still a part of us, only now it has been shared. Thus, all our direct personal contacts and even our indirect contacts through media such as books, films, or TV are part of our total personal space.

Personal space or life space as concepts can help us to understand our relationships with individuals, groups, organizations, movements, and bodies of belief. If you define a space which at its outer limits represents the total you, it is possible to define within that space the part you share with your work (employer), your school, your religious activities, your family, or the goals and objectives of a group to which you belong. Gaining a feeling of how you share your space, from an energy-time-interest perspective, can be helpful in your search for increased satisfactions and positive payout from life. Sharing of your space can probably be thought of best in terms of energy. The concept of time seems too limited and by contrast we can expand energy. It is important, too, to learn to sense the need for change in emphasis, to find ways of compensating in one part for losses or gains in another part, and to set long-range goals for improvement in balance.

Figure 5.1* shows personal space pictorially as a basis for developing and understanding life balance. The outer limit of gray is constantly expanding and changing shape and defines total space

---

* The *Personal Vitality Workbook*, Section 6, contains a personal-space exercise for your analysis of your own life balance. Now may be a good time to do this exercise before you read further. However, it is the sort of projective, personal-analytical tool which can be used at any time.

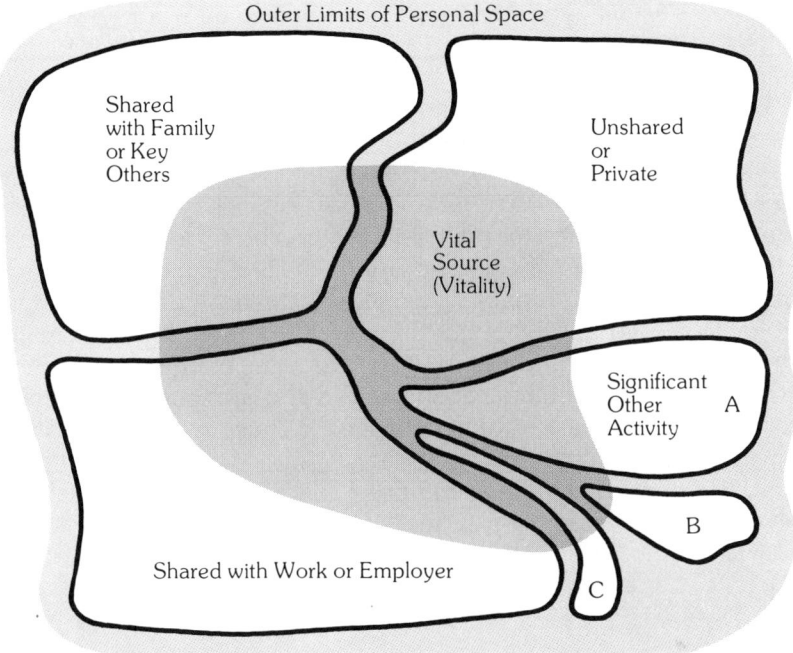

Fig. 5.1 Personal space

at a given time of analysis. You can think of it as a picture of how you spend your energies. Three major activity/relationship areas have been defined.

In our example the relative areas described for family, private, and work-related life show, in this case, the portion of space devoted to that activity by one hypothetical individual. The central portion designated as vital source is intended to show the relationship of satisfactions or payout to each of these applications of personal energy. The vital source is the psychological income and reinforcement, the amplification of energy we feel when we spend our energies successfully and gain a sense of growth and accomplishment. Payout or vital source can also be thought of as the recharging of motivations, or an energy supply. The overlap portion of vitality related to an allocation of personal space reflects how well that segment is paying off.

Other activities and relationships can also be pictured. For example, community service, religious, and special organizational memberships can be shown as needed to define your individual space properly. In our example, these are shown as significant other activities A, B, and C. Although it is important to reflect your major uses of energy, it is also important to keep the picture as simple as you can. Putting in too many activities may overwhelm you with the complexity of life balancing. The pictorial representation is best drawn as of a particular time in life. Usually this is longer than a day, for you don't engage in all activities in one day, but it probably should not be longer than a few months. In this way you can look both back and to the future to highlight changes. In other words, these areas change in shape and relative proportion dependent on your interests, your perception of needs, and the satisfactions you get from them.

Now consider Fig. 5.2. Suppose an individual has just taken a new job. The probability is that as a result a larger portion of energy, time, and attention will be given to the job. This means the

PERSONAL EXPERIMENT 8

Identify a period in your life when your job (your main activity) was very demanding of your time and energies. If possible, pick a period when this lasted long enough that you felt you were out of balance, and perhaps others commented about it or you lost opportunities to do things you really wanted to do. An example might be work that interfered with a vacation, or work which caused you to drop out of some activity or group, or family activities so demanding that you gave up something else you wanted to do. Now try to identify what actions you took or what happened which helped you to rebalance your life. Did you consciously do something to rebalance? Are the techniques you used ones you would use again? Can you discover other techniques or activities which you could have used to reestablish balance? What are the conditions which lead you to feel your life is in balance?

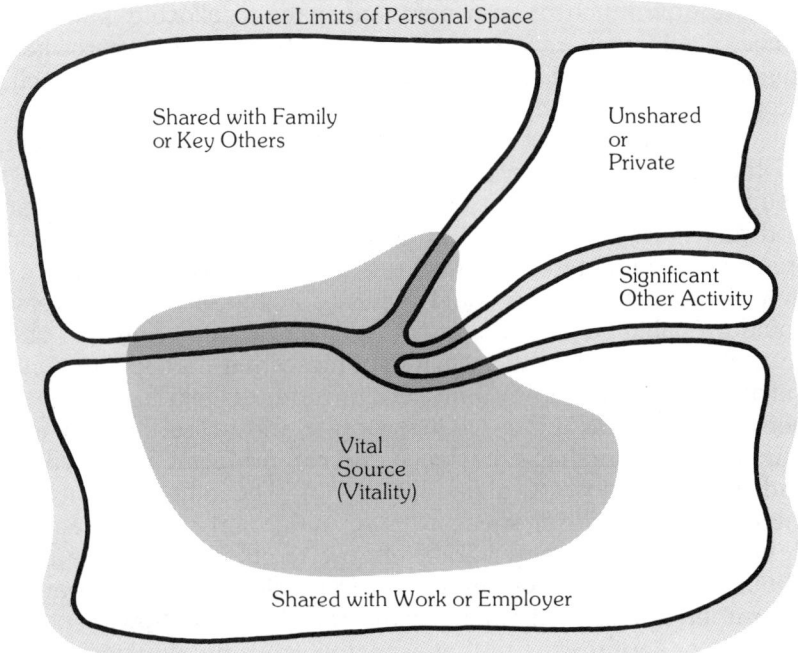

Outer Limits of Personal Space

Shared with Family
or Key Others

Unshared
or
Private

Significant
Other Activity

Vital
Source
(Vitality)

Shared with Work or Employer

Fig. 5.2   Personal space

"shared with employer" space will be larger at least for a time. If this greater expenditure is paid off by increased satisfactions it probably will grow some more as will the portion of vitality shown related to that work segment. If this space grows too much it will impinge on other areas. Figure 5.2 shows a possible life-space picture with large energy devoted to work, and a resultant major contribution to that person's vitality. As an example, a lot of overtime could cause that kind of growth of the work segment of your personal space. The time shared with the family thus will decrease. You might, however, devote more energy to family relationships. Something may be gained or lost in this relationship as a result of the change. Achieving a new and satisfactory balance will require adjustment and change on the part of the individual and probably each member of the family. It may require rebalancing of other segments of your life space. How to achieve these adjustments and how to determine how much of your personal space to allocate is the challenge of achieving a work/life balance. Life balance requires keeping all the segments in proper relationship to each other and each in proportion to its contribution to your vitality.

The outer limits of the personal space are defined by the edge of the gray area. For the growing, vital, alive person these boundaries are constantly expanding. As we make new contacts and gain new interests and knowledge, we enlarge our personal space by including in it the new relationships, new information, or new skills. In fact, if we could measure it, the vitality of a person could probably be judged by two aspects, the rate of growth of life space and the size of the vitality source within that space. Action initiated by others can also invade, intrude, or help to enlarge our personal space. Whether we incorporate and utilize this new input is up to us. We manage the space and can protect it from invasion, and we can choose to expand it or not. The other person may, therefore, expand our space or may make part of our space less desirable to us. We may literally choose to cut off or eliminate part of our space as no longer useful. Usually this is not a deliberate act but rather a kind of dimming with time. It could, however, be a blocking or suppressing of that aspect which is not working well for us.

If you think about some friend out of your past with whom you shared pleasant experiences but whom you have not seen for a long time you can experience this dimmed, unused personal space. This is probably a positive piece of your space. Recalling a painful incident and/or relationship which didn't work out well and which you have deliberately blocked will help you experience a negative part of your unused space. The blocked or dimmed part is totally lost but it is not easily activated. It can be revived by recalling it or making fresh contact. You have the power of choice.

The private part of personal space contains the unshared aspects of your life. It may include time spent on hobbies or in activities in which you are alone. It includes contemplation or meditation time. It includes daydreaming time and sleep time. You should be careful, however, to exclude sleep time since it may distort the picture and give the feeling of more private activity than is truly the case. Private space contains the time you spend thinking about yourself. Such expenditures can be a source of exploration and satisfaction as well as strength. For example, the person who loses a job and makes a successful adjustment usually draws heavily from the content of private space, perhaps by moving an activity from hobby status to serve as a major life purpose.

Private personal space is drawn upon for study and enlargement of skills and knowledge. If one takes educational course work in the evening, it is private space which becomes enlarged. Extra-hour study can also reduce the time available to share with family, work, or other activities. It requires adjusting goals and rebalancing priorities. Each time we enlarge or change the balance we are making growth possible but not assuring it. To the extent that we change balance consciously, we are making the judgment that by investing more energy and time in a given segment we will get more in return. Getting more psychological income should contribute positively to vitality. Sometimes the balance is shifted for us by events such as illness, change in family status, or loss of work. Even when the shift appears to come from outside, what we make of it—how it affects vitality and growth—is the result of decisions we make and how we change emphasis in our life.

The primary front between us and the world is at the outer limits of personal space. Secondary fronts exist at the boundary of each subsegment of life space. One can think of the boundary of the private personal area as representing a more sensitive or tertiary front in the relationship of the self to the world. This inner interface bounds that part which includes inner thoughts, desires, and goals. It includes our subconscious and the storage of our beliefs and knowledge. It can be thought of as representing a risk boundary as we attempt to gain personal stability. Those parts of us we've put into active service are in the work-shared, family-shared, and activity-shared space. Those parts we've chosen not to risk are in the private part. *

A life-balancing story

John was a successful young engineering professional. He had graduated from a top-ranking engineering college and gone to work

---

* A discussion of this aspect can be found in Donald B. Miller, "Privacy: A Key Issue Between Employees and Managers," *University of Michigan Business Review*, Jan.-Feb. 1976, pp. 7-12.

for a small electronics firm. The company was growing rapidly and John grew too. In a few years he was promoted to manager of a small engineering group, he got married, bought a home, and became involved in the community both through church and a local good-government group. After a few more years the young family had two children and John had been promoted to a higher-level engineering-management position. Although there were often hot projects and meetings which took many evenings and weekends and he had to give up his involvement in the community, he felt his life was well balanced. His wife did not share this view and felt she was bearing too much of the home responsibilities.

The small company was bought out by a large organization. New management came in above John from the parent company. There were many new rules and limitations, and he began to feel he had less and less opportunity both to influence the direction of the company and to grow in responsibility. In fact, he was gaining less satisfaction from his work. He seemed unable to do anything which pleased management and began to think about leaving. At this time, however, there was a recession and several engineers in the community were out of work. Home life wasn't going along too well either, in part because his lack of satisfaction from work often brought him home in an ugly mood. He felt he had no outlets or alternatives and didn't feel right about getting reinvolved in the community. Community work also didn't increase his pay and provided little outlet for his engineering talent. He was beginning to feel trapped.

What does this brief narrative suggest about life balance?

1. It is probable that John had devoted too much of his personal space to work. Therefore, when work provided too little satisfaction he had poorly-developed alternative interests.

2. As far as the story goes, we have no evidence John has tried to re-tune or change the work situation where he is. Rather, he seems only to be thinking about a major change.

3. It is probable that John moved or was moving from one phase of his life to another and had not thought about or reassessed his goals.

4. A distortion of one segment of his personal space (work) impacted other segments (family) and (significant other activity).

5. John's personal-space diagram just before his company was bought out probably looked much like Fig. 5.2.

Balance and phase of life

Life may be divided into phases. What we call these phases and how long they appear to last depends on your particular interest and perspective. For this chapter, the concept of phases is more important in sharpening our sense of change in life balance and understanding how we can manage it than the number of phases or their names. For our purposes therefore I've chosen the phases as defined by Havinghurst.

Life phases

0-10	Coming into independent existence
11-20	Becoming a person in one's own mind
21-30	Focusing one's life
31-40	Collecting one's energies
41-50	Exerting and asserting oneself
51-60	Creating a new life-style
61-70	Deciding whether to disengage and how
71-	Making the most of disengagement*

Phases tend to define the central life purpose for that period. This does not mean that the phase is necessarily defined by a unique segment of personal space. Instead it might be better to think of the phase as a pervasive theme. The theme affects life-balance choices and may be instrumental in creating and defining new life-space segments or modifying old ones.

By taking a broad look at the phases of life we can see how this theme changes in emphasis. At birth, personal space is entirely represented by the private personal area. Early development begins by finding one is a being in physical space and that one can move and command use of part of that physical space. For the child, segments of space begin to take on definition and the whole expands as it relates to the family. The child learns to manage life balance as it finds capability to influence mother, and as it identifies toys as its

---

* Robert J. Havinghurst, "Dominant Concerns in the Life Cycle," in Morton Puner, *To the Good Long Life* (New York: Universe, 1974), p. 40.

own. The physical sense of space begins with the crib or playpen as one's area and later expands to one's house, yard, and street. An early-childhood interaction with another child is often an argument about these boundaries.

As schooling comes along it becomes a major life purpose. It fills an area of major importance, similar to work for the individual later in life. Schooling is a major life work. It becomes a source of learning and new experiences which dramatically extend the boundaries of personal space. The end of formal schooling used to be seen as limiting this kind of expansion. With today's moves toward lifelong learning, we know this type of expansion can and should continue.

On taking our first job we develop a new life purpose. The job becomes a new source of expansion of our world. By enlarging our income, it becomes possible for us to satisfy desires for acquisition or perhaps a change in life-style. By providing a potential source for satisfaction, it can become a major stimulus for growth. By providing new associates, it can open doors to new relationships and new interests. These are the positive aspects. Like a two-edged sword, work can also provide disappointments through failure to meet expectations and through sapping of energy out of proportion to perceived return. In some senses what it becomes has to do with circumstances external to us. For example, the physical requirements or the technical process can determine how we are expected to behave. In some senses what that job becomes has to do with our expectations and how we manage our relationship to it, how we attempt to alter its character, and take the responsibility for choice and action. If we find ourselves unable to alter it, to make it positive, we can change jobs. If it is positive, we can work to make it more positive. In fact, the probability is that if the first job is a positive experience this will establish a lifelong positive orientation toward work. Work can provide the individual with the first sense of real, meaningful achievement, a major source of the feeling of becoming an identifiable self. It may become the base of future reference to identity. This is exemplified by a person who answers: "I am an artist;" "I am an engineer;" "I am an attorney;" etc., to the question, "Who are you?"

With marriage the family space enlarges and changes. As with major changes of status in any segment, marriage provides opportunities for growth, change, and expansion of life space. The new family can provide satisfactions and a source of vitality. It can pro-

vide crises which open the space for change. By giving the individual the opportunity to share the self on a very intimate basis, it can
add deep meaning. Like other segments, the family part of personal space also contains negative potential. Failure in interpersonal relations in the family can reflect negatively on work. A simple
example is that an argument at the breakfast table can lead to
trouble with relationships at work. A financial need or crisis at home
can cause the individual to emphasize pay at work. The segments
are not independent—they are all part of total life space.

In our story John had moved quickly from the 21-30 period
into the 31-40 period. Apparently the change took place just as he
needed to exert himself and feel capable of impacting the organization. He has several balancing activities to consider. First, changing
the nature of his work where he is. Second, changing employers.
Third, building some alternative activities for immediate satisfaction
or as insurance and bridges for later change. Fourth, reestablishing
the strength of his family relationships. He may do these singly but
most probably will do several.

At retirement the "shared with work" segment disappears.
This can be a major crisis and, like other crises, provides opportunity for growth or defeat. For one who has centered life interest
on work, gained positive growth from work, and experienced satisfaction, moving from being needed one day to not needed the next
requires a shift in life balance. How one negotiates this shift depends on previous successes and failures in managing life balance.
The change is affected as well by expectations of retirement as good
or bad and the existence or lack of plans. Strength in other segments of personal space can help in this adjustment.

As an example, the individual who has not achieved a good
balance, who has devoted too much life space to work, will have
more difficulty in replacing work with a satisfactory alternative than
one who has many interests. This is where hobbies can help as a
source of new activities. However, one may have plans for travel,
for instance, and then find that health or finances are not compatible with travel. One then finds achieving a new balance difficult.
Plans and goals must be realistic.

On the positive side, retirement can provide the freedom to
develop new aspects of self, to achieve a new sense of being, and
to find new satisfactions. Setting up reasonable expectations,
understanding the life-space balance concept, and having a rich
source of alternatives will contribute positively to life's quality. An

example is the individual who finds an opportunity to serve others in new ways. One way might be in running the business aspects of a cooperative housing arrangement. Another might be in teaching hobby skills to other seniors. Still another might be in becoming a consultant, making use of one's life-work expertise to advise those starting out in the same activity. The opportunities are boundless but succeeding in them takes ability to identify a need, project oneself into a positive relationship, and gain satisfactions, results, and vitality from the effort.

Tuning the life balance

Tuning and managing balance are two necessary aspects of putting the personal-space concept to work for you. Tuning can be thought of as proper adjustment within work, or of family relationships. Balance can be thought of as achieving the proper relationship between segments such as private, work, and family life. It is necessary to identify inputs, feedback, and outputs to achieve tuning. These are shown in Fig. 5.3, which is a more detailed look at a portion of Fig. 2.1. Neither the list of inputs nor outputs is complete. Nor is it the only list. These are samples we will use to help us understand the need for tuning and some other possible adjustments. Some are defined as inputs—things we bring to a relationship or activity. Others are defined as outputs—things we take from a relationship. Still others are represented in the feedback loop which affects an adjustment and tuning.

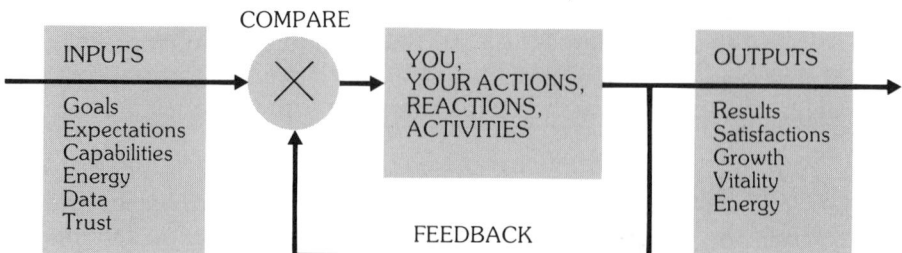

Fig. 5.3 Tuning a part of your life

Outputs which are positive help generate inputs. Outputs which are negative tend to reduce what we input. Failure to achieve outputs of value leads to "turning off" on that segment. Success in achieving outputs of value leads to "turning on." Turning on or off in one segment can affect our attitude toward and expectations from other segments of personal space.

As one tunes a radio one seeks the strongest signal with the least interference. So it is, too, in tuning an aspect of life. For an example, we will use "capabilities" as the aspect to be tuned in the segment of life space called work. Each of us has capabilities which are combinations of skill and knowledge. Their application is affected by interest or motivation to use, our expectations of success which reflect our experiences, self-knowledge and self-confidence, trust, goals, and the other inputs. Their application is reinforced or strengthened if we feel we are gaining a desired payout in the form of accomplishment, growth, and other satisfactions. Let us suppose, for explanatory purposes, that we have artistic ability and interest. If we alter our job to create conditions utilizing these abilities and as a result we gain satisfactions, this should result in a sharpening of our abilities and a desire to use them more. The tuning process consists of making a change in what we are doing and/or what we expect and sensing feedback of the result. Based on the result, tuning requires making a decision as to whether the result is an improvement and we want more, or a worsening and we want less. Tuning requires that we be conscious of what we are doing, sensitized to measure the results (feedback), and willing to experiment with change. In our example, John retuned the work segment but apparently was not sensitive to feedback of dissatisfaction in the family situation.

Balancing the elements of personal space

Achieving balance is like tuning but adjustment is made between elements such as work and family life or family life and private, unshared space as opposed to adjustments internal to an element or segment. As we start out on our working career, if the expectations are for success and satisfactions the tendency is to commit large amounts of energy and time toward making a work beachhead. The purpose is one of searching for results and the desire is to find out quickly whether we made the right choice. Early reward for our efforts provides psychological or other income and probably rewards the employer with additional commitment on our part. Failure to receive reward pays off in disillusionment, question, and perhaps decommitment. John was experiencing this under the new management. The work initiate is anxious and often struggles too hard, thus stumbling over personal desire. When this is the case other elements of life space probably shrink in time and energy devoted to them.

If at some later time the individual gets married, it is probable that family will take on significant importance and more energy and time will be devoted to the members of the family. Balancing is the attempt on the part of the individual to keep expenditure and income or payoff in proportion. When our satisfaction falls off in one element, we have two choices. First, we may try to adjust the tuning in that segment. Second, if we fail at tuning or we perceive (feel) that tuning won't pay off in increased satisfaction, we can try balancing. We compensate by seeking satisfaction in another element of life space. The process of balancing usually changes conditions so that changes in tuning must occur within several elements.

When we recognize the complexity of the process, we may wonder that anyone makes this juggling act work. Certainly being conscious of our personal-space elements, what balls are in play, should help. But as with the juggler the process must eventually be maintained at the feeling/sensing level, for eye contact with each ball is not only impossible but self-defeating. So too with too much cognitive attention to life balance. So too when we feel we are succeeding and succumb to the tendency to keep doing more of the same. This may be the worst thing we can do—only by checking feedback will we know.

Summary

This chapter has discussed achieving life balance as a process necessary to meet the challenge of achieving personal vitality. Being successful at balancing the various segments of life, tuning each segment and managing one's total personal space, can contribute to achieving vitality. Balancing and tuning are an art, not a science. However, creating a personal-space picture as used in this chapter may, by making the process more evident, aid each of us in achieving life-balancing skill. By increasing or decreasing the amount of time, energy, and interest applied to a part of our lives we make new investments in the hopes of new payouts. If by investing more energy and time in work or defining a new work activity we can increase our psychological income, this leads to increased motivation and personal growth. Increased investment in any segment with increased psychological income can lead to personal growth. The nature and direction of our growth varies with the area of our life in which we are changing the investment. Growth and vitality are closely related. Creating a new life segment and investing in it is an alternative to increased investment in an existing segment. This is the sort of change that can result from study of a totally new area. Knowing how to recognize when a change in tuning or balance is needed is as important as designing and executing the change. Vitality depends on developing personal techniques and skills for managing balance. Development of skills requires experimentation. Personal techniques can be discovered for continuing the expansion of personal space, increasing vitality, and developing new segments. Growth and vitality require investment in and continued expansion of personal space. Growth requires taking responsibility for making life work or not work.

Suggested readings

Gardner, John W. *Excellence*. New York: Harper & Row, 1961.

Miller, Donald B. "Privacy: A Key Issue Between Employees and Managers," *University of Michigan Business Review*, Jan. 1976, pp. 7-12.

Paulus, Trina. *Hope for the Flowers*. New York: Paulist Press, 1972.
> Who would think that the story of a caterpillar's life and struggles could teach us about life purpose, balance, and tuning? This is a charming book which as a result of talented writing and interesting artwork opens doors of understanding for the reader. You cannot help but ask yourself important questions about your life as you read this book.

Shon, D.A. *Beyond the Stable State*. New York: W.W. Norton, 1971.

Sommers, Robert. *Personal Space: The Behavioral Basis of Design*. Englewood Cliffs, N.J.: Prentice-Hall, Spectrum Books, 1969.

Vickers, G. *Freedom in a Rocking Boat*. England: Pelican, 1972.

Sources of
solution

6

Personal-growth concepts

Introduction

Personal growth results from full confrontation with life. Growth is the process of adding new experiences and data and using them. Growth is both the reordering of priorities and values and the adding of new ones. Growth is being capable of doing something tomorrow that you cannot do today. It can result as much from the unleashing or unblocking of capabilities already within you as from your gaining new powers. Growth requires learning, change, and movement.

An exciting aspect of our times is the explosion of new growth processes and aids. We are also rediscovering and applying old techniques for growth. Meditation is the application of an old technique. There seems to be an increasing intensity of personal search for growth in our era. This may come from disillusionment with "the system" as well as increased leisure and a reduction in personal energy used up in work. There is an increasing understanding of the need for growth as an element of survival and vitality. We humans have become aware of our power to shape events. Today we have increased choice of life-style and life philosophy. Today we have new freedoms and are growing in our acceptance of variations in life-style which makes it possible for each of us to explore and change. While many of the techniques cannot be called scientific in the sense of twentieth-century rational science, some can. An example is biofeedback, which is emerging as a way to increase the individual's sensitivity to previously unconscious activities. This feedback provides a basis for training and control of body functions not heretofore considered controllable.

Providing each of us with a framework for viewing the broad perspectives of growth opportunities is a primary need we are trying to review. No chapter can present all the alternatives; whole books are written on what we will mention only in passing. But if by example we can provide a technique for the reader's personal sorting and personal analysis of possibilities, this will be an important first step.

I will also try to provide some criteria for your personal experimentation and for self-guidance through the maze of alternatives. There is no map, for the terrain is individual, but this discussion may begin to provide a compass and also a can of paint for putting your mark on some of the trees in the forest.

How we approach future growth is based to a large extent on what has happened to us up to now. Our past has shaped our beliefs and values. How we approach growth depends on our goals, on what we want and expect.

Personal responsibility is necessary to personal growth. Only when we take charge, only when we stop being the victim, does real growth take place. Once we take a step to increase our awareness and once the growth process accelerates, then it is as though opportunity opens up before us. Growth happens—it is like being drawn toward some greater destiny. Castenadas* speaks of this feeling of being drawn toward a new sense of being.

Concepts of growth

Our approach to growth is closely related to our belief about the purpose of life. Beliefs about why we live and what we live for come from values; and our values are shaped by early family life, religion, philosophy, experience, education, and membership in groups and organizations. For example, one group influencing values is the family. For these value inputs to influence an individual the individual must come in contact with them. The family impacts the individual through intimate and daily contact and through offering and withholding rewards. For a group to influence values we must either want to be part of the group or deliberately want to be different from the group. We must confront and reject or integrate the values. For example, if, as in Japan, some hold the belief that management should be paternalistic, this can have little influence on us unless we know about it. Even knowing about it won't be of much influence unless we decide to try the approach or deliberately move in another direction. Our approach to growth shapes our exposure to techniques for growth. If we go along a particular road, we are not exposed to what is happening on another road. The very fact that you are reading this book and this chapter means you are increasing your exposure. This exposure increases the probability of your acceptance or rejection of the values and the kinds of alternatives presented.

Growth requires both a desire for growth and an exposure to experience or new information. Conceptually, growth can be approached from many perspectives, some of which are shown below. Associated with each perspective are some possible activ-

---
*   See suggested readings.

ities or techniques to assist in interpretation. In reading this table, notice how the perspective, or outlook, tends to shape the type of activity.

Growth concepts and activities

Concept	Activities
■ Growth is physical	■ Exercise, muscle building, or coordination-improvement activities
■ Growth is spiritual	■ Exposure to religious training and/or experiences leading to acceptance or rejection and change in behavior
■ Growth is internal	■ Meditation, biofeedback, or activities like dream analysis or training in logic
■ Growth is gaining ability to control people and things	■ Management training, public oratory, politics, or training in the use of complex and powerful equipment
■ Growth is enhanced knowledge	■ Study, reading, or exposure to someone who has great knowledge—a master, or role model
■ Growth is increased skill	■ Practicing arts, crafts, and activities requiring a high degree of coordination, manual dexterity, or control
■ Growth is necessary for continuation of life	■ Active pursuit of growth until death, including searching out new experiences and learning, and the pursuit of change

These examples of concepts and associated activities show how the growth outlook shapes life. One can, of course, believe in more than one of these concepts. While the outlook tends to shape one's approach to life, it does not exclude growth in other dimensions, nor does it eliminate the possibility that an unforeseen event will alter the perspective.

PERSONAL EXPERIMENT 9

Relax on the floor with your eyes closed. Put your hand gently on your abdomen. Focus on the sensation of touching yourself at that point. Feel both the sensation in the abdomen and in the hand. Remove your hand and sense the feeling of removal. Touch another spot such as your forehead. Try touching ever so lightly or by contrast push and sense the difference. Try other parts of your body. Try touching in different ways. For example, brush your hand across part of your body rather than touching a specific part. Feel the difference. Continue the exercise trying to become increasingly sensitive to your body through this process. You may at first rebel at this idea, but knowing your own body and how it feels for you to touch it is part of self-knowledge. This is a kind of activity you may have turned off since childhood. As you progress you should find that it is interesting to take pleasure in sensing your own body. How did it feel to you? Is this an activity you have denied yourself? Think of ways in which this type of activity might help you to become more attuned to life.

Philosophy and religion

From Greek and Roman times onward, the thinking and debate about great questions has had a profound influence on the course of life. A king or leader who traveled months to visit the Oracle at Delphi had to believe very firmly that the Oracle could see the future. Present-day analysis of the supposed technique used in making Delphic predictions further intensifies the role of belief and expectations. Predictions were made in unpunctuated associations of words that could be interpreted many ways that were dependent on the frame of reference of the recipient—the one reading the prediction. What one did after receiving a pronouncement certainly was influenced by it, and thus the exposure to experience and learning was in a sense shaped by the belief. A modern-day parallel is the influence of the horoscope on those who believe in horoscopes.

Western philosophical thought, although having many branches and forms, has at its core a rational, logical form. It provides a base for our science and the materialistic accomplishments of our world. Through these beliefs we have demonstrated that we can influence and shape the world but with some, perhaps serious, costs. Eastern philosophical thought, by contrast, has at its core a belief in control by destiny and a search by humans for "the natural way."

As a consequence, there is in the East a greater emphasis on the individual's internal development. Powerful as these two philosophical themes are in shaping the growth and development of people, we can find similar but different development in each sphere. There have been creative artists both in the West and in the East. There have been achievements of great physical prowess in both cultures. In other words, although the philosophy has a great effect, it does not exclude developments which might be more easily reinforced by the other sphere of belief.

Included in growth concepts are philosophies. Can there really be a new philosophy? Philosophy can be new to the individual if it represents a change and a different perspective. Philosophy can be new in the sense that it is newly described or represents a unique combination of concepts. One of the most applicable philosophies to the topic of growth in our times has been given the title "existentialism."* As applied to the nature of the human it holds to some specific themes such as the "field theory." It is interpreted to mean that individuals do not exist in isolation but as part of a large system. Change in any part affects all other parts. The philosophy also holds that there are four modes of consciousness: individual, intimate, cosmic, and eternal now. The theme of personal responsibility for what happens, good or bad, is also central. Although we are all part of a large system, there is uniqueness. Another of the tenets is that it is right for the individual to seem different from other human beings. That one's life is an endless process of growing,

---

* A source of explanation of existential philosophy is Peter Koostenbaum's *Managing Anxiety*. One can compare it with Eastern philosophy by reading some of the writings by Alan Watts, such as *The Book*, or *Nature, Man, and Woman*. (See suggested readings.)

emerging, and reaching out is also central to the existential philosophy. One can, therefore, say the philosophical base for this book is existentialism. Since there is great similarity between these tenets and the philosophies of the East, one might also say it is Eastern. But, because the definitions and embodiment of the vitality theme are newly brought together here, one could also say it is new.

Choosing a growth experience

The right growth activity for us is one which matches our stage of growth. That is, in a true Sufic* sense we must be prepared or ready for an experience to be able to integrate it with ourselves, to learn it. Knowing where we are and who we are is a prerequisite, therefore, for choosing what we should do to enhance our growth. A possible road map for insight to our stage of growth has been provided by Albert Bellante (*Personal Growth*, Number 23, 1975). He suggests there are eight stages of growth:

1. Boredom, vague discontent—slowly growing awareness.
2. Problem eruption—the individual is embroiled in a threatening situation, a crisis, which turns on the biological alarm system.
3. Coping behavior—reduction of the apparent cause of stress.
4. The dark night—the personality has been affected but there is realization it is not over.
5. Latency period—normal behavior returns but something is happening internally.
6. The "aha" period—we become conscious of the new aspect of us, we become aware.
7. Externalization—we begin to use the new aspect.
8. Inflation—completion of the cycle and integration of the new into the personality. †

---

* Indries Shah's writings are a good source of information on Sufism. An essential belief in Sufism is that you cannot teach one who is *not ready*. Robert Ornstein has written a chapter on contemporary Sufism in Charles Tart's *Transpersonal Psychologies* (New York: Harper & Row, 1975).

† Used with permission.

These stages of growth are both a problem-solving outline and a demonstration that growth is iterative. The stages are cyclical and repeated. They vary in length. In Stage 1 we have an awakening and a free choice of the aid or assisting experience we choose to help us with our change. In fact, some growth experiences are designed to create Stage 1. Encounter is an example. Stage 5 is another time when we may find assistance from some growth-aiding technique or experiences.

Readiness can be determined in the sense of Bellante's growth stages, relative to a given period of change, or in a broader context of compatibility and acceptability of ideas. This broader context probably is related to life stages and values previously referenced. Readiness is the ability to take and to use because it is what we need and it fits with our perspective. An example illustrates this.

In my own life I have been twice exposed to Eastern philosophical thought at two widely spaced periods, about 20 years apart. The first time I felt myself totally confused and turned off. The second time I felt as if I had found something I had been looking for all along. The first time I was not able to integrate the "new" with my approach to life. The second time the "new" philosophy reinforced some conclusions I had reached on my own and added to my ability to move ahead. It is necessary, then, in choosing a supplementary growth experience to know where we are in the course of life, for both the long-term growth cycle and the short-term growth cycle. Testing by continually exposing ourselves to new issues and seeing how they feel to us and whether we can see a way to use the "new" are the basic ways of determining where we are in the long-term cycle. Increased consciousness of ourselves and our feelings is the way to determine where we are in the short-term cycle. You are probably well aware of the Stage 1 and Stage 6 phases. You may have to work to achieve consciousness of the others.

Assuming for the moment that you know where you are in both growth cycles, is there anything further you can use to tell what new experience is right? One way is to share with others like you where you feel you are and how you feel. Finding someone who is compatible does not mean doing what they are doing but rather expanding your exposure to alternatives by adding the experiences of others to your own.

The problem of choosing the right growth experience, the one that fits you, is summed up well in the following quotation from *Shifting Gears:*

The problem is that we learn to grow according to arbitrary plans set up by society rather than growing as individuals according to our own internal needs. There was a time when the societal plans worked — our growth and development were synchronized with society's development. Under these conditions you can safely measure yourself by society's yardstick. But society now presents us with such a bewildering number of options that we cannot relate them to our inner selves. And when our inner selves are not synchronized with society, then our attempts to measure up to external yardsticks become exercises in self-contradiction that may lead to a sense of isolation and anxiety. *

What is available — what's happening?

More than ever before there are opportunities for growth-enhancing experiences all around us. This is not to discount the growth which occurs from experiencing our day-in, day-out living, but to say we have the choice of supplementing these experiences to accelerate and enhance growth. The opportunity to supplement is not new. The multiplicity of alternatives is. During earlier times it was possible to spend time with a teacher or philosopher or to travel. These were supplements. Modern communication has expanded these opportunities, and the contemporary intensity and magnitude of the search for personal growth has made the development of such opportunities good business. Our ability to reduce the portion of time we must spend just surviving has also increased the time we can spend on psychological growth opportunities. The local community or junior college, high school or community adult classes probably represent the foremost opportunity for new growth experiences. Exposure to new interests and new information is now inexpensive and convenient. What's more, it is socially acceptable and relatively safe to look at change in these environments. Taking a course does not commit ourselves beyond exposure. We still maintain the choice as to whether we integrate and use the new information. In the San Francisco Bay area we have almost arrived at the point where the adult who is *not* taking a course is the exception!

Four of the suggested readings at the end of the chapter provide lists or introductions to a broad cross section of growth-en-

---

* From *Shifting Gears* by Nena O'Neill and George O'Neill, p. 14. Copyright © 1974 by Nena O'Neill and George O'Neill. Reprinted with permission of the publisher, M. Evans and Company, Inc., New York, N.Y. 10017.

hancing activities.* Some are unique, or basic growth areas; and within each of these there will be many varieties and practitioners. Some are proprietary and bear the name of the creator or inventor. In searching out growth experiences, the motto is "Caveat emptor." In fact, it would be good to stay away from any which are advertised as improving everything. You must be the judge of quality and meaningfulness. Referring you to such listings is intended to introduce you to the dramatic range of activities. It is not necessary to understand them now. Some of them will be addressed later in the book when they help to make a particular point.

Growth experiences versus normal life

What then are growth activities and how do they differ from our daily experiences? In broad concept, they are activities which increase the probability of learning new behavior. They supplement

---

PERSONAL EXPERIMENT 10

Sit in a chair, preferably a straight chair. Close your eyes and relax. Now start exploring your space. First try to identify the farthest sound you can hear. Next identify the closest sound you can hear. Next explore your space with your hands. Feel the floor, the chair, and any objects near you. Next try to sense the pressure of your body on the seat. Next try sensing the room around you. Try to picture the room, the ceiling, the wall in front of you and the wall behind. Try in any way you can to sense where you are and how you relate to where you are. When you feel like it, open your eyes. It is probable you will see your surroundings with new clarity. Is it possible that in your life you have denied yourself inputs from some of your senses? How would it change your life to become more sensitive to your surroundings? Is this desirable?

---

* See especially Ornstein, Rozak, Petersen, and Yee.

or complement the normal activities of life. They are often pursued in a fashion which increases the awareness of what is different or the awareness of our feelings or reactions to what is going on. A growth activity would, therefore, be any process which enhances our self-perception, or our sensitivity to external events, or aids in the process of personal integration of new information or experience.

The growth activity to which we have been most exposed is the lecture. We sometimes wonder about its effectiveness; however, when it works we can grow as a result of the exposure. A good lecture is one which engages our attention, sharpens the differentiation between alternative actions, and motivates us to new experience, or aids us in internalizing the information. A good lecture gets us emotionally involved. A good lecture presents material in a way which captures our involvement and interest. A good lecture disciplines our use of time and our actions in a way we cannot or have not done for ourselves.

Biofeedback is a good example of a supplemental growth experience because it makes it possible for us to be aware of an aspect of ourselves about which we were previously not conscious. Barbara Brown in *New Mind, New Body* puts it this way:

> *Biofeedback is a curious mixture of startling simplicity and challenging complexity. It is deceptively straightforward: tap into the mysteries within directly from the surface of the body, use a simple device to convert the activity of the body system into a form which can be sensed, and voilá, the person can identify the feelings he has when the body is signalling the monitor device to say "blood pressure up," or "blood pressure down," or "heart rate up," or "temperature down," or "more alpha."* *

Thus biofeedback meets our definition of a growth experience. It enhances self-perception, our sensitivity to internal events, and aids in the process of personal integration of the new experience. Two other aspects of a growth experience should be stressed: preparation, both psychological and through study, and persistent practice.

---

* Barbara Brown, *New Mind, New Body* (New York: Harper & Row, 1974), p. 9. Reprinted with permission.

Personal-growth concepts

Perhaps the most important concept for enhancement of growth is the idea of engaging in growth games. Personal Experiments 9 and 10 are representative of growth games. Growth games provide for the adult the learning experiences that a child creates naturally when playing house, experiencing a puddle, or sitting on a bike exchanging feelings with contemporaries. Growth games are drawn from humanistic psychology, and they are constructed to provide positive experiences which will yield increased self-understanding. Games are processes which heighten the learning which should take place in normal activity by causing you to focus on your feelings, by providing enhanced feedback for self and others. The games described vary from activities you can engage in alone to activities which require a group. Some provide sharpening of senses, some provide a basis for getting in touch with your body, some are designed to short-circuit normal inhibitions, and some are designed to build interpersonal trust. All are designed to stimulate growth and make the process fun.

As an example, a growth game which I have used with managers and industrial designers may make the point clearer. Because the process of living requires limiting our inputs to remain stable in a world which seems designed to overload our input circuits, adults generally have "detuned" their sensory inputs. To demonstrate this and to build on the concept of increased sensory awareness as a way of improving interpersonal relations, the "orange experience" was conceived. In a class situation each student is given an orange. For three minutes they are instructed to look at the orange, feel the orange, smell the orange, and anything that would help them to get to know their orange. Then for two additional minutes they continue the process with their eyes closed. During both periods they are instructed to be conscious of what is going on within them. Next they are paired off and given a period to introduce their orange to their partner. All oranges are then put in a basket and the participants asked if they feel they will be able to pick out their orange. Usually about one-third believe they can. Actually no one has any real difficulty in picking out his or her orange. Next the group peels and eats the orange, going slowly (about fifteen minutes), examining texture, taste, and all characteristics as if they had never eaten an orange before. For most this is a pleasant experience. It was also felt that it was a learning experience. Most achieve the realization that they have turned off sensory input but are reassured they can turn it back on. After the experience an opportunity to discuss it usually brings out a felt need to be more sensitive to what they do in life.

From these few examples we see the principles of growth-enhancing experiences. By some technique they make the individual more conscious of what is going on within his or her body and mind while engaging in some relatively normal activity. Growth-enhancing experiences sharpen or amplify the feedback to increase the chance we will break through the numbness built by a life of inattention and retreat to security and safety. These activities are designed to make the risks of growth more comfortable, to catch the individual unaware, and to let the reward of the experience enhance growth.

How to increase
your growth

Increasing your growth is a matter of preparing yourself, understanding yourself, setting up positive expectations, experiencing change, practicing the new, and gaining satisfactions from the process. It requires choice, responsibility, and action. Increasing your growth requires setting goals and building learning into your life pattern. This can be enhanced by using some growth-aiding processes of the type discussed earlier. More importantly, growth is enhanced by anything which increases your understanding of self and your sensitivity to what you are doing in your life.

The secret of enhancing personal growth is to devise your own growth games. It is necessary to find ways of turning your normal activities into growth-amplifying experiences by finding ways to sharpen feedback and increase awareness of what is going on. A simple example of a managerial technique may illustrate the point. A manager who was conscious of the need to make work experiences growth experiences and learning situations devised two techniques. The first was to take two minutes at the end of each meeting to discuss what had been learned during the meeting. Sometimes this was something about the subject of the meeting. Sometimes it was something about the people in the meeting. At first he found the technique a bit uncomfortable, but after a while it became natural; and he found that his subordinates and his peers caught on and took part whole-heartedly. The second technique was to ask his assistant to report what he saw happen between the people such as missed cues, turning off, or evidences of anxiety. At the end of the day the assistant fed back anything significant he had observed about adequacy and understanding of communications, about the quality of agreements, and the accomplishments of the day. This process became a learning one for both assistant and manager.

Another growth game is to pick some aspect of life and highlight it for a day or several days. One can highlight an activity by requiring that it be noted in some way. An example might be to become conscious of the unnecessary words one uses which have no meaning like "mm," "huh," "yup," "ayah," etc. Another might be to try to become conscious of agreements between yourself and others, both spoken and silently understood. Still another might be to keep track of how many times you interrupt others in the middle of their comments. Special things to keep track of should be drawn from your experience. These examples highlight communications.

Growth games can be invented which elicit the help of friends and thereby add to the interest and motivation. One way is to follow the suggestions previously made but make a pact to record and comment on the other person's behavior. Another is to engage in word games as groups. Still another is to take a topic and expect one member of the group to research it and enlighten the others. Related to this would be the practice of modifying your lunch-time conversation so that by prearrangement you discuss a certain topic. These latter examples might be called boot-strap learning in the informal group.

The point of these examples is that each of us can make some creative inventions for our living process which will enhance our learning. The techniques we devise should be ones which fit our style and, therefore, quickly become a part of our life pattern. Experimentation is the way and should lead to the right growth games for you.

Recording your changes

Growth is change in behavior and capability as the result of learning from experience. Sensitizing yourself to change, becoming conscious of how you are changing and growing, can accelerate growth. A technique for understanding how you are growing is to record your new perspectives, ideas, and capabilities in a diary. In this day of inexpensive cassette recorders a tape recorder can be your diary if you feel comfortable with this technique. Any notebook, however, will do.

What to record depends on what kinds of growth you see as important. Looking for things to record will increase the things you have to record. It is best, of course, to record positive accomplishments or changes, for this reinforces the positive. Recording negatives, by contrast, will probably accentuate the negatives and contribute less to growth.

Suppose you have determined you need to improve your ability to teach. After each of several teaching experiences think back over what worked well, and how you determined it was working. That is, did you get any feedback which indicated success or failure? Then ask yourself what conditions seemed to indicate these results. For example, was your attitude going into class different? Were you more confident? Did you relate the material to your personal experiences and share more of yourself? Did you have too little material and work to gain class participation? Or were you rushed with seemingly too much to cover? Did you find some new device or point of view for gaining attention or participation? These are but a few suggestions of questions you should ask. In each case taking a few minutes to record your feelings about something which worked for you will sharpen your understanding of what happened and increase the probability of its happening again. It is probable that the frequency of successes will increase without consciously planning to use the techniques. Recording your changes increases your consciousness of self. Recording your changes provides you with some self-reinforcement for positive progress. This technique requires no training, no new set of philosophies or scientific instruments. It requires only your personal commitment to periodically concentrate on and record what is happening to you. The frequency of your record of change may be daily, weekly, or just every once in a while. Your frequency should fit your pattern.

Summary

Growth is both frightening and fun, stress-creating and stress-relieving, energy-using and energy-creating. Accelerating and managing our growth can result from opening up our philosophical beliefs or finding a fresh perspective. It can be accelerated by exposing ourselves to one or more of a number of processes designed to increase our awareness of selves and assist in integration of new experience and new information. Growth-assisting experiences abound and range from newly packaged philosophies to technological or educational experiences which enhance our ability to learn. Growth and learning are closely related. Growth requires the use of the new learning.

Suggested readings

Koostenbaum, Peter. *Managing Anxiety, The Power of Knowing Who You Are.* Englewood Cliffs, N.J.: Prentice-Hall, Spectrum Books, 1974.

Lao Tsu, *Tao Te Ching.* Translated by Gia-Fu Feng and Jane English. New York: Alfred A. Knopf, 1974.

LeShan, Lawrence. *How to Meditate.* New York: Bantam Books, 1975.

> *One of the easiest things you can do to enhance your personal growth and your success in life is to find a time or two each day to be alone, quiet, and contemplative. Author LeShan takes the mystery out of meditation. He points out that there are simple ways to create a meditative state and describes the benefits in the form of increased energy and ability to withstand the "slings and arrows" of life. Meditation, he says, is learning to do one thing at a time. Such a capability leads to fulfillment and effectiveness in life.*

Lewis, H. R., and Streitfeld, H. S. *Growth Games.* New York: Bantam Books, 1972.

Morris, Taylor. *The Walk of the Conscious Ants.* New York: Warner Paperback, 1973.

Ornstein, Robert. *Psychology of Consciousness.* San Francisco: W. H. Freeman, 1972.

Ornstein, Robert, ed. *The Nature of Human Consciousness.* New York: Viking, 1973.

Peterson, Severin. *A Catalogue of the Ways People Grow.* New York: Ballantine, 1971.

Pirsig, Robert M. *Zen and the Art of Motorcycle Maintenance.* New York: Bantam Books, 1975.

Rogers, Carl R. *On Becoming a Person.* New York: Houghton Mifflin, 1961.

Rozak, Theodore. *Sources, An Anthology of Contemporary Materials Useful for Preserving Personal Sanity While Braving the Great Technological Wilderness.* New York: Harper Colophon Books, 1972.

Schutz, Will. *Joy*. New York: Ballantine, 1973.

Watts, Alan. *The Art of Contemplation*. New York: Pantheon, 1972.

Watts, Alan. *The Book: On the Taboo Against Knowing Who You Are*. New York: Random House, 1972.

Yee, M. S., and Wright, D. K. *The Great Escape: A Source Book of Delights and Pleasures for the Mind and Body*. New York: Bantam Books, 1974.

7

Learning to learn

Introduction

One of our most important tasks in life is to learn to learn. Yet, as individuals, we seem to assume that learning is an inborn skill. We pay little attention to the process of learning. Most of our attention is on the content we learn. This chapter is intended to call your attention to the process of learning.

Motivation to learn is self-generated. There is some evidence, however, that we can set up conditions for increased personal motivation. If in a hobby sense we become excited and interested in a project and intent upon accomplishment, then we have established conditions for motivated learning. Learning of this kind suits our purpose and our goals.

Often in a learning situation we try too hard. This is exemplified by the typical home scene when Johnny is having trouble in school. The usual comment is: "You are not studying hard enough—you are not putting in enough hours." While it literally may be true Johnny is not grunting enough, it is probable that Johnny doesn't understand why he needs this information or that he skipped over a basic principle or concept which would clear it up. Learning to learn, therefore, has something to do with how we approach the task and our learning from our own experience with the task.

The objects of our learning vary with phase of life and our goals, and are affected by our culture. Cultures differ in their emphasis. Our Western culture has emphasized cognitive learning—the accumulation of facts and processes for pursuit of activities. The Senoi, a culture of Malay peninsula, teach their children that dreams are the way to work out life. The breakfast table in this culture is a place to recall dreams and to plan to live out aspects of the dream during the day. The Sufi learning tradition, which developed in Greece, Turkey, and Pakistan, emphasized learning through the parable. Readiness on the part of the learner was important in their emphasis on catching the learner in an illogical extension of past information. Our educational emphasis is thus in the broad sense established by our culture.

Learning is also affected by the media. Again in Sufism the media is a short story normally told out loud. Much of our education has been built on the book and now television. More recently we have enhanced the opportunities to learn through participation and reintroducing learning through hands on contact. Since each of us has different capabilities and each of our senses is not equally efficient, the media can make a difference in learning effectiveness. We may find learning difficult because we don't understand how we learn best.

Here we will suggest that both the individual and the organization need to question, to discuss, and to understand how they learn. For the individual this means deciding whether eyes or ears, private study or group study, theoretical or practical approaches work best and why. For the organization it means study of feedback systems, learning where and how organizational experience is stored, how data is transmitted, and how to differentiate between learning by people and that of the organization.

We will explore together some possible ways of improving our learning capabilities. The aim is to help you create a learning environment where all activities supplement and complement the learning process. Part of this environmental design must include an understanding of your motivations for learning as well as of your needs for learning.

Learning—what is it?

The experimental psychologists see learning as that process which causes changes in behavior. They see its purpose, then, as modifying what people do, improving it by some standard—the teacher's or the manager's goal. Kinds of learning include, for example, stimulus-response training where we build an association between two events. This is the sort of learning we hope takes place when we reward or recognize the type of behavior we want to occur.

Another kind of learning takes place in acquisition of a skill like riding a bike, typing, or driving a car. Most of us were introduced to still another form of learning early in life when we were expected to memorize a poem, a multiplication table, or a part in a play. Later in education we were expected to understand the substance of a written passage and explain it in our terms. Lastly, in the psychologist's terms, is the learning which provides us with the basis for applying previous experience to the solution of complex problems or to develop concepts.

Despite the fact that this is already a complex view, it does not account for other important aspects of learning. For example, where do religious experiences fit into learning? How do we explain the kind of learning which happens because we become part of a group of people who work, play, and share experiences together?

Another way to look at learning is to see it as divided into positive and negative experiences. Positive learning results from spontaneous curiosity and response to needs. It is the growth of skills and power to handle life. Negative learning, by contrast, is the product of anxiety or fear of disapproval. Negative learning is avoidance.

Learning, then, is a complex process which although not totally understood can be extensively described. These descriptions are sufficient to provide for each of us as individuals a start in learning about our learning. Learning consists of the individual with a set of expectations and stored experience coming into active contact with new material, taking this material in through one or more sensory inputs, evaluating the material, and adding it to other information so that it influences his or her future behavior.

Elements of the learning process

A further attack on the issue of how we learn and how we can improve our learning depends on breaking the process into definable, discussable steps. The following listing presents these elements for discussion:

Elements of the learning process

- Set or perspective—includes openness, images, and expectations.
- Drive—the motivation for learning.
- Exposure or stimulus—the active contact with an event or new information.
- Involvement—the nature of the relationship, the emotional content and contact.
- Response—the immediate result of exposure and involvement.
- Evaluation and generalization—integration of the new information.
- Experimental use—testing and using the new information.
- Feedback—observation of the results from use.
- Review, revision, and repetition—comparing expectations with results leading to integration and skill-development and modification.

Understanding our set or perspective requires that we approach each new experience understanding what we know and our expectations. That is, it is necessary to know what assumptions we have made, because these can affect the outcomes. Assumptions can both change outcomes and alter our perception of them. It is necessary also to know whether we are more concerned with maintaining our security by holding on to what we already know than in acquiring new information. Closely related is the necessity to understand or project possible outcomes and to know whether we see these results as desirable or not. Therefore, the first element in the learning process is understanding our condition and our approach to a new experience or new data. This condition or perspective probably exists at several levels of consciousness and some will be easier to determine than others. For example, the state of our knowledge about the experience or data can be determined. Our emotional stance may be more difficult to determine. It will be harder to determine generalizations from previous experience which may have been forgotten but which affect how new information can be related. So the several levels of perspective or approach are definable in terms of levels of consciousness.

Our drive or motivation is the next element it is necessary to understand. Wanting to learn can make a great difference. If learning is part of our plan, our objective, then there is a higher probability we will put forth the energy necessary for the process. Our motivation can come from needs and goals (internal plans) and it can be enhanced by the environment in which we find ourselves. It is easier to study, for example, when we are with others who are also studying. This enhancement of our drive comes from the environment. Environment can affect motivation by changing the threshold at which we will be moved to action.

Learning is not a process which can go on in absentia or by sending someone else in our stead. Exposure to the new data or new experience must be our own exposure. We must come in contact. True, we can do this through a secondary medium such as a book. In this respect the author's experience is passed on. The strong suspicion is, however, that this secondary exposure of contact is never as good a learning mode as first-hand experience and contact. It may, however, be more efficient in the sense of expanding our range and depth of exposure. In some way there must be personal contact with the new experience or data for lasting learning to take place.

The quality and extent of the involvement is the next factor. Whether or not we put ourselves into the process is important. Whether or not we let the information through our many defenses and barriers is important. Whether or not we participate actively as opposed to passively is important. It is the involvement that differentiates a lecture, in which we listen, from a discussion, in which we express our reactions and thoughts.

The discussion provides the setting for active involvement although it does not guarantee involvement. One can be an active listener in a lecture and thus be involved, but that is probably more difficult to do than to be involved in a small-group discussion. Yet one can be a passive participant even in the discussion situation. It is the individual's activity, not the situation, which makes the primary difference.

Response, or what happens to us as a result, or what we do as a result, is a confirmation that we were involved and did receive the message. The discussion, for example, provides the opportunity for quick confirmation. Quick feedback or confirmation strengthens learning. We state what we feel we heard on our terms and we get feedback from the group. Another kind of response or affect can be confirmation or the "aha" of getting it. In this case, the response does not require the presence of others for confirmation. It is an internal occurrence.

Evaluation and generalization are probably two separate activities. Evaluation is sorting out how the new material relates to other inputs and to old material. Evaluation includes the decision making. Do we throw out the old and keep the new? Do we keep the old? Do we reject both? Generalization is the process of associating the new in such a way that it is usable in a variety of ways. Generalization means that when we see or are exposed to another occurrence which is similar we will relate it to the data that we just took in. These two activities are associated. The results of the evaluation process determine the character of the generalization. These processes are not necessarily conscious. Sometimes they are deliberate and definable as when reconciling the addition of a column of figures when we have arrived at two different answers. Sometimes they are subconscious as when we react favorably, seemingly spontaneously, to a panoramic view or a painting.

The test of learning is our ability to use the information in a new situation. We have learned when we can utilize data of experience to accomplish what we want or to better understand new information. We have learned when using the information makes us more effective and/or increases our satisfaction. Experimenting or trying to use the learning, therefore, is an important part of the learning process since the feedback from experimental use tells us whether we have integrated and stored the information—whether we have mastered it or not.

Review, revision, and repetition are the parts of the process which assure retention. If we can recall the information over increasingly widely spaced intervals, then we have it for more or less permanent use. With repetition we become more expert and more sure in its use.

These elements have been presented as a way of categorizing the steps in the learning process. By understanding what is supposed to happen and becoming more conscious of ourselves in the process, we should be able to improve the process of learning. But a caution is in order.

We really know very little about learning. If these elements have sounded like facts, they are not. If I sounded as though I know the answers—I do not. We do know that human progress has been dependent on setting up hypotheses and using them until something better is discovered. That is what these elements are—ideas to use until better ones come along.

For both personal and organizational productivity and effectiveness and for the pursuit of vitality, learning about learning is an exciting frontier. Progress at this frontier can reap many dividends. Both individual and organizational energies should be addressed to this challenge.

Improving your learning

Learning to learn more effectively requires the desire to do so. It requires becoming conscious of the process. Learning to learn also requires experimentation. By setting up games or experiments one can become more conscious of what works best, what conditions surround effective learning and how to motivate oneself for learning. To improve learning, personal feedback of results must be part of the experimental design. Setting up the experimental outlook is akin to restimulating childlike curiosity. Childlike curiosity is akin to vitality. The experimental situation supplies a portion of the motivation and commits you to push for outcomes. Part of the experimental outcome can be a checkout of your various input channels and a better understanding of whether they need resensitization and resharpening. An example of such a checkout is to try delegating a project to someone else in several different ways with different follow-up techniques. Set up your experiment so you will learn about sharpening your communication, learning about balance between specification and freedom, and the relationship of

---

PERSONAL EXPERIMENT 11

In this experiment the intent is to use some part of your work or life experience to heighten your understanding of how you learn best. An example might be to pick an article describing new developments in your field, a lecture or seminar, or some specific new task you must learn on the job. Pick something you are motivated to learn either from work, a hobby, or other activity. Choose a self-contained learning experience of not too long duration. Rather than tackling it in your usual way try to be sensitive and alert to the following:

1. What senses or modes of input you are using and how you feel about using them (i.e., a strain, moderately stimulating, no particular feeling).

2. What evidences there will be that you have learned the material. If they are not built into the process, like questions at the end of a chapter, then devise some interesting ways of testing yourself. One way would be to try to utilize the information in a conversation. Try to create an atmosphere of experiment. Try to do those things which will make the process fun.

After this experience ask yourself what you have learned about your learning. Would it have been easier to have read instead of listened, or listened instead of read? Would it have been better if you had had an opportunity to do it; that is, actually handle pieces and parts or try the process that was being described?

these criteria to effective follow-up and appraisal techniques. The purpose of this kind of experiment is to understand how you gain information and which ways contribute most to improving your effectiveness.

With these examples, the experimental approach to learning to learn better can be understood so that you can design your own. The experiment can be a comparison between learning techniques. The experiment can be a planned learning experience during which you try to become more conscious of what is happening and how it feels. What the experiment is probably makes little difference. *The prime principle is to entice yourself to play the game of learning more about your learning.* Part of the value from the experimental outlook also comes from the additional attention you pay to everyday events as a result of your attention to setting up the games or experiments.

Another way to approach the subject of learning about your learning is to concentrate on your daily activities. Here the intent is to understand the level and frequency of your exposure to new experience and new data and how you are reacting to it. It is probable that you will discover you can perform most of your routines without learning anything new—that is, your day requires mostly the replaying of previously learned experience. An example of activities with little learning is your morning routine of brushing teeth, washing face, dressing, and such activities. It is also possible that your day contains a large exposure to new experience and learning of new behavior. Such would be the case if your major activity was going to school.

To concentrate on your daily activities it is suggested you first record and then analyze the activities of your day. Next roughly divide these activities into those which are routine and require no new learning, those which are some combination, and those which require almost totally new learning. A combination experience of using old habits and experiencing new things might be answering your mail. The process is not new but the subjects of the letters require different approaches and introduce you to new material. Still greater variety and learning might result from trying to answer someone else's mail. After becoming conscious of the kinds of learning in your daily experiences, ask yourself how you feel about what learning is going on. Are these activities where learning is taking place interesting, comfortable, and satisfying? Is learning taking place in the areas necessary to improve your performance in life? What would you do to improve the learning in your life? Could you increase the number of daily activities which expose you to new material and require learning? Do you feel this would be desirable?

Another approach to understanding how you learn should concentrate your attention on learning about yourself. First, do you devote a time every day to consciously learning about yourself? When and how do you add to your information about your strengths, weaknesses, skills, interfaces with others, etc.? Are you conscious of learning about self? Again, taking the experimental approach will lead to greater understanding. Check up on your learning about self by seeking out those experiences where the probability of increased self-knowledge is high.

One technique is to take a small notebook or reference record and record insights about yourself as they occur. When you record the insight in whatever personal shorthand you choose, also note the circumstances surrounding the learning incident. After recording several that seem to have taken place under similar circumstances try to set up those circumstances and see if you can increase the probability of new learning. This is experimenting with learning about self.

An example will clarify the concept and the technique. Suppose that you record an insight about yourself occurring as you are driving home from work. Later you record an insight about yourself which occurs as you are taking a long walk. Still later you record an insight coming as you are playing tennis. Two of these incidents involve physical exercise. Two of these incidents, driving and tennis, required concentration on the activity in which you were engaged at the time and one probably did not—walking. None of these activities required intense mental activity or conversation. Probably all of these activites were undertaken after a period of active engagement with life, undertaken as relaxation in the case of two and escape or changed environment in the case of one. As a result one might devise an experiment to test these findings. One could regularly take exercise like walking at the end of the day and see if this leads to a meditative, insightful, personal-learning experience. But an important thing to remember is not to force it!

Of all the suggestions about learning to improve your learning the latter has the most risk. Too much attention to self is probably self-defeating. It should probably come in bursts and then you should relax and let life flow. The goal is to create a curiosity about life, events, and self. The goal is experimentation as a way of life. The goal is not incessant examination of self.

Expectations

What we expect shapes what happens to a great extent. Therefore, if we are interested in learning about our learning, setting up expectations, goals, or objectives can help in this process. Establishing the goal of becoming more conscious of your learning process and improving your ability to continue learning can have a strong positive effect.

Building learning into life

Setting up experiments is one way of building learning into life. Setting up growth expectations, goals and objectives, is another. When you have some insights into what creates a good learning situation, then it is possible to design your life to include more of these activities. The third process is, therefore, redesign of your lifestyle. Knowing when redesign is necessary and learning to sense a decline in your learning rate is an important aspect of learning. Decline in learning is an early warning of decline in vitality. Thus, sensing the need for increased learning, the need for alterations in style and activity, and knowing how to design or create learning situations are all important parts of maintaining vitality.

One of the simplest and most effective ways of quickly increasing your learning experience is to increase your reading. Establishing a deliberate reading program, increasing your exposure to the new, either in a field you already know or in a new field, can increase the learning in your life. Aggressive reading is a route to expansion of interests and keeping up with change.

Deliberately seeking new experiences is another relatively easy way to increase learning. This can be a visit to a nearby historical site, a visit to a museum, or travel. It is actively reaching out taking an action to increase your exposure. It can also result from involvement in a new organization or activity. Such activities range from scouting and community service, to hobby-oriented activities or group social experiences such as play reading. The range is extensive and inexhaustible. New involvement can also result from giving more of ourselves to something in which we are already engaged. Seeking new experiences, then, means either striking out in an entirely new area, or strengthening and deepening our involvement in what we are already doing.

Enrollment in an educational activity is another good way of quickly increasing learning exposure. With the plethora of offerings by local high schools, community-service organizations, junior and senior colleges and proprietary educational organizations, there is literally something for everyone. Education can also come into the home over television or some correspondence program. Engaging in new and continual formal-educational experiences is relatively easy and builds bridges to new experiences and extended exposure.

Redesign of career or job are also powerful ways of increasing learning. These are discussed in Chapters 11 and 14.

Summary

Learning is part of growing, staying alive and vital. Most of us take the process of learning for granted. We treat it as something which comes naturally, a process about which we do not need to do much of anything. This chapter suggested that it is important to learn about learning and specifically how we learn best as well as how to find ways of deliberately increasing our learning.

Learning was defined as the process of taking in new information and integrating it in such a way that it can modify our future behavior. Various ways of looking at learning, including stimulus-response and conceptual understanding, were discussed. The fact that learning can be positive leading to increased ability, or negative leading to avoidance or restriction was also covered. Different perspectives of learning included the presentation of the idea that if we choose, we can take an active part in the learning process. We can indeed manage it.

Elements of the learning process were listed and analyzed. They were presented as a hypothesis which will aid us in managing learning. They range from our set or perspective to our motivation or drive. Included in the review of the elements was a discussion of the roles of involvement, experiment, and feedback in the process of learning.

It was suggested that the reader take an experimental outlook. There are two purposes for this: first, to set up expectations for learning about learning and to become more conscious of the process; second, to increase the probability of learning about learning by deliberately designing situations which provide personal feedback on the process.

Once one has increased personal understanding of the learning process then it is possible to use these data to redesign elements of one's life. Increasing the learning activity in life and doing it in areas of importance to the individual is a positive way of influencing vitality. This does not mean one must go through life constantly worrying about learning. Nor does it mean that every experience must be a learning experience. We need to do some things based on past experience. We need to have times when we don't have to be alert to the new. It does, however, mean that an increase in the consciousness about learning and a deliberate design of improved learning situations is something we can do to improve vitality. In fact, being conscious of a decline in new learning may be the first sign of the onset of a loss of vitality and the first step in turning your life circumstances to an increase in vitality.

Suggested readings

Boulding, Kenneth E. *The Image.* Ann Arbor: University of Michigan Press, 1959.

> *Boulding says that what we perceive is related to our store of knowledge and experience or our image of the world. What we do depends on this image. The meaning of a message is the change it creates in this image. He applies this concept to a range of things from the organization to the political process. Finally he suggests partly in jest but mainly in all seriousness a new science based on the study of the image.*

Bruner, Jerome S. *On Knowing.* Cambridge: Belknap-Harvard University Press, 1962.

Bruner, Jerome S. *The Process of Education.* Cambridge: Harvard University Press, 1962.

Cantor, Nathaniel. *The Learning Process for Managers.* New York: Harper Brothers, 1958.

Downing, Joseph. *Dreams and Nightmares.* New York: Harper & Row, 1973.

Ouspensky, P.D. *In Search of the Miraculous.* New York: Harcourt Brace World, 1949.

Shah, Indries. *Thinkers of the East.* Baltimore: Penguin Books, 1972.

8
Unlearning *

*   Portions of this chapter were delivered as a paper at the Frontiers in Education Conference, Atlanta, Ga., October 1975. See conference proceedings, pp. 208–213, published by IEEE.

Introduction

If we think of some learning as the buildup of tendencies toward certain reactions, then it is easier to understand the need for unlearning. Such a buildup causes us to live much as a program unfolding in an automatic fashion. Our reaction to experiences in our lives establishes the conditions which control how we will face new experience. Not all our experience is adaptive. Maladaptive experience can, therefore, build conditions for future failure. Even adaptive learning which represents knowledge or techniques that are no longer valid can block new experience. Organizations as well as individuals can store experience and build up tendencies to operate like machines. Both organizations and people need techniques of unblocking—unlearning.

Since we live in a time of pervasive change which requires new learning, we must be able to disconnect past learning from its consequences, or we must be able to discard parts of previous learning as a prerequisite for new learning, adaptation, personal growth, and change. Vitality probably depends on learning how to unlearn.

Formal education and training has done very little to address this issue of unlearning or the undoing of programmed tendencies. This chapter presents a concept of unlearning and explores some ways to achieve it. Whether the individual can be taught these techniques is an open question, although there is some positive evidence since unlearning does now exist. Most of this experience and information, however, comes from disciplines and approaches strange to the career-management, work and business world. Here is a first attempt at bringing what we know about this into useful form for the individual and the organization.

The concept

If the process of learning is the buildup of experiences in some type of storage and retrieval system, it then follows that the information which is stored affects future storage. In the simplest sense, if we think of a finite storage, medium blocking can occur because the space is already full. In a more complex sense, it is possible that we are dealing with some type of probability concept. The fact that certain patterns have been learned may set up neural circuits which have a greater probability of carrying a given message because they have been used before. In another sense, previously stored experience may in effect bias or filter what can get in by setting up expectations. When we expect something, we are sensitized to see and hear those things which coincide with our expectations and tune out those which don't fit. Another possible storage concept has to do with the weight or percentage of all related experience represented by an event. If we expose ourselves to something new, the first instance of experience is our whole experience and, therefore, very important. If we expose ourselves to something at which we've spent days or years, the next minutes of experience weighed against previous experience have little chance of effecting a major change in our behavior. Which of these concepts of brain function is right is not important. It is not the function of this discussion to argue the merits of these various hypotheses. What is important is that the addition of knowledge and experience seems to follow these principles and leads us to the next point.

Blocking can and does occur. How the process of living, for some, seems to dull the senses, impede the acceptance of new experience, and interfere with new learning is an important issue in maintaining vitality and openness to new learning. If we can find a way to unlearn or rid ourselves of the effects of previous learning on a selective basis, we can improve our ability to continue learning and extend vitality. The exploration of unlearning or breaking the blocks created by past learning and experience evolves from this logic.

I have identified three types of blocking for our discussion. The first is content blocking. This occurs when the presence of a previous answer gets in the way of accepting the idea and eventually the reality of a new answer. This is a storage-media problem. An example of content blocking is to ask $9 + 4 = ?$ For most of us the normal response is 13. But if I tell you I am thinking in terms of clock time then you will readily agree the answer is one. The most normal response is so built in by experience that it tends to block an open view.

The second is process blocking. This occurs when the process used to get answers which worked in the past is replayed to no avail. This may be viewed as a programming problem. Acceptance of the idea that some new process must be used is necessary to get around this block. An example of process blocking can be drawn from a learned behavior which is no longer applicable. For example, people who have driven a car with a gear shift and a clutch will probably catch themselves reaching for a nonexistent clutch in a car with an automatic transmission. Or, in the opposite situation, drivers will often stall because they did not use the clutch.

The third type of blocking is emotional blocking. This may be viewed as a motivational problem. Emotional blocking occurs when the previous experience or knowledge becomes inseparable from ourselves. For example, if I learned physics as Newtonian physics and have successfully applied these principles to create personal successes and accomplishments, I build an emotional bond with Newton's beliefs. If you then expose me to Einstein's physics and argue these new beliefs are better, you are not only attacking Newton—you are also attacking me.

Strong emotional involvement, necessary for learning, may intensify the rigidity of any of these blocks. That is, if breaking the belief that the individual is right threatens the individual, new learning which requires that break will be threatening. This situation is relived each time we catch ourselves vociferously defending a position. Have you ever noticed that the stronger your defense the greater the probability that you are at least in part wrong?

It is important to understand that when we talk of unlearning, we're not primarily talking about forgetting or erasing knowledge or experience. Although actual erasure may occasionally be necessary, what we are talking about primarily is disconnecting with some of the consequences of past learning. One consequence is that some kinds of learning seem to become part of us. We establish a psychological bond with the learning and mistake it as part of our being. When we talk about disconnecting from the consequence we are talking about separating ourselves and our being from the knowledge. The process of unlearning in this sense is a disassociation, a recognition that we are separate. Our experiences are part of us but they are not essentially us. It is possible, therefore, to know something and not to have that data be us.

There are some known techniques which appear to cause a kind of unlearning. Psychotherapy might be one, for example.

Seldom have such techniques been presented as unlearning. Often they have been presented as new learning or in some cases simply some interesting new experience. The question is whether these techniques can be taught and whether people can use them effectively to improve learning capability. Some techniques for unlearning require changes in the personality, role shifts and new life purposes. Some techniques are not selective in their unlearning effects. That is, if what happens is a kind of total dump of disconnection, this will be both threatening to the individual and possibly counterproductive. It is important that, whatever the process, the individual maintain the power of choice over what to discard and what to keep. Unlearning may thus present us with another problem. It may be that the individual does not possess the basis for making a decision about what to discard and what to keep even though some form of disconnection can be achieved. It would appear, however, that to unlearn has the potential for helping us to adjust and grow.

It is important to note that everyone will not see unlearning as unlearning. Many will see it as learning. The difference is subtle and best understood if you think of unlearning as that activity which comes first and makes new learning possible. Even if it is considered a form of learning it is a necessary part of the process and becomes more necessary as the conflicts between what we know and what we experience increase.

Ways to unlearn

Mowrer defines unlearning as "how (the process) learning in either direction (positive approach behavior and habit or negative avoidance behavior) can be undone, counteracted or reversed."[*] Some unlearning occurs normally as part of life. It occurs because of the discovery of new data which destroys the apparent validity of previously learned data. By using a rational approach, we then question our previous premises or points of view and prepare ourselves to look at another perspective. This happens for the scientist when the results of an experiment don't confirm previous theories or concepts. Here the unlearning process is usually one of reexamination, retest and discussion with others in search of some explanation which will rationally explain the difference. Failing to find the explanation, we tentatively set aside the past and experiment to see if we can gain further verification for the new. Unlearning in this example consisted of examining the past knowledge, trying to rationalize the difference with new data, and tentatively or temporarily setting the old aside to make further exploration of the new more comfortable and more compatible with what is known. This is the standard method of science—the scientific method.

---

[*]   O. Hobart Mowrer, *Learning Theory and Behavior* (New York: Wiley, 1960), p. 388. Reprinted with permission.

It is also possible that unlearning occurs simply when the weight of new evidence is overwhelming and we are forced to accept change. This setting aside of the past is probably not the scientific method. It may be that sometimes all we do in this situation is to repress or sublimate the old without really giving it up. Much psychoanalytic theory and practice is built on this premise; that is, that problems occur in life because we have failed to understand, in the context of the new evidence. Although unlearning does happen by rational decision based on the weight of evidence, it can appear to happen when we just repress previous data, blocking it by new information.

Unlearning may also occur in life because we set up the expectations for it. This is done when we enroll in a course of formal study and expect results which can only be achieved by accepting the new. In these cases we open ourselves to change. A form of unlearning is, therefore, opening up. We can unlearn by expecting to learn something new and thereby create the conditions for acceptance.

With these brief introductory thoughts we will explore several possible additional ways to unlearn and mention techniques which may be transferable to the task of unlearning.

1. *Behavioral Training.* Behavioral scientists have given us a body of experimental information which demonstrates that people can be retrained to behave differently. That is, by providing a positive reinforcement for the new behavior, and generally no reinforcement for the old behavior, we can diminish the old response. From this it is possible to propose that unlearning could be accomplished by depriving the individual, or by the individual setting up self-deprivation, of positive reinforcement for old behavior. This unlearning could be separated from the acquisition of the new behavior. This loss of the old without acquisition of the new should set up a condition of openness and readiness to accept new information. As a result of this technique the individual might be likened to a sponge which has been squeezed but not yet allowed to expand.

An example of unlearning through behavioral training exists in weight-loss programs and several of the programs designed to help individuals stop smoking. First, these programs associate negative rewards with the act of smoking. One system suggests buying another brand you do not like. Second, these systems often associate positive reinforcement with nonsmoking. This is done by the individual setting up a reward to be self-given when certain goals are reached. There are, of course, many other aspects of such programs which depend on other principles like support from others.

2. *Breaking Neural Patterns.* Psychiatry has used shock therapy for serious unlearning. This is very drastic action. By apparently overloading or overstressing previous neural connections, these connections seem to be broken thus forcing the individual to learn anew. Similarly, a stroke is an internal accident which can destroy neural connections and recovery is dependent on building anew. For our purposes, both of these occurrences are undesirable, but it is conceivable that the concept is applicable to some milder form of unlearning cognitive knowledge. For example, consider the possibility of using a simple device such as a pair of glasses which distort perspective and force the learning of new patterns. The glasses in effect break or block the former transmission route.

3. *Surfacing, Sharing, or Reliving Past Experience.* Psychoanalysis gives us a clue to unlearning through the process of bringing past experience into conscious thought. By this process the individual becomes able to make a conscious choice as to whether this previous knowledge or experience will be allowed to continue to influence or affect future life. This surfacing of the past can be done on a verbal or cognitive level or at a feeling, sensing, reliving level as in Gestalt dream analysis. It is part of the reason group encounter works, and it is a basis for much pastoral and social-service counselling. Admittedly, most often this process is dealing with material not closely related to the knowledge base of a professional career but it is conceivable the technique is applicable. Such a technique may require the cooperation of another person.

An example may be found in some of the activities included as part of career planning for working adults. In these workbooks or sessions one of the activities is to draw a lifeline and cite and chart major positive and negative events. Unburdening oneself of past experience both positive and negative is a necessary and desirable precursor to thinking about the future.

4. *Training in a New Mode of Thinking.* Study of Eastern philosophy and religion suggests that the practice of meditation, Zen, and various forms of yoga may represent a process of unlearning. Certainly the openness, the absence of internal or negating struggle, and the acceptance of the concept of "one way" all tend to make the student better able to accept new knowledge. Some of the experimental reports published by those marketing meditation techniques certainly tend to demonstrate the power of this approach for unlearning and suggest that productivity and success in life are greatly improved for many people.

5. *Creativity Training.* Those who have studied creativity have developed many exercises or processes devised to make problem solving or arriving at new answers a more probable outcome. These processes cause the individual to face a problem from a new perspective. They also provide ways of trapping the individual in the negative results of past experience for the purpose of helping him find new ways. Normally creativity deals

---

PERSONAL EXPERIMENT 12

Experiencing unblocking a free flow is probably the best way to understand this type of unlearning. Take pencil and paper and list all the uses you can dream up for old tires. Think of yourself as a consultant to a used-tire lot. Don't forget humorous uses. Really let yourself go and don't evaluate the practicality of the idea. If you really succeed in reducing your inhibitions you should easily list more than twenty uses. Here is a start:

- filling drained and unused swimming pools
- crash-landing pads for airplanes in distress
- beach erosion control
- replacements for Jack's beanstalk

How many did you come up with? Did you notice how not stopping to evaluate the practicality, if you were able to do so, unleashed a flow of ideas? Now look back at the list. If you had a surplus of old tires, are there some you would go on to investigate?

---

with process blocking. Creativity processes are designed to free up inhibitions and set up expectations for wild ideas. Individuals are encouraged to express what otherwise would be unacceptable ideas. Creativity is enhanced by restricting evaluation of ideas until a later stage. The process lowers the threshold of inhibition and is a form of unblocking.

6. *Sensory-Awareness Training.* Some people in search of a fuller and better life have pursued the reawakening of deadened or dulled senses as a route to openness and new learning. Their thesis is that in order to maintain stability in a life filled with too many stimuli we have learned to detune our receptors. Those teaching sensory awareness have demonstrated that training can enhance the individual's contact with the world and enrich life. Thus they escape a world of stimulus deprivation. Included in this concept is the possibility of heightening the individual's awareness of bodily activities and responses through the amplification and feedback of body responses. In other words, biofeedback expands this concept beyond the response of senses normally attributed to humans. In any case, heightening sensory awareness is a form of unblocking for new learning.

Because of sensational press coverage some of the examples of sensory-awareness enhancement emerged as faddish and avant-garde. A simple example will stress the point of enrichment which is possible. Think to a time when you visited a beach and responded to the urge to take off your shoes. How much more of the experience comes through when bare feet touch the sand, a rock, or the water!

7. *Work-Group Restructure.* Those who are pursuing industrial democracy and improved quality of working life are experimenting with work-group restructure. Because the individual gains values and establishes beliefs with respect to the group, and because of the individual's desire to belong which brings conformity to group norms, it is possible that restructuring groups may be a key to unlearning. Unlearning here is related to changing the patterns of previous interpersonal relationships and establishing new relationships. For example, some experiments substitute group accomplishment as norms instead of individual achievement and interpersonal competition. What goes on when a person joins such a group is new learning. The restructure is the precondition which changes the rules, unblocks, and opens the possibility for new learning. An example could be a managerless group. Suggestions, participation, and decisions which were previously repressed because the manager was in charge are now desired and rewarded.

8. *Intellectual Understanding of Learning.* Most of our education has been based on the concept that exposing the individual to new data will of itself cause learning or the displacement of the old concepts. This is an old-fashioned educational theory. We teach believing that learning is adding knowledge much like a child building a tower of blocks. It is possible that if we could demonstrate that knowledge acquisition is like filling a crate with eggs and that removal of the knowledge from one compartment neither hurts nor destroys the whole, we can establish an intellectual basis for unlearning and changed behavior. In other words, one approach to unlearning may be to teach new concepts of learning.

An example of an educational approach which stresses the structure rather than the content is theme teaching. A teacher who picks a theme like the Mississippi River and teaches social studies, economics, and mathematics only as ways of understanding the impact of the river is using this approach. Such an approach is not in itself unlearning but accepting the different concept of the learning process may require unlearning.

9. *Controlled Irrationality.* Life consists of learning socially acceptable behavior. We learn to play our roles and to do those things which are expected of us. This process causes a dulling of instincts and a rejection of the natural or spontaneous. Possibly this practice of closing off part of us needs to be broken in order to open us to new experience. In this context the philosopher Alan Watts suggested building a bit of nonsense or controlled craziness into our lives to extend life, enhance vitality, and restore

creativity. His suggestion was that we set aside a portion of each day when doing anything is acceptable to get the nonrational, nonordered activities flowing. One example may be setting up conditions which make reliving dreams acceptable and desirable. What is suggested here is the recreation of childlike behavior under controlled conditions. To do this one must either be alone and safe from interruption or with a group which is sharing the experience.

10. *Direct Biological or Physiological Processes.* There are many beliefs and evidences in our culture which support a relationship between body health and the health of the mind. It is possible that there is an inverse relationship between one's mental openness and muscular tightness. If one accepts the concept that a body in balance with good muscular tone supports openness, then training to acquire this is unlearning. An experimental way of dealing directly with the physiology or biology of unlearning might include Tai Chi, Rolfing, osteopathic or chiropractic manipulation, calesthenics, group games, individual exercise, breathing exercises, diet, and vitamins.

Tai Chi is meditation in motion. By training oneself to assume a carefully prescribed series of positions in a flowing sequence one exercises every muscle and increases the mind-body relationship. The process requires concentration. Practice of Tai Chi seems to enhance energy and vigor and open the individual to a fuller and more successful life.

These concepts are not the only applicable ones. However, for a start, they provide sufficient opportunities for suggesting a range of possible activities and for starting on building a plan for personal exploration of unlearning in relationship to maintaining vitality.

The relationship of unlearning to learning

In trying to understand the relationship between unlearning and learning we have a sort of chicken and egg problem. Early learning by the child presumably is not dependent on unlearning. Adult learning, however, must represent some displacement, breaking of connections with or setting aside of previous information. Is this setting aside part of the learning process or a precondition? Does strong motivation to learn make unlearning less necessary? Does the type of learning, the subject, or the relationship of learning to self-concept or image have an effect on the necessity for unlearning? Is emotional involvement the key? Certainly emotional attachment to previous knowledge could be presumed to make unlearning difficult. But emotional involvement is also necessary for new learning. It is not easy to sort out these relationships without experiment. Even with experiment it is conceivable that we will find that individual differences are more significant than general principles in influencing outcomes.

The desire for learning frequently occurs in adults when they discover something they have supposedly learned doesn't fit the facts, doesn't work, or doesn't supply a satisfactory explanation for what they have observed. The adult says, "I thought this was true, but obviously it is not. I'll have to find out more about that." Here unlearning creates the desire for learning because one of the eggs has been taken out of the crate. The adult has consciously set aside a previous answer and created an opening. There is a felt need to replace it. This is a powerful motivation for continued learning and study. When we find we haven't enough knowledge to understand what we have observed, our picture of the world has a hole in it.

Some people are ashamed or self-conscious about admitting this kind of intellectual curiosity. This insecurity often causes the substitution of a plausible reason for continuing education. Such reasons include: I want to make more money, or I want a better job. It is not yet socially acceptable to say, "I want to get turned on by learning."

Clarification of the relationship between unlearning and learning will come through setting up hypotheses and testing them. Our hypotheses are as follows:

1. The need for unlearning as a precondition for taking in new knowledge increases with the rigidity of the individual's position with respect to the subject or skill to be learned.
2. The need for unlearning grows with increase in the rate of change of the applicable knowledge base and the need for personal adjustment or change.
3. The need for unlearning is inverse to the individual's depth of understanding of self, comfort with self, and clarity of self-concept. Probably the better integrated and more open the personality the less the need for unlearning as a separate capability.
4. Techniques and processes for unlearning can be taught.
5. Adults can improve their vitality, capability to continue learning, and adaptation to change by learning to disconnect from the consequences of previous learning.

It is suggested that each of us in our own ways set out to test these hypotheses for ourselves. We can do so by making slight changes in our lives and embarking on relatively simple, non-threatening experiments. Or we can set out in a more aggressive way. In either case, as good "scientists" engaged in the process of learning about ourselves and improving our vitality, we should record what happens and make personal comparisons between learning when we have tried some unlearning process first and learning when we have not. Such a process is, of course, scientifically unreliable because we will want to show that a technique works. The purpose is to get us all to experiment.

Moderate personal action and experiment

Some simple test of your need to engage in unlearning activity is a desirable first step. Here is one to try. I really do not know whether saying "yes" or "no" to a specific number of these questions indicates a need for unlearning. Generally I believe the underlined answers indicate some need for unlearning. Try answering the questions for yourself. Then see if you will join me in the conviction that we all can use unlearning to offset some of the negative consequences of living and learning.

A writer in the *New Yorker* magazine several years ago suggested a simple but effective form of unlearning which provides another starting exercise. List all of those things you have always been thinking about doing but never seem to get around to doing. For example, I've thought I would like to learn to play the organ, write a book, take a series of photographs to illustrate activities in America, make a contemporary movie, and so on. List those things you've been carrying around as baggage, feeling you want to do. Next, systematically decide you will do them or that you are not going to do them. Stop worrying about and beating yourself up about those things you are not going to do. Cross them off your list and stop carrying them as desires. By doing so you may find a great weight is lifted from your shoulders. For those things that you really want to do—start doing them a little at a time. Try to make a little progress each day. Use some of the time you usually waste to do this. This process requires self-discipline. While it seems a simple method of straightening the record with yourself, it can open new spaces for accomplishment. By eliminating nagging, negative wear

PERSONAL EXPERIMENT 13

Unlearning Check List

- Do you sometimes find yourself in the position of saying something won't work because of previous experience?   (<u>Yes</u>) (*No*)

- Are you sometimes considered by others to be fixed and unbending in your perspective?   (<u>Yes</u>) (*No*)

- Do you enjoy solving puzzles like mazes or word puzzles?   (*Yes*) (<u>No</u>)

- Can you list four or five new ideas, thoughts, concepts, activities, skills you've acquired or tried in the last few months?   (*Yes*) (<u>No</u>)

- Would you be willing to try eating a new delicacy based on octopus?   (*Yes*) (<u>No</u>)

- Have you read one or more books in the last month?   (*Yes*) (<u>No</u>)

- Do you tend to get together with the same people for social activities?   (<u>Yes</u>) (*No*)

- Do you remember, discuss, or analyze your dreams?   (*Yes*) (<u>No</u>)

- Do you put a high value on personal vitality and new learning?   (*Yes*) (<u>No</u>)

- Did you change your first reaction to any of the questions above as a result of seeing the underline?   (<u>Yes</u>) (*No*)

and tear on you and your energies it frees energies. This process represents an example of the necessary unlearning activity of facing up to and disconnecting from the consequence of previous experience, data, or decisions. Unblocking or opening occurs when we let go of something we have been carrying around. This technique is of value in clarifying our career objectives. For example, someone who has always wanted to become a vice president but knows it is practically impossible in reality could make life more effective by giving up that aspiration. Do you have an unrealistic career aspiration to clean out?

At work many of us who are knowledge workers and professionals frequently engage in communications and problem solving in groups. We call meetings to review problems and plan action. A way of trying a simple form of unlearning or unblocking in this situation is to ask each person before the meeting begins to tell the others in the group what perspective, biases, preconceived notions, or answers they carried into the room. If at the beginning of each such session we each unburden we can open the channels for communication and avoid some of the blocks or misfires normally occurring. These blocks occur because we don't admit, even to ourselves, these preconditions and certainly don't reveal them to others. We communicate inefficiently or miscommunicate because of the assumptions we have made about where others stand on the issue.

Here is another form of personal unblocking or clearing. This technique consists of pushing oneself to remember a series of things and dredging up memories associated with them. The suggestion is to record these dredgings and at the end free yourself by some symbolic destruction like burning the paper. There is no presumption that any specific item in the series represents a problem, only that its blocking effects may end by bringing it into consciousness, thus allowing you choice about its future impact on your life.

As an example of how it works, one chooses two or three categories. Typical categories might be people I've known, experiences I've had, concepts I believe, techniques I use, or projects I have worked on. These are just examples and the categories you choose should fit you and your unlearning need. For each of these categories, list a number of separate items or incidents. In Arica I understand they would suggest five hundred. I believe two hundred will work. The important thing is that the number be large enough to stretch your recall. For each of these entries then list at least five attributes, aspects, memories, associations, or relationships. A completed item might look like any of the following. These examples do not represent items from a consistent category but rather a random group:

- Amsterdam visit, 1970—canals, candles, wine, friends, pictures, flea market

- Rose garden, Wappingers—don't put a $4 rose in a 10¢ hole, scent, trials, failures, beauty
- James Kip Finch—philosopher, stacks of paper, double desk, pen and ink sketches, wassail, waiting for attention, 1906 Columbia, creative woodwork, gentle

Whatever notes you make, they are yours and for your eyes only. One might liken it to a diary all written at one time and created in retrospect. A diary which is created to push recall and thus aid in unblocking and unlearning is an example of our third category of unlearning technique. Remember to destroy the list in a somewhat ceremonial way.

A third example of a moderate personal-unlearning project is meditation. In its simplest form meditation consists of learning to turn off our constant activity both mental and physical and let happen what will happen without trying to control the outcome. It is relaxation but with an undirected alertness. It is not accomplished by trying. The meditator is not asleep but rather quite sensitive to things which are normally not able to get through to consciousness because of our ongoing barrage of mental activity. A good source of information on meditation is *How To Meditate* by Laurence LeShan.

Why is meditation a form of unlearning? First, because it seems to cause a new openness, an enhanced ability to accept what is. Second, because there is extensive evidence that meditation opens the individual to personal growth, increased learning, reduced anxiety, and increased effectiveness. In other words, if unlearning means disconnecting with the consequences of previous learning, some of the things which happen to meditators seem to be like that. Meditation is suggested because it is relatively easy to try as a personal project and because you can be the judge of improvement or change.

These examples of moderate personal experimentation with the idea of unlearning are just that—examples. You are a better designer of experiments for yourself than anyone else. The impact on you results more from the concept of experimentation than from the particular experiment. In designing an experiment you should review the ten types of unlearning starting on page 156 for ways which are applicable to your unlearning need. Behavioral training, type 1, can be tried by picking some minor but desirable reward for yourself and giving it to yourself for each recognized demonstration of new openness on your part. Surfacing and sharing types might be experimented with by agreeing with some friend or a member of your family to take five minutes a day to listen to them and five more minutes for them to listen to you. The topic in this example might be to describe some past experience. In any case, experiment!

Aggressive personal action

Making the decision to change outlook, behavior, or role and actively seeking experiences which accelerate change are examples of aggressive unlearning activity. There is no one way; and processes which work well at one stage of a person's life are not appropriate at another. Because one system allows one person to move to a new level of self-awareness doesn't mean it is the right process for you. Each of us must understand our personal process of learning and be ready for a specific experience to have value for us. We should be ready for that experience.

A selection of possible activities listed below fall into the broad classes or types of unlearning described earlier. The list represents primarily those things you can find at a nearby educational institution or nontraditional learning center. The numbers referenced, therefore, refer to the earlier list which starts on page 156. Many activities include aspects of several of these categories and where this is true the several numbers are referenced.

Courses or activities which may contribute to unlearning

Autogenic Training—1, 2
Biofeedback—1, 2, 6
Encounter—3, 4, 10
est—Erhard Systems Training—1, 2, 3, 6, 9
Meditation—4
Arica—1, 4
Yoga—4, 8
Tai Chi—4, 10
Rolfing—2, 3, 6, 10

Creativity Workshops—4, 5, 8
Team Building and Organization Development—1, 4, 7
Massage—3, 10
Growth-Movement Activities—3, 4, 9, 10
Psychoanalysis—3, 4, 9
Retreats and Monastic Activities—1
Gestalt Dream Analysis—3, 4

The fact that these activities are listed does not mean endorse-
ment. Variation in quality and competence of the people running
seminars in these categories is great. The listing is neither complete
nor representative of all the ways which may work. More complete
listings can be found in suggested readings.

Another way to design an unlearning activity is to concentrate
on the measurable outcome. Figure 8.1 shows the desired outcome
graphically. A successful unlearning activity makes a significant
change in the rate of growth which is discontinuous in relationship
to both prior growth and growth after the event. Can you think of
an activity or a process which will put you on a new or higher learning and growth curve?

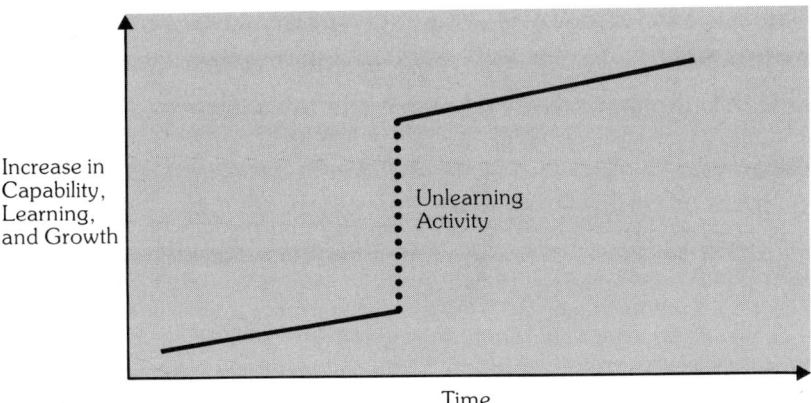

Fig. 8.1   Outcome of successful unlearning

Summary

Unlearning is descriptive of activities which open the individual for new learning and growth. Unlearning for the adult is a desirable precondition for improving the capability for additional learning and growth. Unlearning is the process of disconnecting from the consequences of prior learning and experience. Unlearning is probably increasingly necessary with increasing age and with greater intensity of emotional bonding with one's experiences. That is, when it is difficult to separate yourself from knowledge, then unlearning is most necessary to expand your ability to accept new knowledge and experience.

Activities which produce unlearning are those which help the individual to get in touch with self, share feelings and attitudes, and increase flexibility of perspective and problem-attack technique. Such activities range from those which break physical or neural connections to those which teach new philosophies or life perspectives, to those which reduce your fears of change and those which raise your level of consciousness to the consequences of previous learning. Ten categories or types of unlearning activities were presented.

Responsibility for unlearning is personal. It must become a part of your life-style. This chapter suggests that as individuals we can be taught or teach ourselves improved unlearning techniques. The message of the chapter is that we must all experiment.

Suggested readings

Adams, James L. *Conceptual Block Busting.* San Francisco: W.H. Freeman, 1974.

> *James Adams presents the reader with a distillation of the ideas he has found help him to teach Stanford University students how to be more creative. The book concentrates on improving your conceptual abilities — abilities he feels have been underemphasized in most of our education. Of particular interest to those thinking about unlearning are the chapters on perceptual blocks, cultural blocks, emotional blocks, and both conscious block busting and unconscious block busting. This is a particularly good book for designers and engineers.*

Feldenkrais, Moshe. *Awareness through Movement.* New York: Harper & Row, 1972.

Lewis, H.T., and Streitfeld, H.S. *Growth Games.* New York: Bantam, 1972.

McKim, Robert H. *Experiences in Visual Thinking*. Monterey, Calif.: Brooks/Cole, 1972.

Ornstein, Robert. *Psychology of Consciousness*. San Francisco: W.H. Freeman, 1972.

Rozak, T. *Sources—An Anthology*. New York: Harper Colophon, 1972.

Schutz, W. *Elements of Encounter*. Big Sur: Joy Press, 1973.

Yee, M.S., and Wright, D.K. *The Great Escape: A Source Book of Delights and Pleasures for the Mind and Body*. New York: Bantam Books, 1974.

9
Continued learning

Introduction

Early universities were established to educate gentlemen, or non-workers. Later the universities moved to education for service—frequently government service. In the twentieth century much education became preparation for career-oriented work. In the last twenty years we have moved from the concept of education as being a preparation for life and work to education as being part of life. Although the move has been more dramatic in the scientific and engineering fields in which the rate of change of knowledge has been well chronicled, it has become evident in all fields. In those fields where public safety or public welfare can be jeopardized by the failure to utilize new knowledge, there have been trends toward building continuing-education requirements into the law. Relicensing, revalidation, or recertification has become required in many professions. For many lifelong learning has become a natural adjustment to the changing culture, and evening or part-time study has become the popular thing to do. Such continued study may or may not be related to today's work. Some of the study is oriented toward hobbies or supplementary interests as opposed to work. However, any study apparently keeps the mind active and challenged and thus benefits many aspects of life.

Maintaining vitality is directly related to the continual acquisition of new knowledge and skills but it is not limited to only the acquisition of knowledge. The search for the economic justification of continued education goes on daily. However, most individuals and some corporations share the perception that to stop experiencing and adding new data is literally to die. Each of us can cite from personal experience the names of people we feel have maintained their energy, vitality, and aliveness without even going near formal education. But this does not mean they have not engaged in study through continued learning. Continued learning is broader than continued education or formal study and includes reading, listening, trying, face-to-face exchange, and all forms and media for continued learning. In today's world even watching TV is a form of continued study, though one may question the quality of the input and the amount of real learning because of the passivity of the viewer. People learn more quickly and better by active participation.

Critical problems for the individual who accepts the need for continued study are: What should I study? How should I engage in learning? When is it appropriate to add new knowledge? and What will be my payoff for the investment of myself, my energy, and my time?

Should the study relate to the job or to a hobby? Should the study relate to what is needed today or what's anticipated as tomorrow's challenge? Should the study relate to the acquisition of knowledge about the world or about one's self? Should it be on the cognitive level or the feeling level? What about skill improvement versus new information? Is training different from education? All these are important questions.

Obviously, we can't answer all these questions for every reader and every condition. What is presented is a way to look at continued learning and to make decisions about continued study. Our expectations which determine whether we study and the quality of our study are influenced by our previous personal experience with study. The kind of study and the priority we assign also relate to our goals and needs. Continued learning and study is presented as one technique, but not the only one, for maintaining vitality.

The challenge

Historically, learning was something expected of the young. The understanding that general learning continued through life was accepted but not stressed. The need for lifelong learning was dulled by the fact that, to live in a relatively stable world, it seemed that one didn't need to learn many new things. A slow rate of change did not stimulate continued formal study. The need for continued learning was further depressed by the feeling that the ability to learn falls off naturally with aging. In fact, there were studies that confirmed a fall-off in learning ability. Even under these conditions there were people who were leaders at least in part because they kept alive a natural spark of curiosity and extended their learning through life. Since we now conceive the state of being alive as requiring continual learning, all people must learn but adults may learn at a slower rate without conscious concentration on the need. What has changed is our understanding of the continued life-long need to adapt. The "future-shock" aspects of our times require that old ways be left behind and new things learned just to permit us to remain stable. Despite these findings, the correlation between formal learning and success in life is not easily found. John Gardner cites the dilemma by saying: "Many whom the world counts as unsuccessful have continued learning and growing throughout their lives, and some of our most prominent people stopped learning literally decades ago."[*]

We can't prove continued learning is necessary for success. We do, however, believe it is necessary for staying alive and vital. We also believe that the probability of success of an enterprise or total system is enhanced if we can create an environment which supports and encourages everyone to continue growing. Growing, by definition, includes learning. Here is how John Gardner describes the challenge:

> *Perhaps the greatest challenge in education — and the most puzzling one — is to discover what it is that keeps alive in some people the natural spark of curiosity, eagerness, hunger for life and experience, and how we may rekindle that spark when it flickers out. If we ever solve that problem, we will be at the threshold of a new era, not only in education but in human experience.*[†]

Note that Gardner equates hunger for experience with learning. It is probable that with further study and experiment we will find a correlation between maintenance of that hunger, good health, personal perceptions of success, vitality, and a longer length of life. The challenge, then, is for each of us as individuals to find a way to maintain our hunger for experience and learning. The challenge for the organization and the nation is to do what can be done to stimulate that hunger.

Learning

Learning is defined as anything which results in changed expectations or behavior. It takes place when the individual accepts and integrates new knowledge or experience and, as a result of this acceptance, changes expectations, modifies skills, and initiates new actions. Acceptance of new data or experiences can result from planned activity or from any of the unplanned activities which occur in the process of living.

---

[*]   John Gardner, *No Easy Victories* (New York: Harper & Row, 1968), p. 107. Reprinted with permission.

[†]   Ibid., p. 107.

Being exposed to new experience or information does not assure its acceptance. The individual must approach learning with an openness and a feeling of sufficient self-assurance that the risk of change does not cause blocking. If, for example, the individual fears the change that may result, the new input will be resisted and will probably not be made a part of his or her memory bank. Or, if the individual approaches new experience with a feeling that past experience or learning is still relevant, the old knowledge may literally block the acceptance of the new. Blocking can occur both in content and in process. Blocking can also occur as the result of generalizing from two previous experiences which were associated in memory or the emotional relationship to a skill or knowledge. Motivation to learn is the overall phrase we use to describe openness and the desire to change as a result of additional knowledge and experience. Motivation to learn or to change is usually built from a combination of the conditions listed below. Continued learning is based in part on becoming sensitive to and understanding these conditions in ourselves.

Conditions which can create openness to change and learning

Challenge	An opportunity to take a risk and win something we see as desirable raises our energy level and opens us to any new data we can use.
Fear of loss	Fear of aging, fear of loss of job, fear of not being needed can cause us to do more of the same or can cause a reexamination and openness to learning.
Goal desire	Picking a goal which requires change and requires study, like a new career, or teaching someone else, or writing, creates openness.
Repeated disappointment	Acknowledgment of the fact that present knowledge and skills are not working can motivate the search for new ways.
Crisis	A total failure can cause the questioning of self and the openness or vulnerability necessary to set the stage for learning.
New information	Sometimes the acceptance of a new piece of knowledge or experience which doesn't fit with previous experience opens a sequence of events which motivates further learning.

Personal assessment	The process of reflection and self-analysis can lead to the conclusion that new goals requiring change and new learning are necessary.
New environment	Immersing oneself either by plan or by chance in an environment where change and learning are both acceptable and desirable is a strong motivation for learning.

While these conditions may be the immediate causes for the initial or preparational learning, they are much more necessary as stimuli for continued learning. Whether the initial stimulus results from a positive or negative incident makes little difference as long as the individual turns it into positive outlook and action. The negatives are sometimes viewed as something which seems to happen to us. The positives seem to reflect action on our part. Learning and change stimuli may result from deliberate action on our part, even though it may not have initially had a learning objective, or by contrast may reflect our analysis of some feedback. Learning to manage these preconditions is part of managing our continued learning.

Continued study

Motivation for active, self-initiated, continued study, whether this means formal education or planned experience, is in part dependent on one's previous experience with study and the values gained. It is also based on the individual's perception of self and personal goals. In the extreme, for example, if one sees oneself as "perfect," this does not lead to much motivation for change and learning! On the other extreme, if one sees oneself as hopeless or beyond help, this also does not lead to self-initiated change and growth. Your goals for the particular phase of life you are in and your expectations are primary determinants of motivation. The environment can be supportive or not. As an example, a retired person who views his or her useful life as past, completed, and over will not be motivated to study. But a retired person who lives in a group or community where everyone is studying will be encouraged by the group and have an increased tendency to study. Following are some of the reasons an individual might develop as the basis for engaging in continued formal learning. Motivating ourselves is providing ourselves with reasons for action. This is a positive form of rationalization.

Reasons for continued formal learning

Payoff from previous study	The individual who feels that education was a major reason for current success will be more motivated to continue study than one who feels previous study was of little value. In other words, one who actively continues education will usually, on being questioned, respond with feelings that past education contributed significantly to achievements.
Absence of accepted certification	The individual who is working in a field or in a position usually attained through formal study and who lacks formal certification may feel a strong need to gain that certification. The non-degreed engineer often goes through life feeling he or she would have been more successful if the degree was part of personal armament. Similarly, the experienced professional who anticipates job change can develop a feeling that revalidation of credentials will improve marketability. In some fields legislation is contributing to this need.
Career change desires	The individual who wants to move to a career where academic preparation is generally accepted as necessary will tend to be motivated to engage in that study. Similarly, even though education is not required, it will frequently be chosen as a vehicle for change because it is socially acceptable and provides an environment for mobility.
Acknowledgment of changing knowledge base	Acceptance of the idea that the field of knowledge on which one's work is based is changing can motivate continued study.
Upward aspirations	An individual with a strong desire for upward mobility will engage in continued study if this activity is perceived to be an important element of success in moving up.
Need for credentials	The individual who perceives a high risk of loss of job is often motivated to study since it is understood that his or her past work experience may have little value to a new employer. Recent educational accomplishment is often viewed as having a higher value in supporting a job change than previous employer-related experience.

| Employer expectations | An employer can create an environment which motivates continued study by relating desired rewards to this activity. For example, the massive summer institutes for public-school teachers have been built on the base that such study leads to salary increase and position change. |

These seven reasons are but representative of the kinds of reasons the individual develops for continued study. If you have engaged in study beyond the basic preparation for your career, what has been your reason? Do you fit in one or more of these categories? If you have not been active, has it been because you don't see yourself in one of these categories? Can you now accept one of these reasons as a base for stimulating your continued learning?

Function of learning

As searchers for vitality, the extension of our personal productivity and the increase in satisfactions from life, we first ask, what is the function of learning? Learning takes place as a result of interaction between the individual and the environment. Learning is, therefore, a way of working toward satisfaction of the basic needs of security and safety. By learning that a hot stove burns and burns are painful, the individual learns to avoid touching hot stoves. By learning how to relate to other people, that is, how to communicate with them and receive responses from them, learning contributes to the higher-level needs of belonging and self-esteem. Learning the values and mores of a group makes it possible for us to choose either to join the group or reject it and seek elsewhere for satisfaction of our need to belong. By learning how to learn and by sensing those things which contribute to our personal feeling of well-being and success, learning contributes to our self-actualization needs.* If you learn that you gain a sense of satisfaction and purpose from helping someone else to learn, you have moved to what is termed the self-actualization level. Therefore, a function of learning is to

---

* In this sequence of examples learning function has been related to A. H. Maslow's Hierarchy of Needs, which starts with food, shelter, and security and moves to self-esteem and self-actualization. See A.H. Maslow, *Motivation and Personality* (New York: Harper Brothers, 1954.)

make it possible for us to satisfy needs and to grow toward achieving satisfaction of higher-level needs. In the sense that life provides the space for reaching and satisfying higher need levels, continued learning is a part of life. Learning is a precursor to need satisfaction.

Choosing what to learn

Broadly speaking, one can learn things which support his or her current roles or one can learn things which provide support for achieving a role change. Learning can be for today or for the future. Learning can and does support many different purposes and goals. For example, it may be in support of the work element of life or to extend and improve satisfactions from the family or personal segments of life. It can thus affect life balance or the "tuning" of a particular element.

Choosing what to learn is based on goal priorities and how we see learning as related to these goals. As adults we tend to become more results-oriented about decisions to expend time and energy. In other words, we need to see a payout for our commitment and expenditure of energy. Thus when we have a choice our learning must support our goals. Goals which involve learning can include increased job capabilities, expansion of a hobby, or enhancement of a skill which has broad applicability. Such directed learning is usually called study. The time for study must usually be taken away from some other activity, so life-balance decisions affect the choice. Figure 9.1 shows possible effects of adding study to a life-balance personal space picture. In this picture continued study is shown as being job-oriented and thus is shown as borrowing energy from job space, family space, and private space. While this continued study is a use of energy, if it is successful it should lead to a larger life space, a more satisfying job, and an increase in vitality. It may also contribute to vitality before completion, if the education process is in itself providing psychological income.

It is also possible to engage in learning for learning's sake alone—that is, to engage in the process for the satisfactions which flow from the process itself. It may be a way of balancing for a part of life that is not satisfying. A related balancing approach is the choice to use education as a diversion. A woman might choose an educational activity as an excuse to get out of the house and meet others. It could, therefore, fill a primarily social need. Or study may

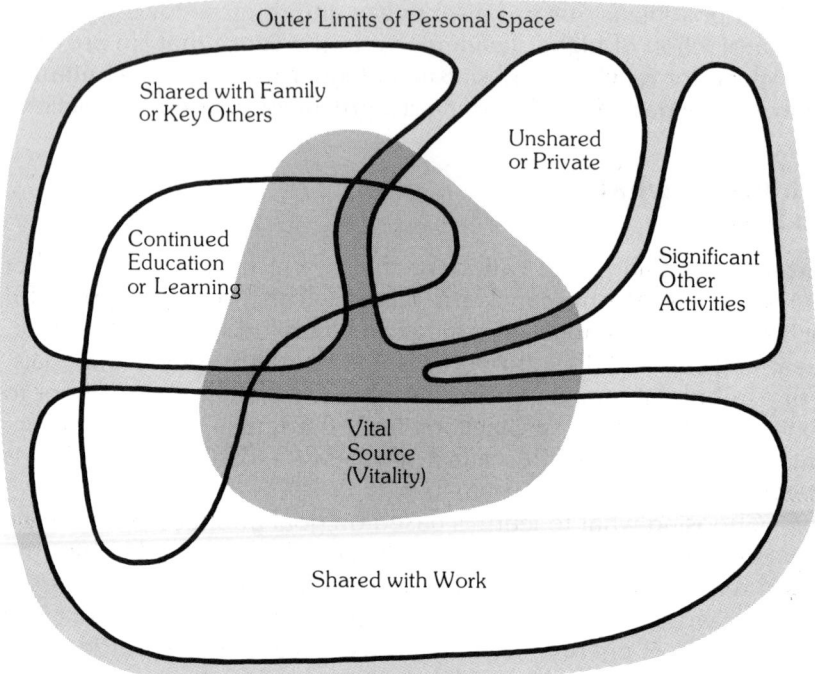

Outer Limits of Personal Space

Shared with Family
or Key Others

Unshared
or Private

Continued
Education
or Learning

Significant
Other
Activities

Vital
Source
(Vitality)

Shared with Work

Fig. 9.1   The effect of continued learning on life balance

become the central life purpose—"work"—for that person. Retired people are increasingly using education in this way.

There is also learning which takes place without conscious choice. This variety of learning is not usually referred to as study. As one varies the time one starts out to work in the morning one learns the effect of time on traffic patterns. This learning does not usually result from a desire to study traffic patterns. It may result from being late or frustrated by traffic. It may just happen. In the process of living, of doing the many little things that make up life, we are constantly learning. We learn, if our soil is clay-like, that it can be worked better wet than dry. We learn about the idiosyncrasies of devices we use and how to compensate for them. If our car brakes grab, we learn to push gently. While what we learn in these circumstances is not the result of a topical learning choice, by changing our activities and environments we can increase our learning rate. Increase in the amount and kind of this unplanned learning has an effect on vitality and our readiness to learn other things. Taking a vacation trip is an example of a choice that exposes us to many new inputs. Vitality is improved by increasing our exposure to change, to increase the probability of this unplanned learning. Vitality is improved by increasing or changing exposure to increase our hunger for planned learning.

Sensing the need for study

If we consider that study is recreated experience designed to help people learn, that it is directed, goal-oriented learning, how do we know if we need it? We learn to decode body signals that tell us we need food or physical exercise. Are there some signals we can learn to decode that tell us when study is necessary? One possibility is that some aspect of our life isn't working and we observe that others are able to do better than we can. We also observe that those who have been through a particular educational experience are the ones who do better. This decoded signal tells us we need to study, that our capability could be improved by study. Another clue to needed study is a desire to do something for which we have no information and no skill. For instance, if one has an interest in leather working and no knowledge, some learning is necessary to pursue the interest. These are internally generated needs and education is shaped by what a person is.

Need for study can also be influenced by the environment. Instead of interpreting personal signals in this case we interpret environmental signals. That is, the need is externally rather than internally generated. Examples of this might be new government rules or regulations or the change of some system with which we work. Such a case could be a change in a manufacturing process in which we take part, or conversion to new record-keeping systems in the bank where we have an account. Or it may be that we are in an environment which generates anxieties which can be reduced through study. In other words, one's need for study may be to reduce internal sensations of stress! This is a good motivation for learning. It is possible all needs for study can be sensed at this level. Sensing internal stress which can be relieved by study may be a key to discovering the body signals which suggest further learning. By

PERSONAL EXPERIMENT 14

Collect the catalogues of nearby institutions providing evening, one- or two-day, or weekend offerings of educational programs. Select some subject which entices you because it sounds interesting or one about which you have had some interest but have not followed up with enrollment. It is preferable that you pick a new area of interest. It can be a hobby interest or associated with some idea of future career or job. The course need not be a long one nor an extensive one. Enroll in the selected program. During and after the program ask yourself the following questions:

- What motivated me to pick this course? Has it fulfilled my expectations?
- What were the benefits to me? Were there some immediate benefits? Will there be some long-run benefits?
- Does this experience lead me to consider further continuing education? If not, why not? If it does, why?

understanding our stresses which can be reduced through study, we may find the way to become as similarly sensitive to ourselves as we are to other needs like eating. Learning and study can be stress reducing or stress creating! If we think of these activities as stress reducing we have a basis for determining when study is needed.

Do you need to study?

How do you know whether you need to study? It is easy to say yes, you do because we all do. It is more difficult to say you must learn to sense the need as we have discussed. Some or all of the sample symptoms listed below may be present and help you to determine that you do. These symptoms are related to the motivations listed earlier. Here they are more closely related to you.

Personal symptoms of the need for study

Symptom	Test
Reduced interest	Active study rekindles interest.
Insecurity and anxiety	Improvement in self-worth through study.
Confusion	Sense of direction comes through study.
Anger	Improved calmness and self-control through study.
Discontent	Study provides way to gain sense of accomplishment and meaningfulness.

The important lesson is that determining whether study will contribute to your vitality requires becoming sensitive to yourself. It is necessary next to try study or some other activity to determine if the activity contributes positively to improvement. You must take action and then measure and analyze the feedback. Whether you get some satisfaction, some improvement in capability or some reduction of tension is a key factor in your motivation and determination of the benefit from continued education.

Form, media, and relationship

Another aspect of continued study and learning is discovering how you learn most effectively. The form and media which shape your learning experience must match you. A couple of examples will help explain this concept. We all have five senses. For each of us, however, these senses rank differently in providing us with input. Some of us are eye-minded and, for those, reading or visual media will be more successful forms than listening. Some of us learn best by doing. For those, the kinesthetic learning of practice processes will work better than reading. Which medium works best depends also on content. It is impossible to learn how to ride a bike from pictures or reading. It is learning by doing it in the presence of a teacher. Some of us need the stimulation of a group. For these people group or class learning situations will provide a better medium than private study.

It is important to understand that all study does not bring the same results. It is not solely the subject matter and the motivation which can make a difference in success but also the form, timing, and nature of the study. Time of day makes a difference for people whose peak performance is in the morning or late in the day. Concentrated versus periodic classes make another difference in timing. Total immersion, concentrated study of only one subject as sometimes used in language study, works for some and not for others. In our primary and secondary schooling, we most often did not have free choice of timing and form. In continued learning and study we have much greater freedom. Choosing the form, medium, timing, and relationship is, therefore, critical to whether continued learning is fun and successful or not.

By relationship we mean the integration or nonintegration with practice and life. Much study is separate from life. As youngsters, we were willing to study something because it was required. Separate study disassociated from life has a more significant place at that time. As adults, because of a more results-oriented outlook, we require a practical application. This need to use the learning when satisfied provides reinforcement for the learning. When we have the opportunity to put our learning into use we are motivated to learn. Adult learning occurs when there is a problem to solve.

Summary

The function of continued learning is restimulation and renewal as well as the addition of new knowledge and skills. By integrating learning and study into our lives we extend our growth, improve our productivity, and contribute to our personal vitality. What we should study is determined by our knowledge of ourselves and our learning habits. An important part of the process is to become sensitive to the signs both internal and external which indicate the need for the stimulation and expansion. We must become sensitive to ourselves as part of the process of managing our continued learning. Continued learning and study is as important to life as eating, sleeping, or exercise.

Suggested readings

American Society for Engineering Education. Continuing Engineering Studies Division Monograph. This series of annual publications began in 1966. The monographs are available from ASEE Suite 400, One Dupont Circle, Washington, D.C., 20036.

Baldwin, L.V.; Collins, A.J.; Davis, C.M.; and Schmelling, G., eds. *Workshop on Continuing Education for Engineers at Mid-Career*. Published as a result of an NSF-sponsored conference, August 21–22, 1974, held at Dallas/Fort Worth Airport.

Bruner, Jerome G. *On Knowing: Essays for the Left Hand*. Cambridge: Belknap Press of Harvard University Press, 1962.

Gardner, John. *Self-Renewal*. New York: Harper & Row, 1964.

Grayson, Lawrence P., and Biedenbach, Joseph M., eds. *Proceedings from Annual Frontiers in Education Conference*. New York: IEEE and Washington: ASEE, 1975.

Hanau, Laia. *The Study Game: How to Play and Win With Statement-Pie*. New York: Barnes & Noble, 1974.

Knowles, Malcolm. *Self-Directed Learning: A Guide for Learners and Teachers*. New York: Association Press, 1975.

> *This is a book which can be used to develop your own competence as a self-directed continuing learner. It is not a book which can just be read—it requires your participation. It thus sets the tone and spirit for its title. Knowles presents you with the need-survival, with the necessary competencies, and with a way to develop your learning plan. He helps you solve the question: What should I learn? I recommend this book to anyone who is seriously interested in enhancing his or her vitality.*

10
Job and organization design

Introduction

In the search for a better working life, for an environment which contributes to vitality, an important element is the job itself. Each of us wants and needs different psychological income from our work but we also have needs in common. Here we take a hard look at some of the techniques which have been or are being used to improve the individual's relation to work. These insights should help each of us to achieve increased individual vitality and growth.

The objective of organizational design is to create a system which can achieve organizational goals, be self-correcting and modifying, make the best use of human capabilities, and contribute to quality of life. This requires participation of the human beings who are part of the system in its learning, design, and modification.

Design or redesign can be approached at several levels. The broadest level is environmental. By changing the philosophies, the fundamental principles and the beliefs to which the organization or group subscribes, one can change the probability of specific events occurring in that environment. Changed behavior seems to flow from change in values, reward systems, and expectations.

One can also change the design of the organization from a structural point of view. For example, what happens to people and how they feel are different in a functional organization than in a project-oriented organization. A functional organization is one where people doing like things are grouped. People in a project organization are grouped by end result rather than specialty. Structurally, some organizations seem to express a feeling of permanence and others a feeling of transience. How the individual behaves and relates is strongly affected by his or her perception of permanence and stability. Temporary systems seem to accelerate individualization or separation of the individual from the group or, even more severely, contribute to alienation. It is as if the individual senses the temporariness and compensates for it by retreating to self or seeking alternative organizations and systems with which to relate.

Redesign at the next level of detail can be found on the work group or team. Here the emphasis is on the relationship of the members of the team to each other and the team to the process or activity. Successful team redesign depends on the relative difference between skill levels and knowledge levels within the group being minimized. Group design also emphasizes the relationship of the social environment to the work and suggests new patterns of reward and new distribution of leadership authority.

The most specific level of design is at the job level. At this level, by varying the characteristics of the task, one can influence the job holder's response to the job. Job design depends on understanding the individual's needs and capabilities as well as the work processes and goals. Characteristics which are amenable to job redesign include the complexity, the time to feedback of results, the types of results fed back, the amount and character of decision making, the social purpose, and many others. Understanding job and organization design is essential to help you improve the payout from your job.

Characteristics of a good organization

If we are to design for improvement, we need an understanding of what is good and bad. Criteria for judging the quality and performance of an organization depend on point of view and desired outcomes. For example, an organization is good from the perspective of ownership when it returns good dividends and grows in value—how good depends on comparison with other investment alternatives. So, too, from the viewpoint of an employee, an organization is good when it returns good income and psychological payouts for the investment of personal time and energy compared with other available alternatives. From the perspective of a citizen and customer of an organization, it is good if it supplies good quality services or products for the price and does not contribute unnecessarily to a loss in quality of the environment.

Albert Cherns, who has been studying ways of improving the operation of organizations and groups and increasing the quality of working life, has evolved a set of principles. These principles, which define the concepts of sociotechnical design, also set up specifications for a "good" organization. A discussion of a few of these will help to sharpen our concept of the goal of redesign and establish a definition of a "good" organization.

His first principle is "compatibility." This means that the design of an organization must reinforce and support the objectives of the organization. Such a design should provide for self-correction and learning so that the system can take best advantage of the human capabilities and adapt to change.

His second principle is that the organization design should specify and limit activities as little as possible. That is, a good design is one which leaves humans free to do what is necessary to make the system go. Several times in recent history the air-traffic controllers have demonstrated the negative aspects of over specification. By working to the rules they have managed to all but eliminate the possibility of flying, meeting schedules, and handling the many passengers who need air transport.

Another of Cherns' principles suggests that errors or malfunctions should be handled as close to the point of origin as possible. This is another way of stating the management principle of delegating decision making to the lowest possible level. He suggests too that information flow in the organization should make this close-to-source action possible. This means that the reports of function, quality, and quantity in a productive process should go to the people who have to make the decisions. Again, the impact is to free humans to do the creative things of which they are capable.

In another principle Cherns suggests that the design of an organization should provide quality working life for its members. In other words, an organization which meets its objectives at a human cost that seems undesirable is not a good organization. *

The transcendent concept inherent in all these principles is that the organization should take advantage of human capabilities to react creatively to changed conditions and thus enhance the organization's ability to adapt, change, and grow.

The quality of a job is more specific. For example, an employee could feel that he or she is working for a high-quality and supportive organization. This would be one with good overall policies, which generally provides high pay and psychological income for the employees, but a given individual might have a job within the organization which he or she does not see as satisfying. In a hospital, which generally qualifies as an organization of worth, the job of surgeon would normally have a high position in the hierarchy of job values. In the same organization, the job of dishwasher would usually rank low in job values. Either, however, could rank low or high for a particular person because of specific work-condition variables. The operating room might be small and old, thus providing less than adequate support for the surgeon; or the nurses could, because they see their jobs as providing low

---

* Albert Cherns, "Principles of Sociotechnical Design," to be published in *Human Relations.*

satisfaction, be hard to work with. Either situation might contribute negatively to an individual's view of the job. The dishwasher, by comparison, might work in a newly equipped kitchen with outstanding equipment and have a supervisor who is understanding, supportive, and fair. Organization quality and job quality are, therefore, not necessarily parallel. A job which, by position in the social or skill hierarchy, might often be considered good or bad may be either because of specific circumstances. One would expect, however, that the probability of having a satisfying job is higher in an organization which places high value on human satisfactions than in one which does not. This is supported by the fact that if it truly values human satisfaction, bad job characteristics will eventually be recognized and rectified.

The characteristics which are judged good or bad depend not only on specific work conditions and personal perspective but on values and goals. In the earlier discussion of organization value we suggested the stockholders look at increased corporate value and dividend income as outputs of value. A retired person might be more interested in income because income is what is important to him. A young person earning sufficient income from her own job would probably be more interested in growth in value of the investment. Similarly the employee who highly values learning and growth will examine the possibilities of achieving these values in the organization. The individual who cannot pay his or her bills will feel salary is most important. One's values and desired incomes are not constant. These values or goals change through life.

To simplify this discussion we must set limits. By limiting our interests to vitality and growth for the individual within the organization, we can make some general statements. Keep in mind that the relative priority of these values will vary with the individual. What is of primary importance to us is how the organization or the job measures up to *our* criteria, not how it meets some general criteria. An organization which provides one with opportunities for growth and vitality is one which has the following characteristics:

- Recognizes individual capability and rewards those who apply it
- Respects the individual
- Provides challenging work
- Has a positive purpose which contributes to society or to human betterment
- Does not invade the individual's privacy

- Has a healthy, open, adult environment
- Supports growth and learning by providing facilities, time, and monetary support for self-development activities
- Provides freedom to change activity, career or job, and interests without undue loss and without leaving the organization
- Has a minimum number of rules and limits but administers what it has firmly
- Provides for individual participation in goal and direction setting
- Provides for participation in the rewards or profits of the organization
- Establishes fair means for resolving conflict and differences
- Has open communication channels, both up and down

An individual may not wish to take advantage of or equally value each item on this list. Often, however, the existence of these positive aspects provides a sort of blanket, or umbrella, which augurs for a positive individual relationship. In other words, if one finds an organization with these beliefs, it is probable that the organization puts a high value on and supports its human assets.

Characteristics of job quality

The characteristics of a good job have been defined by many social scientists. Most of these lists deal primarily with the psychological payouts. These are higher-level payouts, in Maslow's terms. In defining a good job we must understand, therefore, that the organization also must provide the more basic (hygenic, in Herzberg's terms) needs. Hygenic needs are those which provide support and contribute to the broad quality but are not in themselves directly motivating. Examples might include working facilities, a good general level of pay, sufficient medical benefits, and vacations and holidays. Therefore, a set of typical entries for a good job might be:

Hygenic and basic — first order

- Pleasant physical working conditions
- Fair reward and punishment
- Pay in proportion to contribution
- Benefits which protect against excessive personal costs for medical problems
- Firm and supportive management

Psychological — second order

- "Challenging or demanding work
- Learning on a job
- Decision-making freedom
- Social support and recognition
- That the work lead to social good—meaningfulness
- Work that leads to some desirable future" *

Specific and individual — third order

- A sense of impact on the organization
- A sense of closure on specific activities
- Proper timing and feedback of results in a way which matches the individual's needs
- A sense of accomplishment and achievement
- A sense of belonging

While I believe these characteristics of sound organizations and good jobs are representative and realistic, it is not my purpose or position to defend a specific list. Rather, the import of this section is to show that, for the purposes of design, a set of criteria can be drawn up. When you decide to design or redesign an organization or a job you should have a set of values in mind. You must determine the values that are important to you.

The individual and the group

As individuals at work we are usually part of a group. Our perception of the problems of organizational malfunction or poor work organization is affected by the group and our membership in it. Our ability to redesign, to fix job and organizational problems, is also affected by the group. Understanding the dynamics of the relationship between the individual and the group and the group and the organization is a critical first step in organization and work redesign.

If in examining a poorly functioning organization you determine that your group needs to take a stronger stand on the quality of material it receives, you need group support and organizational

---

* This list is drawn from the work of Einar Thorsrud of Oslo, Norway, and can be found in ROSOW (see suggested readings), p. 6.

support to make the change. Your relationship to the group will affect this acceptance. If the group accepts you in your role of suggestor of a new approach it will help. If they do not see that as your role you will have a hard time in gaining group support. Not only your role but how the group sees its role and how management sees the group will affect ability to change.

If job redesign or task shifts or changes will make your job better, then your ability to effect change will depend on the willingness of someone else to adjust. We do not live and work in insulated and separated activities. What we do affects what someone else has to or can do. In improving work, your job, you must gain the support and acceptance of others who are affected. Often a switching of tasks can make everyone more satisfied. But it is possible to come up with tasks no one wants. These are good candidates for elimination through redesign or automation.

Where does design start?

The dream of any designer is to start with a clean slate, a new enterprise with no previous history. This may be done in design of a new facility or a new organization which does not exist. Most of us, however, are faced with slow and painstaking modification. The redesign of a complex system is changed by our very entry into the system. Design, therefore, can start at any of several levels, and social scientists often discuss ad infinitum the best place to start. No value judgment is intended here; instead, this is a "map" of the places where one can start. Entry levels in concept are as follows:

- Purpose of organization
- Policies, scope, and practices of the organization
- Design of the work environment
- Design and management pattern of the functional or project department
- Design of the work group
- Design of the job
- Design of the tasks

Starting from the bottom of the preceding list, the design of the task has been the approach of industrial engineering based on the principles handed down from Frederick W. Taylor and Frank

Gilbreth. This approach has led to simplifying tasks and movements so that they can be measured, planned, and predicted. Much of the productivity progress of the last seventy years has been based on this approach. Because it has led to extremes in which the human advantages have been eliminated or sacrificed for the machines' efficiency, it may have reached a point of diminishing returns.

By contrast, the more recent "quality of working life" approach started with job design. Here the attempt was to balance the needs of the worker with the needs of the organization. In manufacturing endeavor this led first to job enlargement, job enrichment, and job development. Job enlargement meant adding to the number of tasks or increasing the scope of the job to add variety and challenge. Job enrichment meant adding to the quality of human involvement allowed by providing the freedom of choice, participation in decision making, and goal setting. Job development is a current term encompassing both. This may still be a valid place to redesign, especially in non-manufacturing areas. However, the primary emphasis in the movement for better quality has shifted from the individual job level to the group level.

At the group level it is possible to question some of the values and assumptions of the past relative to cooperation and competition, supervision and group authority, and division and organization of work. The autonomy of the work group and making the tasks of the group a whole process with control of inputs, feedback on accomplishment, and control of the output interface has been the area of emphasis.

At the functional level it is possible to deal both with the interpretation and embodiment of the mission or assignment and with the style of management. At the functional level it is possible to establish new values and to buffer the suborganization from the rest of the organization.

To a great extent, our values are shaped by the values of the organization of which we are part. One way to change organizations is, therefore, to work at shaping the values of the organization as a whole. For example, if we wish to build an organization where study is highly valued we might consider investing in a library, supporting educational programs, and rewarding growth through study. Such changes directly impact the values of the organization which in turn influence those who work in it.

In a classic article in the *Harvard Business Review*, Theodore Levitt discussed the impact of the definition of mission on the scope and values of the organization. He pointed out how different the

PERSONAL EXPERIMENT 15

You are a member of some organization where you and others get together for some shared activities. Pick one of your relationships of this kind — it may be work but it does not have to be — for this experiment. Approach the group about participating in an experiment which can make the group more effective. If you can get agreement, start with a session of an hour or so when you all suggest and list the problems you see with your operation. Be careful to set ground rules that accept any problem anyone sees without question or evaluation. After about an hour try to agree as a group on some order of priority for these problems and combine those that are really different ways of saying the same thing. Try to pick one, or a maximum of three, of the problems that the group agrees to work on. Next brainstorm for solutions. Accept any idea, no matter how peculiar it sounds, and list it. Only after you have listed all the proposals should the group start sorting out and analyzing to find the appropriate and effective solutions. If you can, find one solution to one problem on which you can all agree to implement. After you have done this take some time as a group to look at how you worked on this problem. Were you effective as a group? What would make the process more effective? Was this a satisfying process? Was the solution successful?

development of the railroads might have been if they had defined their business as transportation rather than railroading.* Today we have the argument in reverse with the oil industry defining their business as energy, much as Levitt would want them to; and we have Congress arguing about forcing a narrower definition of their business, such as oil recovery and refining. The purpose and the specific statements about purpose are an important way to shape the environment, values, and outcomes of the organization.

---

* "Marketing Myopia," a 1960 *Harvard Business Review* classic, rewritten and reviewed in *Harvard Business Review*, Sept.-Oct. 1975, p. 26 ff.

All of these places of impact for change are legitimate places to modify the organization. Which is right depends on the capabilities and relationships of the persons making the changes, the change readiness of the organization, and the history and culture of the organization. Making changes at several of these levels is probably better than changing only one. For our emphasis on vitality the purpose of any change should be to improve the satisfactions and growth possible through the individual's participation in the organization.

Congruence

An integrating concept for all aspects of job and organization design is congruence between the individual and the organization. The aim of any design should be to increase the congruence between the members of the organization and the organization itself. By increasing congruence, the loss through friction, differences, and inefficiencies should be reduced. There are many aspects of congruence but a few will serve to demonstrate the power of the concept.

The organization and the individual bring needs and capabilities to each other. Examples of needs each brings are goals and purposes. If the purposes of the organization and the purposes of the people who make up the organization are in alignment, then congruence exists. When this is true, the probability of achieving the objectives of the organization is enhanced because the people are pushing toward the same end. When congruence doesn't exist, the individual and the organization are at cross purposes. Working together requires alignment of purpose. Such alignment is built on shared values, clarification, direction, and communication about goals and objectives. The ideal of perfect alignment is probably unachievable, but if the organization designer builds in systems and techniques which enhance clarification of objectives and open communication about them, then the process of organizational improvement is built into the design. Not only should there be mechanisms for improving the organization, there should also be mechanisms for improving the people. Opportunities to change one's work and opportunities for education are examples. These opportunities enhance the probability of achieving congruence by supporting human change. A good organization, then, has abundant processes for gaining alignment or congruence between its members and itself.

Alignment of values is probably harder to achieve than alignment of goals and purposes. Two major problems exist. Many organizations fail to make their beliefs and values explicit; and people, having formed their values over their whole lives, are neither articulate about them nor often conscious of them. Some experimentation has been done with the design of new organizations and making values explicit. Members are not asked to accept the values, merely to understand that these are the rules by which the organization will play. The work of Carl A. Bramlette, Jr., is an example. He set up training programs for management and workers which presented new values for work, like group rewards instead of individual rewards.

Job and organizational design

Bramlette's programs included values like the following:

- Acting interdependently with others
- Sharing tasks and purposes cooperatively
- Defining the individual's work needs and activities
- Solving problems of increasing complexity
- Choosing from among a wide range of alternatives
- Taking the initiative
- Controlling personal behavior and responsibility
- Continuing personal growth toward achieving maximum individual potential

The people were asked not to believe in the new values, but rather to understand that, in playing the game, the rules would be based on these values. His experiences demonstrate that the ability to work in groups where new values exist can be increased through training and education.*

Another area in which congruence is desirable is between rewards and punishments the organization uses. Rewards should be appropriate for the individual and punishments should seem fair

---

* See the Proceedings of the Frontiers in Education Conference sponsored by IEEE and ASEE at the Georgia Institute of Technology, Atlanta, Georgia, October 20, 21, 22, 1975, "The Design of Work—Eliminating Organizational Blocks to New Learning," pp. 206-207.

and proper. For a reward to be motivating to the individual it must fit the individual's values. To the extent the organization is able to incorporate personal values and adapt reward schemes to fit them, motivation is improved because of congruence of the individual's need with the organization's reward capability. If, on the other hand, the organization views employees as economically motivated while the employees' true interests have moved to psychological payouts, then there is lack of congruence. The people and the organization are "out of phase." An organizational design which includes this capability to adapt and fit company rewards to individual reward needs is moving toward a design of improved quality.

What can the designer do?

To decide what to do, one has to decide what the problem is. Problem definitions, to a great extent, shape changes and progress in our world. It must be a real and acknowledged problem which is shared by those to be impacted by the change. For there to be action and change there must be "ownership" of the problem. Ownership of a problem occurs when the problem is your problem, when you acknowledge that solving the problem is important to you. Those having to act must "own" the problem. A simple example may clarify the point. We know that we cannot help the person who is sick unless that person admits sickness and wants to be helped. So too with an organization. It is not enough for the designer to determine that the problem is a lack of learning leading to a deficiency in skill and knowledge which in turn contributes to low productivity. This may be the real problem but it will not be dealt with and fixed until others agree with this perception of the problem. If by this point you, the reader, do not share my point of view that vitality for individuals and organizations is desirable and can be improved through understanding it and managing it, no motivation will result. You will have read the book but nothing will have changed. Unconvinced, you will not take new actions. If you share the perception of the problem, if it becomes yours, you will probably make changes in your life to increase your vitality.

Three groups need to share the problem with the designer or "change agent" who intends to change organization and job design. First, higher management must give its support and acknowledge the problem. Second, the group managing and responsible for the part of the organization to be redesigned must accept it as a problem. Third, the people who work in that segment of the organization must agree to the need for change. Which of these supports is most important depends on both the nature of the problem and the "culture" of the organization. Gaining the support and selling the concept is the responsibility of the designer or change agent.

The designer must decide on strategy and technique, based on some concept of motivation, work design, and individual payout needs. Is the approach to come from the outlook of the industrial engineer enriched by the study of Maslow? Is the approach to be that of the quality-of-working-life groups and emphasize enhancing psychological payouts, or is it to come from the concepts of job enlargement or job enrichment? This subject is far too complex for this book; however, the references at the end of the chapter may help. Suffice it to say the designer must have, in addition to a definition of the problem, an understanding of the counter-pressures and the backing of various groups, a hypothesis or set of hypotheses on which to base the design. A design concept is a necessary next step and from it can flow a strategy for change and techniques for implementation.

For example, George F. Farris, in discussing productivity improvement, thoroughly reviews the importance of the designer's viewpoint. He suggests that we are at the point of being able to make three tentative statements about causality for productivity.

1. *Organizational characteristics cause productivity*
2. *Productivity causes organizational characteristics*
3. *Certain organizational characteristics are more important psychologically for high producers than low producers* *

These examples typify the kind of working principles which are necessary as a designing point of view. Following such broad precepts, the designer would have to set forth a set of experimental hypotheses to be tested. An example might be: if we improve the capability of our human resources, productivity will increase.

What the designer can do, therefore, depends on understanding the culture or nature of the organization. It depends also on the nature of the perceived problem and who owns it. To

---

*   George E. Farris, "Chickens, Eggs, and Productivity in Organizations," in *Organizational Dynamics* (New York: AMACOM, Spring 1975), p. 6. Reprinted with permission.

manage change one needs some principles and hypotheses to be tested. There are many levels at which one can make changes, ranging from the job to the organization. The designer must be clear about where it is best to make changes based on past experiences and his or her ability to communicate and influence. The characteristics of the organization are a primary determinant of what happens.

What can the individual do?

You and I are the designers. You and I are the causes of many of the problems since we have allowed our organizations to evolve without designing them and we have taken our job as fixed and immutable. In the words of Pogo, "We have met the enemy, and he is us."

Chapter 14, Redesigning Your Job, is a "how to" approach which discusses this subject from the point of view of the individual. A couple of points should be made here, however. First, we as individuals make up the systems of the organizations of which we are part. Many of the limits and blocks to change, many of the inefficiencies and lacks of effectiveness reflect our creations. Organizational and job change for improvement in quality, vitality, and growth start with us. If we value improvement highly, we set up conditions which encourage change. If we are defensive and holding on tightly to our prerogatives, our niche, and our job, we will impede change and growth. An organization's ability to change is highly dependent on the attitudes of the people who are part of it. So the primary thing for the individual to do is develop an open, positive, growth- and change-oriented attitude. The individual should be asking what he or she can do to make the organization better, rather than asking what the organization can do for the individual.

It is necessary first to select changes which are small and relatively certain of success—not biting off more than one can chew. This is important because it builds positive accomplishment. Part of determining the size of the change includes choosing a particular change where we can be assured of feedback which will tell us whether improvement is occurring. It is not good to pick a change where someone else is the first to know what happened as a result. All this argues for starting with small changes so you build self-confidence and a reputation for success.

Summary

Redesign of organizations, redesign of work, and redesign of jobs are powerful processes to help us gain improved productivity, learning, and psychological income from work. As in all social design, the relationships are not one-to-one and the outcomes are not entirely predictable. Nevertheless, it appears that work can be made more positive and growth-oriented when we make it possible for humans to contribute those things which they do best. We can increase the congruence between organizational goals and individual goals and by so doing increase the probability that individual energies will support organizational objectives. Increased congruence should also positively affect the perceived quality of work.

Redesign depends first on definition of the issue or problem to be solved. Secondly, the priority of need for change must be shared by management so they provide support and by those who must implement the change. Where one enters the system and the type of changes to be made depends first, on the problem definition; second, on the culture of the organization; and third, on the disposition and capabilities of the designer or change agent.

Can organization or job redesign positively improve organizational and individual vitality? The answer is emphatically, "Yes." When the organization can improve its ability to decide on goals and communicate these objectives in a way to gain employee commitment, the organization becomes more vital. When work can be redesigned so that it stretches people, motivates learning and the application of human capabilities, then individual vitality is enhanced.

Suggested readings

Davis, Louis E., and Cherns, A. B. *The Quality of Working Life*, Vols. I and II. New York: Free Press, 1975.

Davis, Louis E., and Taylor, James C. *Design of Jobs*. England: Penguin Books, 1972.

Ford, Robert N. *Motivation Through the Work Itself*. New York: AMACOM, 1969.

Francis, Dave, and Woodcock, Mike. *People At Work: A Practical Guide to Organizational Change*. LaJolla: University Associates, 1975.

  As its title suggests, this is a practical, usable guide for organization redesign. The authors identify eleven problems or blockages which they see as reasons for organization malfunction. They guide the reader in how to determine if these are problems in the reader's organization and then suggest techniques for fixing the problem. It is a workbook with many suggested forms, questions, and processes.

Gooding, Judson. *The Job Revolution.* New York: Walker, 1972.

Hersey, Paul, and Blanchard, Kenneth H. *Management of Organizational Behavior—Utilizing Human Resources.* Englewood Cliffs, N.J.: Prentice-Hall, 1972.

Herzberg, Frederick. *Work and the Nature of Man.* Cleveland: World Publishing, 1966.

Herzberg, Frederick. "The Wise Old Turk," *Harvard Business Review,* Sept.-Oct. 1974, pp. 70-80.

Hinrichs, John R. *The Motivation Crisis Winding Down and Turning Off.* New York: AMACOM, 1974.

Katz, Daniel, and Kahn, Robert L. *The Social Psychology of Organizations.* New York: Wiley, 1966.

Loftquist, L. H., and Dawis, R. V. *Adjustment to Work.* New York: Appleton-Century-Crofts, 1969.

Miller, Donald B. "Changing Job Requirements—A Stimulant for Technical Vitality," *American Society for Engineering Education, Continuing Engineering Studies Division,* Monograph #7, 1972.

Rosow, Jerome M., ed. *The Worker and the Job: Coping with Change.* The American Assembly, Englewood Cliffs, N.J.: Prentice-Hall, Spectrum Books, 1974.

Sheppard, H.L., and Herrick, N.O. *Where Have All the Robots Gone? Worker Dissatisfaction in the Seventies.* New York: The Free Press, 1972.

Schein, Edgar H. *Organizational Psychology.* Englewood Cliffs, N.J.: Prentice-Hall, 1970.

Terkel, Studs. *Working.* New York: Avon, 1975.

Vough, C. F. *Tapping the Human Resource—A Strategy for Productivity.* New York: AMACOM, 1975.

11

Career management

Introduction

There can be, and probably should be, several careers in one's lifetime today. The individual is in charge of what happens. Career
management is about how to plan and gain satisfaction within a
career as well as negotiate the transition between careers. The
process has several stages. They are sensing the need for change,
assessment, matching, negotiating, trying, and navigating.

Our thesis is that understanding the process has a greater
impact on our ability to manage our careers than specific techniques. Some useful techniques are suggested, however, and their
probable effects reviewed. The need to negotiate with your
employer or potential employer is covered as well as how to
determine the issues for negotiation. Obviously this chapter can't
present all the techniques, but it should show you how your career
management and maintenance of your vitality are related.

When you leave your lifetime employment, the action is
normally called retirement. I consider the concept of retirement to
be obsolete. Improved health is extending the human life span.
Increased safety and our greater sensitivity to our environmental
ecology will probably further extend the human life span. If work or
some activity is central to life, what happens after age sixty-five?
How does one adjust to retirement? Is retirement necessary or
desirable? These questions are addressed.

A primary suggestion of this chapter is that we should replace
the term "retirement," which suggests giving up, with a concept
that suggests moving into a new and exciting phase of activity.
"Second career" won't work as the title since life could be made up
of many careers. To point us to the positive, "Career of Choices"
has been chosen as the term for extending life, extending vitality,
and assuring meaningfulness after Social Security begins.

What is career management?

Career management means taking responsibility for the choices
and direction of the work aspects of your life. It is the process of
navigating through the several stages of a given career in order to
gain the maximum growth and satisfaction. It is also the process of
managing the transition from one career to another and navigating
through the phases of your life as your values and objectives
change. For our discussion a career is pursuit of a coherent role
with an associated set of activities, a common group of skills, and

an identifiable knowledge base. This does not mean that all people who can be identified as being in the same career will carry out the role in the same way. It does mean that when you look at these several individuals in the same career you will be able to identify some common characteristics.

To understand the concept of career management, let us start by examining a career. Suppose we select the career of a doctor. The first major step in career management requires commitment to the objective of becoming a doctor and successful completion of the required education and internship. This initial decision is usually made in adolescence and assistance in deciding on a career comes from career counselors and in early success and interest in related academic subjects. Often such a decision is strongly influenced by a friend or role model.

Career management, in the sense we are discussing it, begins with the beginning of practice as a doctor. Some preliminary signals and early course-of-life adjustments probably begin during internship. For example, the individual gets a chance to sort out the activities in the doctor's role which are most interesting and rewarding. If the young doctor finds genuine interest in childbirth, then assessment should take place. Assessment includes understanding the pros and cons from a personal point of view, the cost and time commitment required by additional specialization, and the potential need for this specialty. Assessment merges into matching. Do these requirements and the individual's interests and capabilities match? Assuming a decision to pursue that direction, the individual then tries it out. This means commitment and the application of energy, time, and study. Once qualified, navigation requires sensing the inputs by trying the role. Is it working? Is it satisfying? How well am I doing? Do patients react well? Am I adding something of value? Based on these inputs it may or may not be necessary to change direction. The management process begins all over again. Many of these activities, although made explicit here, merge into one another and are usually not consciously identified.

Career management requires, therefore, a sensitivity to how you are doing, some estimation of the future, choice about direction, commitment, and trying. This process may go on within a career or between careers. Our hypothetical doctor, for example, might later on in his career sense that the satisfaction is no longer worth the strain and input. At this point alternative careers might be considered; for example, moving to a related or nonrelated activity in which the individual has control of the hours and the time which must be devoted. A choice of joining a company as an industrial doctor might fulfill this requirement. So also would a complete change of career to leatherworking craftsmanship. These are typical kinds of career-transition decisions.

Many people believe that their careers have not been or cannot be consciously managed. To them, being in the right place at the right time and knowing or having the right connections seem to be of primary importance. Certainly these can be important factors. However, a personal philosophy which says "it is done to me" is not a growth-oriented, vitality-motivated outlook. In essence, part of the secret of career success is taking charge, being responsible for your life. This does not deny the applicability of luck but encourages you to take advantage of it by knowing yourself and your objectives when luck occurs. It also suggests that some of those incidents which appear to be chance can be managed or created.

Generally what we believe about careers simply isn't so. The usual belief is that a career is the result of educational preparation, rational choice, and diligent pursuit. Careers evolve and are managed by people who have in addition several other characteristics. First, belief in oneself; pursuit of a career requires selling and often overcoming logical and rational objections. Second, a capacity to take risks; pushing oneself into situations where the chances of success are questionable is often the success factor in a career. Third, a sense of timing; good careers—those which match our needs and capabilities—are made, not found. But to create them we must time our thrust to respond to a need others feel. Fourth, ability to go on for extended periods without external reward; this means both learning to live with self-recognition and to live through times of boredom and lack of challenge. Fifth, creating a reputation as a doer; this does not necessarily mean doing it yourself but it does mean being seen as the creator of action. It does not mean taking credit for the accomplishments of others but it does mean enlisting their help and giving them recognition. Sixth, taking responsibility; this is the ability to fight, stand up and be counted, and admit when you are wrong.

Career stages and
life phases

Not only does the process of career management require an understanding of your interests and capabilities, but it also requires understanding the phases of a career. There have been several attempts to describe career stages, life stages, or phases. They probably are separate but related phenomena. Sometimes, especially historically when a single career matched a single life, careers and lives were seen as synonymous. It is possible, therefore, that separation between careers, career stages, and life phases is a growing and changing aspect which reflects the variety of opportunities and the multiplicity of careers we now can have.

Life phases are probably best described by looking for the dominant objectives of a life stage. Havinghurst's* life stages represent a sequence with such objectives. They describe a logical dominant theme such as gaining acceptance, climbing the responsibility ladder, or deciding to disengage. While these can be helpful in assuring that the kinds of feelings one is having are normal and in recognizing it is no longer appropriate at age 60 to continue to expect promotion, career management requires a more detailed relationship with work. Dalton and Thompson, in their studies, have come up with such career stages.

These stages have been defined by examining the activities, relationships, and psychological shifts. Through interviews, they have defined four stages in the career of the engineering and scientific professional. Stage I is essentially working under the direction of someone else; Stage II is gaining the acceptance which permits self-direction; Stage III is providing direction and counsel to others; and Stage IV is impacting policy and direction of the organization.† In their concept, the first three stages are sequential and hierarchical. They also suggest that, with change in assignment, it is possible to recycle or move back to an earlier stage.

For the purposes of understanding the concept of career management I have developed a slightly different model. There is no validation of the model other than its basis in rational personal experience and its usefulness. If it helps you in understanding, much as a map might help in plotting a trip, then it is working.

Career stages

1. Preparing
2. Starting out

---

* See Chapter 5, Balance and the Phase of Life.

† Thompson, Paul H., and Dalton, Gene W., "Are R & D Organizations Obsolete? New research findings indicate it is more the organization than the individual that becomes outdated," *Harvard Business Review*, Nov.-Dec. 1976, p. 107.

3. Becoming accepted
4. Contributing as an individual
5. Contributing through others
6. Decline in impact and satisfaction
7. Choosing and preparing for a new career
8. Transition

For the knowledge needed by working professionals, preparation (1) usually means study at the university level. It may even include an apprenticeship such as internship for a doctor or working as a law clerk for a lawyer. Starting out (2) is the first direct application which includes some freedom of choice and decision-making by the individual. At this stage the individual should be identifiable as such rather than simply as seen through someone else—the principal. Becoming accepted (3) is when one gains a sense of success and acceptance at starting out. This is when the organization demonstrates through task assignment or advice seeking that it can see the individual as a uniquely contributing person with specific characteristics and capabilities. Real contribution or impact upon the organization occurs when one contributes as an individual (4). This need not be working alone—it may be as a team member. It does, however, require an identifiable contribution in both the individual's mind and in the eyes of others. The next stage (5) implies leadership of others, either as an expert in the field or as a manager of others. (This is Stage III in the Dalton and Thompson series.) Contributing through others does not, however, require managerial authority and responsibility. This phase of contributing through others may never occur or it may be skipped. The decline in impact and satisfaction (6) may result from the individual's change in motivation, change in direction of the organization, changing policy, and many other factors. For example, dentists tell me it occurs in their profession based in part on reaching a certain age. New patients are reluctant to start with an "old" dentist and "old" patients move away or die.

Decline in contribution and satisfaction may never occur. If one is riding the crest of a business need and stays vital and up-to-date it is possible to stay on top for a working lifetime. It is, however, becoming less probable that this single sustained crest phenomenon can occur. Those who are motivated to grow, contribute, and remain vital start searching for a new field or career (7) when they sense the decline. This is an often overlooked or unidentified aspect of career and life management. Individuals who are good career managers develop this special type of sensitivity to change. The engineer who goes back to college to graft on a new capability may be expressing this understanding. The individual who seeks transfer within the organization to a new activity or seeks a new job outside may be doing this. It is also possible to seek opportunity and modify capabilities in an attempt to maintain oneself atop the crest. If one chooses and prepares for a new activity, then managing transition (8) is the process of returning to starting out (2) all over again. One very important difference is that, for the experienced person, there is most often some carryover and applicability of past experience; it is not starting out all over again in the literal sense. Transition, however, requires taking a risk and giving up some of the security and support of the currently comfortable, probably successful, role and career. This is difficult to do. It is probable that sensitizing oneself to stages (6), (7), and (8) holds the real key to the continuing management of life and career success.

Sensitizing yourself to the signals which represent the potential for decline or early stages of decline and doing something about it is absolutely necessary to maintain vitality. In choosing a new career, you must be sensitive to and understand yourself as well as the opportunities. Transition requires openness and seeking of new contacts and heightened sensitivity to feedback which may help you adjust. The next sections which discuss the process therefore concentrate on sensing, choosing, matching, and managing transition.

The career-management process

Does your role fit? Are you gaining satisfaction from your work? Will these continue as you project into the future? These are the types of questions which when answered provide the input which sensitizes you to the need to change life course or career. Signals for change which cause modification of your current activity or preparation and search for new activity are like the inputs a ship's captain uses to determine the need for course corrections. Sometimes these signals are very specific and sometimes they are your response to subjective feelings. In career management, often the initial signals are nonspecific to career. For example, regularly oversleeping in the morning, leading to chronic lateness, is the sort of phenomenon which might indicate lack of work motivation. It does not necessarily mean loss of career satisfaction, however, but for the moment let us proceed on that thesis. Such a lack might be caused by lack of perceived importance of work, lack of challenge, lack of impact, lack of commitment, lack of goal congruence, and a myriad of lacks. Analysis and assessment in this case could lead to change in the design of the job or a new job. Analysis could also lead to a need to change outlook, values, or face and change personal characteristics.

These signals are similar to those which would, as discussed in Chapters 12 and 16, indicate need for other kinds of personal change. The inputs are not labeled and identified. The signals don't say to us, "I apply to your job," or "I pertain to your family life." The first step in career or life management is, therefore, sensitivity to inputs and the ability to sort these out for assessment. We need to learn to relate feedback to causes. The feedback results from some problem in the way we are living or in the way we are applying our energies to achieve our goals.

Some of the possible signals which might alert one to the need for change in or migration to another career are shown in the following listing. Some of these signals can be subtle and some can be strong. Some of these signals may also indicate need for other changes. For example, decline in your performance on the job could be health related. Deterioration in vision could on a job requiring reading cause such a performance decline.

Signals for career-change consideration

Be alert to the following signals for career-change considerations.
- Decline in personal-growth rate.
- Decline in your performance on the job.
- Increasing dissatisfaction with work.
- Decline in your feeling of vitality.
- Increased psychosomatic or physical maladies.
- Evidence of an impending end to the need for your function.
- Receiving an unsatisfactory performance appraisal.
- Symptoms of potential failure of, absorption of, or relocation of your employer.
- Evidence of a shift or change in the political power structure in the organization.
- Being demoted, fired, or laid off.

PERSONAL EXPERIMENT 16

Sensing changes in the state of your career is an important part of learning to manage your career. Signals for career change have just been reviewed. Use the following questions to heighten your sensitivity to the need for you to take career-change action.

1. Do you feel you are growing in your career? (Rapidly) (Some) (Slowly) (None)

2. Is this growth more or less than you felt three years ago? (More) (About same) (Less)

3. How would you appraise your performance on your job? (Outstanding) (Good) (Satisfactory) (Poor)

4. Has your performance changed over the last three years? How? (Improved) (Stayed about constant) (Declined)

5. Are you more or less satisfied with your work than you were a year ago? (More satisfied) (About same) (Less)

6. How do you feel about your vitality? (Improving) (Staying about the same) (Declining)

7. How has your health changed over the last five years? (Improved) (Stayed the same) (Declined)

8. Do you see a need for your expertise in three years? (Yes) (Maybe) (No) Is this need growing or declining? (Growing) (Staying about the same) (Declining)

9. Has anyone, your manager or your peers, assessed your performance as inadequate in the last year? (Yes) (I don't know) (No)

10. Do you expect your employer or your business to be in existence five years hence? (Yes, ar.d growing) (Yes, but declining) (Yes, but taken over or usurped by others) (No, it will be displaced)

11. Are you considered to be part of the team or group currently in power in your organization? (Yes) (I don't know) (No) Do you expect this group to be in power in three years? (Yes) (I don't know) (No)

12. Has your potential of a salary cut, a layoff, or early retirement increased over the last several years? (Yes) (I don't know) (No)

Assessment requires finding the cause for the signal. Often this requires making a change in what we are doing and seeing how the feedback changes. Experimentation can lead to understanding. Other times assessment may require seeking counsel or setting up stimulations when we cannot change the real thing without commitment to change. Seeking counsel can range from talking to your manager or a friend to visiting career counsel and testing centers at a nearby university. Simulations can be set up when it is possible to try a change without commitment to a permanent or irrevocable change. Taking a vacation or a leave of absence and trying something else temporarily might be such an action. Much of the material designed to help in careers is applicable to this assessment phase. Workbooks such as those referenced at the end of this chapter or our Personal Vitality Workbook are designed to help you understand what your interests or capabilities are. They can also help you in separating what works for you from what does not, or in sharpening understanding of what is happening to you. One aspect of assessment is analyzing yourself; then, to understand why you feel as you do about some aspect of your work or career.

A second aspect of assessment in career management is finding out about opportunities. Is there a need for a particular kind of capability? Who hires people to do this? Is the market growing or nearing saturation? These questions can apply both to opportunities internal to your organization and opportunities external to the organization. Opportunities may exist as openings or merely as potential needs where the opening has to be developed and designed. More often, real opportunities are of the latter kind—to be developed. This is a significant challenge in career management. It requires understanding the problems of the organization so well you are able to define a need the organization has not yet defined for itself. Upon identification of the need, you must find a way to sell yourself as the solution to that need.

When, on the one hand, you have defined a need and, on the other, you know your requirements, bringing the two together is matching. Matching people with jobs and careers has been thought of as putting pieces in a jigsaw puzzle. This is an inadequate model. First, it is inadequate because it assumes a static person and a static organization. Matching is a dynamic process of bringing together two parts (individual and opportunity) both constantly in motion and changing. Matching, therefore, requires creativity, negotiation, and change. Often it means accepting a partial fit and motivating both organization and yourself to work to gain a better fit or congruence. He or she who takes a job changes the job. People shape jobs and jobs shape people.

The next stage in career management, which is trying or applying one's energy, has within it a continuation of the matching process. By redesigning and changing the characteristics of the job or by changing one's own interests and capabilities, the two can be brought closer together. Another possibility is that, once the need is acknowledged by placing someone in it, the need changes or even disappears. Personal sensitivity to these shifts is an essential element of career management.

The matching process

This process has been briefly discussed under the career-management process. It is, however, sufficiently complex to require more thorough discussion. One of the major problems in matching is that you are matching things which are dynamic and changing. You, your interests, your goals, and your capabilities change. Opportunities change with changing technology, changing culture, and change in organization objectives. Second, you are matching with incomplete data. You will never know all about yourself nor will you know all about an opportunity. Third, the process is like matching apples and oranges. Needs and capabilities are not necessarily described in the same language nor measured using the same scales. Lastly, matching is not one for one but rather interrelated and interdependent. Matching one aspect affects the other aspects you have to match.

One of the ways to try to understand matching is to look at the things we have to match. Figure 11.1 shows a representative group of the things or aspects to be matched.

First, it is apparent that it is possible to match aspects on the left both with those on the right and with some on the left. Placement in the figure does not mean that the adjacent items are the only matchable ones. For example, suppose an interest in art is represented in A. It is possible to be interested in art and not like, or be interested in, or be skillful at, the activities and tasks artists in a particular job or career are required to do, as represented in B. One could be interested in art and not have, or be capable of acquiring, the skills needed, as represented in C. Even if these things could be partially matched, the economic payout might not fit economic

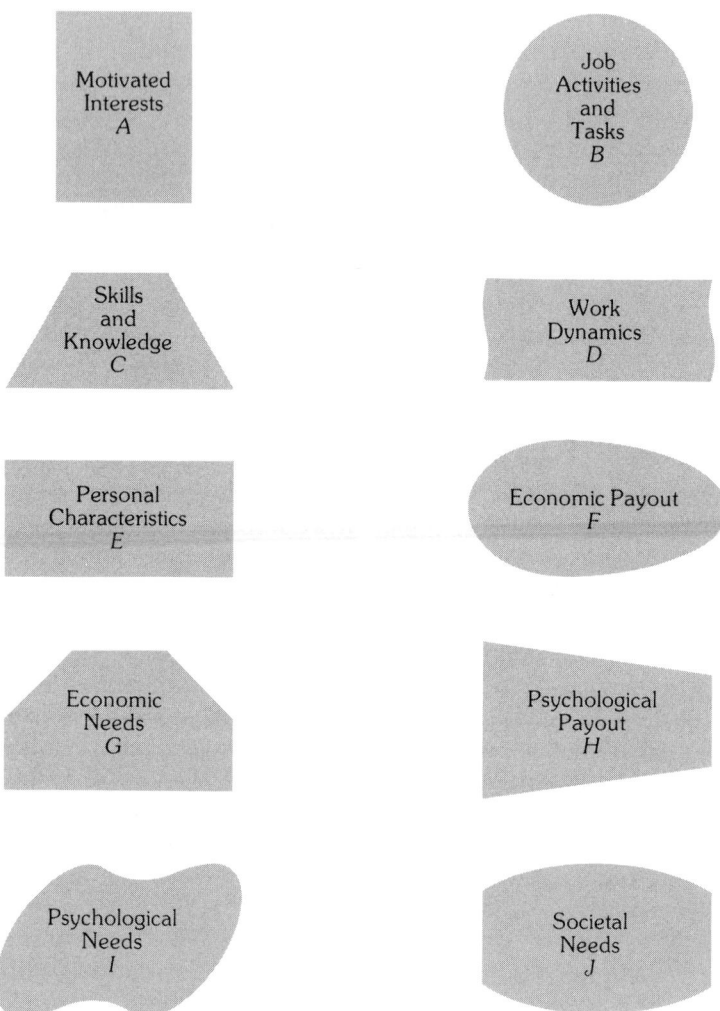

Fig. 11.1 Career matching

need G. Modifying the type of artistic endeavor in B from, for example, commercial art to window decorating and display would change the skills and knowledge C required and might make a better match with interests A. Matching is iterative and interrelated. A particular match becomes input to or shapes another match.

Work dynamics D includes such aspects as whether it is an outdoor or indoor activity, whether it is a paced production activity or a job one does alone, and both how long one waits for feedback and the types of feedback one gets. Societal needs J may put a low priority and thus a low economic payout F on the type of activity in which you are interested. Your personal characteristics might include good muscular coordination or an ability to listen which is or is not required by the job activities B. Inputs to the matching process are therefore variables in themselves.

PERSONAL EXPERIMENT 17

Rather than go through a theoretical discussion, take a moment to see what happens using this matching model and your career. Select some career you are in now or are interested in considering. Next, work through the several matchings and see the complexity of the relationship.

For a block A list interests you are really willing to work at. For circle B list as best you can the activities and tasks in the career you are test matching. For C list your skills and applicable knowledge. For D, work dynamics, list such characteristics as: employed by a company or self-employed, work alone or as a member of a team, requires capital to set up or requires none, requires interfacing with machines or not, is primarily outdoors or indoors, requires extensive communication or not, etc. Under personal characteristics E list five positive and five negative descriptors of you. For F estimate income potential for the activity. For G estimate your economic needs. For H try to describe the psychological income, satisfactions, you might gain from the activity. For I list psychological incomes which are important to you. For J estimate whether society needs this activity and whether the need is recognized and growing or declining.

Now spend a few minutes comparing and seeing if all these segments match. Estimate how you or the career would have to change to improve the match.

From the brief discussion of the picture you should begin to see more clearly than before some of the problems. Each of the objects in the diagram represents both a set of requirements for a particular career under review and a set of capabilities which represents you. It is, therefore, not just matching between aspects but also within each aspect that is required.

It is possible to come through Personal Experiment 17 with the view that career matching is so complex it cannot be done. It must actually be possible, however, for there are many people who are happily matched with their careers and who arrange to change careers and achieve success. Much of the matching activity goes on at a nonexplicit, nonovert level. Matching these aspects can be improved through the negotiation process.

The negotiation process

Assuming your personal assessment suggests you should change career or job, how do you do it? If you have made a trial match and found the differences, then negotiation is the way to improve the match. Negotiation is necessary to make it possible to carry the matching process to conclusion and implementation. In its simplest terms, the negotiation process requires the individual to change what he or she needs from the job in return for the person representing the opportunity (employer) changing some aspects of the job. In the case of the self-employed, the equivalent of negotiation goes on between customers or clients and the individual. In these cases the services are redefined. It requires open communication and a willingness to change priorities and compromise on both sides. In tough economic times or when the individual's needs are very strong and the opportunities scarce, it seems that the individual must bend to the organization or the customer. In better economic times and when certain skills which the individual has are scarce, it seems that the organization is willing to compromise and accommodate the change. When the individual feels weak and inadequate in negotiation, sometimes a third party is sought. For example, the executive moving from one organization to another will often get a lawyer to help draw up a contract. When the organization feels weak, it will often substitute capital investment for human endeavor, thus changing the bargaining base or even eliminating jobs. Such is the case, for example, in the current trend toward more automatic harvesting of wine grapes. This is a partial result of attempts on the part of farm labor to shift the negotiating balance.

Goal setting and career management

No discussion about managing life and careers is complete without a discussion of goals. Goals provide motivation for change, a rationale for choice, and a way to discuss and plan actions. Goal determination is a part of the assessment process. Goal change is implementing one's acceptance of changed conditions and changes in oneself. The basis for a goal is, therefore, new information which suggests establishing a new goal which will reflect one's change in values and which will help to manage improvement. Career-management failures often are based on the failure to identify new goals when old ones have been achieved or discarded. Helpful goals can be differentiated from unhelpful goals. The following list defines the characteristics of helpful goals.

Helpful goals

1. Useful—to the individual, the organization, and society.
2. Realistic—within the potential capabilities of the individual and with a reasonable probability of achievement.
3. Challenging—stretching and growth-oriented; not so easy as to require little or no effort.
4. Specific—able to be defined in terms which can be communicated and in a way which will provide evidence of achievement.
5. Measurable—relates to specificity but adds the need of a standard of comparison.
6. Reasonable time span—the time to completion must not be so short that it contributes little to life direction nor so long as to be unreal and beyond control.

Helpful goals, therefore, are goals which work as destinations in providing direction for activity and a basis for choice. The more useful the goal the greater the potential for satisfaction as a result of its pursuit. It is not enough that it be useful to the individual since all of us need a sense of contribution to something larger. A daydream or flight of fancy in which one wishes one could be someone different does not meet the criteria of realism in goals. A realistic goal is one which not only has a possibility of achievement, but one which will stand testing by other people. Even if you feel you can reach your goals, failure to gain positive reinforcement from others will mean you must spend a lot of your energy just selling rather than working toward your goal.

A challenging goal is fun because achieving it means you have accomplished something. If it was as easy as "falling off a log," then little satisfaction flows from the achievement. One does not achieve a sense of worth from reaching a goal which is so easy that one's capability to achieve it was never questioned. A goal which one cannot define sufficiently to talk about or to discern when it is achieved fails the test of specificity. A goal which is not measurable has questionable value. A goal which is twenty years away is beyond a reasonable time span. Usually short-term goals which are achievable within the current year and long-term goals which are achievable in up to five years work best for career management. If the goal is too far away, it's hard to sustain the drive and direction. If the goal is too near, it represents but a small diversion in life and usually requires little investment. Such a goal probably is not very challenging. Defining the period of time to achievement is an important part of setting a goal.

Some examples of helpful goals will drive the need home still further. A useful goal represents a matching of individual needs and capabilities with the needs of some larger entity. If I had an interest in solar energy and engineering capability to carry out a project, setting a goal to produce a $300 solar hot water heater would be useful. A solar heater at that price would contribute positively to reducing our fuel shortages. Such a goal is realistic only if I have the ability, the facilities, and the finances and there is no evidence that material costs or some other production element makes a $300 goal unachievable. I consider the goal a challenge. Even in kit form the lowest priced solar hot water heater at the moment, to my knowledge, is in the $450 to $650 range. This is a specific and measurable goal. Up to this point we have not set a time span. My guess is that if it can be achieved in six months to one year there will be a market. If it takes longer someone will beat me. These are examples of the issues to face in setting helpful goals.

Goal setting is an important aspect of career management. Adequate goals, helpful goals, have a power to aid us in success which is not true of inadequate goals.

Vitality and career management

Work and career can provide important inputs to vitality. These are: providing a purpose, a sense of accomplishment, and personal growth. Having the right job, therefore, is the key, and career management is the process of continually assuring that you have the right job. If one is in the wrong job, the anxieties and lack of psychological payouts are debilitating and fail to provide motivation for growth and change. Not only does work not pay off but the lack of payoff may negatively affect health and other life relationships.

Work is not the only contributor to your sense of worth and vitality. However, it seems logical to expect the following (minimal) inputs to vitality from your career:

- A sense of purpose for direction in life.
- A way to contribute and gain positive feedback from it.
- A medium and purpose for learning new skills and knowledge.
- An opportunity to grow in self-awareness and understanding.

Career management from a vitality perspective is a constant tuning of your work relationships to achieve these outputs. Which output is most important to you, or the loss of which one triggers the need for change, is very personal. At different life or career phases, different outputs take a higher priority. In part, this is a reflection of life stage, and in part it may reflect how other elements of life are working. For example, failure to gain positive reinforcement in family life will probably raise the priority of positive feedback from your work. Or, in reverse, a very satisfying family relationship can contribute positively to the sense of purpose and direction which flows from work.

The ultimate career: "career of choices"

Although many people view retirement as giving up work, a more positive view is to look at it as a career change. Because work is a source of life purpose, meaning, and understanding of self, the choosing of an activity to replace it is necessary for retirement success. Loftquist and Dawis in *Adjustment to Work* say:

Another group for whom the meaning of work comes sharply into focus is the group of workers who are coming to the end of their work careers. . . . Work is something to do, a way of filling the day and passing the time. Work is a source of self-respect, a way of achieving recognition and respect from others. Work defines one's identity, one's role in society of which he is part. *

In *Working In Retirement* by the editors of *Retirement Living* the need for a purpose in retirement is stated as follows:

But consider this fact: doctors say that more energy is consumed and more tension is generated by boredom and restlessness than by most of the jobs in our country! It may be that you can't afford not to work — from a physical and emotional point of view as well as a financial one. †

If we accept the premise of need for activities to provide purpose and meaning in retirement, how does the process of achieving this differ from career management as discussed in this chapter? The primary difference is the culturally accepted definition of retirement which impedes even the thinking about work. Retirement means giving up work. Secondary differences include the general ideas existing in our culture about older people and work. Examples of these include unsubstantiated feelings of slowed learning, increased illness and absenteeism, lowered energy, and many others. The third difference is that this career shift is often thrust upon the individual and often requires a job hunt, even more often creating an opportunity. In other words, the discovery of work requires the making of contacts external to the organization and the relationships one knows. For the fifty-five to sixty-five-year-old who has been continually employed, the process of job searching is strange and threatening. As a final negative reinforcement, in retirement we face income tax laws which discourage work through loss of social security benefits. With these exceptions which provide a psychological barrier or block to working in retirement, the process of making the career change is similar.

---

* Rene V. Dawis and Lloyd H. Loftquist, *Adjustment to Work* (New York: Appleton-Century-Crofts, 1969), p. 10. Reprinted with permission.

† "Working in Retirement" (*Retirement Living Magazine*, 150 E. 58th St., New York, N.Y., 10022, 1975), p. 3.

We have called this the "career of choices" because for many it is the first time in life that the burdens and constraints have been sufficiently removed to allow response to one's feelings. If work in retirement is required solely for financial support this is not true. If work is in reponse to psychological needs barring societal limits this is true. Career choices for the retiree must fulfill some or all of the following:

- The need to feel needed.
- The need to contribute to society.
- Maintenance of physical and mental health.
- The need to continue growing and learning.
- Maintenance of family status.
- The need for recognition and reward.
- The need to fill the time.
- The need to continue practicing what expertise one has developed.

Summary

Career management is a personal responsibility. The process requires assessment of self and assessment of opportunities. Matching your interests and capabilities to opportunities requires negotiation over goals and the growth of new capabilities as well as new specification and a redesign of jobs. Once you have chosen a career and decided upon its active pursuit, you must be sensitive to feedback representing success or failure and learn to navigate. This requires continual learning and personal growth. When your success and satisfaction decline or when you sense external changes which make a career less attractive, you must decide on change. Change requires preparation for the new activity through study and experience. Transition to a new career requires projecting yourself, taking some risks, and leaving the security of the current position. It requires establishing new goals, hopefully useful ones. Useful goals have a way of contributing to your success.

Career management is a lifelong process because of our world of pervasive change. This world provides many opportunities and allows the individual to gain a variety of experiences in several careers. Even retirement should be viewed as a career transition because of the need for a purposeful and meaningful activity through which one sustains self-respect, maintains health, and prolongs vitality.

Suggested readings

American Friends Service Committee. *Working Loose.* Philadelphia: American Friends Service Committee, 1971.

Bolles, R. N. *What Color Is Your Parachute?* Berkeley: Ten Speed Press, 1972.

Campbell, D. P. *If You Don't Know Where You're Going, You'll Probably End Up Somewhere Else.* Niles: Argus, 1974.

Crystal, J. C., and Bolles, R. N. *Where Do I Go From Here With My Life?* (a work book) New York: Seabury Press, 1974.

Dalton, G.; Thompson, P.; and Kopelman, R. "But What Have You Done For Me Lately?—The Boss," *IEEE Spectrum,* Oct. 1974, pp. 85-89.

Ford, G. A., and Lippitt, G. L. *A Life Planning Workbook. For Guidance in Planning and Personal Goal Setting.* Fairfax: NTL Learning Resources, 1972.

Haldane, B. *Career Satisfaction and Success.* New York: AMACOM, 1974.

Kellogg, M. S. *Career Management.* New York: AMACOM, 1972.

Loughary, John W., and Ripley, Theresa M. *Second Chance: Everybody's Guide to Career Change.* Eugene: United Learning, 1975.

> This is a combination of a text and a workbook. Despite its title, "everybody" means the mature person who has worked at something. The authors divide needs into job needs, vocation needs, and leisure needs. Job needs are for basic survival. Vocation needs are for a sense of fulfillment. Leisure needs contribute to recreation and esthetic pleasure. They see some career changes as forced on people and others as ones we can control. They identify needed competencies for career management as: clarifying problems, translating complaints to goals, increasing self-understanding, dealing with constraints, making decisions, implementing change, making no-change changes, and obtaining career-change information. Their approach is complementary to the one taken in this book.

Uris, Auren. *Thank God It's Monday.* New York: Thomas Y. Crowell, 1974.

"Working In Retirement." New York: *Retirement Living Magazine,* 1975.

12
Personal assessment

Introduction

Life is a continuing process of sensing, assessment, and change. Assessment is measuring and deciding on the value of an action, thought, or communication. The word "assessment" as used here describes that process which helps us to understand ourselves better and helps us to determine how we can improve our success and satisfactions through a change of goals, outlook, or activities. Assessment is aided by comparisons just as measurement of physical characteristics such as length and width are aided by a ruler. In the assessment of individuals, however, we have nothing so precise as a ruler. The simplest personal assessment device is a mirror. By reflecting us to ourselves, it allows us to see the effects of a change in posture, expression, or the way we comb our hair. But our only reference is our ephemeral memory of how we looked the last time.

Assessment, then, involves comparison with a standard or reference. In human affairs we seldom have a standard. But we can compare our reaction today to our reaction yesterday and thus gain a sense of stability or change. We can compare what we are able to do with what we perceive someone else doing. Here assessment involves both trying to understand a difference and deciding whether we want to change that aspect of our lives. We can ask someone else to help us assess our differences or shortcomings. We can be taught by others to improve. This is the relationship we normally have with a coach, teacher, or sometimes a manager. Sometimes this other person's wisdom is embodied in a test or device. Sometimes the person or device acts merely as a mirror. In nondirective counseling, for example, the counselor reflects and provides space for the individual to discover himself or herself. One of the devices discussed in this chapter and a part of the *Personal Vitality Workbook,* is the Personal Growth and Vitality Inventory. It is mostly nondirective; it is like a mirror. It is, however, an active mirror in that it aggressively seeks your reaction.

How do you find out what works best? Trying a change, doing something, and examining the feedback is a continuing process. Feedback provides the grist for assessment. Feedback provides you with the input necessary to know whether what you are doing is working. This chapter suggests ways of assessing personal needs, interests, goals, expectations, and capabilities. Reading the chapter should help in this personal-assessment process. One way of looking at the function of this chapter is to consider that it is designed to help you make your private or internal agenda explicit and communicable both to yourself and to others. Doing this should help you improve the congruence between internal and external reality, and thus move toward improving vitality, growth, and satisfactions. The belief or assumption underlying this approach is that improving congruence of internal and external agendas is part of the growth process and is a key to generating a feeling that life is working and leading to success. In fact, "having your act together" is probably having your internal agenda in alignment with what is actually happening in your life.

Feedback

A process which presents us with a picture, or result of what happened from our action, is called "feedback." Feedback comes normally in the process of living. Sometimes we set up a simulation to get feedback to the question: "What if we do so and so?" Without feedback, without fresh input as the result of our thoughts and actions, assessment, purposeful change, growth, and improvement are impossible. Living without feedback provided by our senses would be like flying blind. In fact, stimulus deprivation, or removal of all feedback, will quickly send the mind into fantasy or irrationality. Immersing people in nonmoving bodies of water is such a process because it eliminates external stimuli. Some kinds of feedback are provided naturally and others must be designed or initiated. Understanding and identifying the feedback mechanism as well as being sensitive to the actual feedback are both important factors in initiating improvement and change.

Following is a listing showing a cross section of sample aspects of our lives from which we need feedback. The listing also provides suggested sources of the feedback and comments on some special characteristics of feedback for that activity. The purpose of the listing is to help us look together at the complexity and variability of the process. Many of the feedback messages have inherent in them a bias or coloration which may or may not match ours. This means there is difficulty, even when the feedback is identified, in understanding, accepting, and evaluating the input. The input may be valuable or may be of questionable value. A simple, everyday example of this confusion is to stop and ask directions to a place

Table 12.1.   Life aspects and potential feedback sources

Aspect	Feedback sources	Characteristics
Athletic Performance	Opponent's action in response to yours	Depends on opponent's capability as well as your actions
	Visual input	Shaped by your expectations and selective observance
	Coach's suggestions	Requires active initiation by coach and acceptance by you
Appearance	Mirror	Reversed image
	Comments by others	Biased by their perspective
	Perception of others' reactions to you	Biased by your perspective
	Personal comparison with your view of other people	Depends on your expectations and the availability of comparative performance
Job Performance	Personally perceived results	Affected by type of work and your expectations
	Manager's appraisal	Reflects manager's goals and may be delayed or unrecognized
	Peer praise or criticism	Reflects their values and competitive posture
Intellectual Capability	Test performance	Reflects standards of test designer
	Results you gain from use of the capability	Variable standards and personal bias
	Comments of other people	Reflects their standards and is complicated by communication difficulties
Brainwaves	Biofeedback device	Requires initiation and design; presents you with data which you may not understand

Aspect	Feedback sources	Characteristics
Interpersonal Communication	Response from other person	Response is affected by relationship, setting for the exchange, listening bias, and both individuals' ability to communicate
	Comment by an observer	Observation is affected by position, outlook, and relationship

you wish to visit. The response you get depends on the experience of the individual you have addressed. He or she may know the street but not its name or may use reference points, like turn left at the Love's house, that may not be understandable to you. You may not receive input which is usable because he or she uses local references, vernacular, or special language. Even assuming you feel you understand the response, you must evaluate the credibility of the source. No wonder the assessment process is difficult when we do not know the quality or the value of the inputs on which we must base our actions.

Feedback provides the necessary input for assessment. Feedback can be the result of really playing the game of life or we can occasionally set up trials or simulations which allow us to play the game before it really counts. Tests and projective, or diagnostic, instruments provide this kind of feedback. The listing just reviewed in addition shows us that feedback itself is a variable and may not be understandable or valuable in the assessment process. It is thus doubly complicated to decipher. It may be distorted in being sent to us and/or it may be distorted in receipt by our coloration or bias. Feedback is, in addition, filtered through our self-image. For example, when the feedback we get comes from another person rather than an impersonal device, it transmits not only a reaction to our action but also represents the outlook and biases of the sender.

Not only is it necessary to understand the variation in the nature of feedback with the type of activity; it is also necessary to understand it in terms of the process. Figure 12.1 is designed to help clarify the feedback cycle. An example of an individual's action

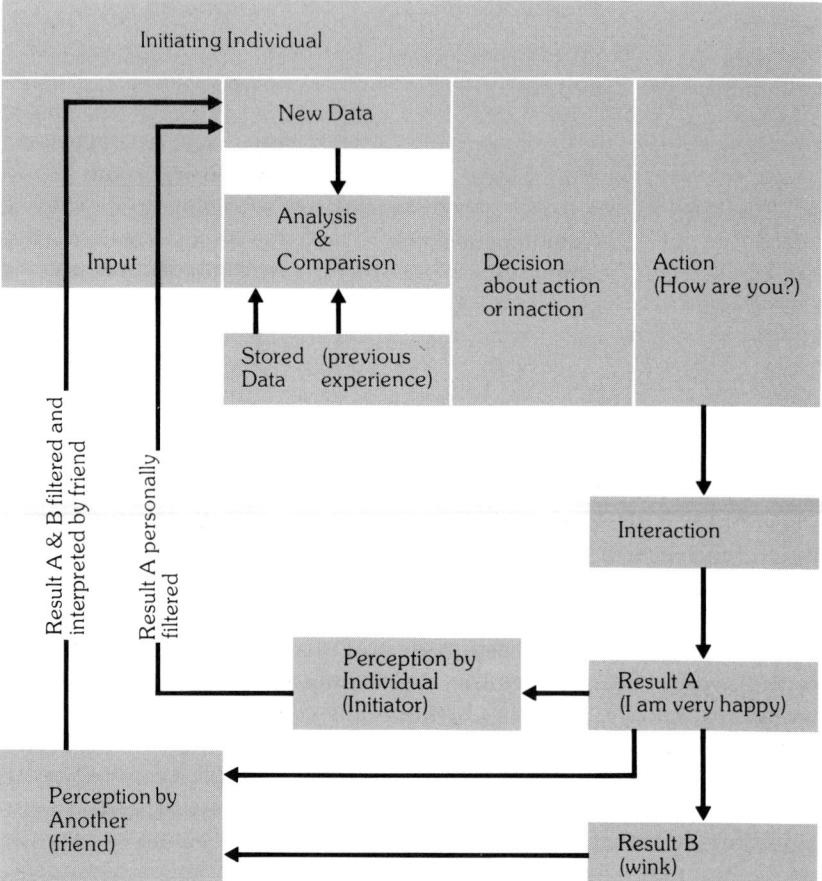

Fig. 12.1   Feedback and analysis cycle

will be used. Suppose the initiating individual is walking along the street with a friend and meets a third person. Our individual greets the third person in a manner which the initiator intends to be cordial. The greeting is the action. The thrusting out into shared space which reaches the other is the box labeled interaction. The third person responds with some reply or result labeled A. Suppose the response is the phrase, "I'm very happy." The initiating individual perceives this as feedback. The friend, who has been just an observer, also hears the response as indicated in the box labeled perception by another and perhaps identifies a secondary result B, not perceived by the initiator. Such a secondary response might be a wink. The friend then comments to the initiating individual that there is reason to question the stranger's response. In this case the originating individual has two feedbacks to compare with stored previous experience. Not only must comparisons be made but the new data must be checked for validity.

The lessons from this diagram are that feedback channels are multiple and perspectives are personal. The result we perceive may not be the only or even the significant one. We must sort out the inputs. We must compare the feedback inputs with stored previous experience and our expectations. We must then evaluate and choose our interpretation. Feedback without evaluation, comparison, and decision will not affect actions. Feedback which is

---

PERSONAL EXPERIMENT 18

Identify a personal activity for analysis of feedback. Ideally it should be of short duration and more or less complete or contained. Examples might be conversation at the dinner table, instruction of another person on how to do something like saw wood or drill a hole, taking a walk, playing a tennis game, or repairing some device. The activity can be one you do alone or one you do with others. The intent of the experiment is to identify all the kinds of feedback. Do whatever it is you have picked as your experiment trying to answer the following questions:

1. **What kinds of feedback are available to me for assessing my performance?**
2. **How did I determine the quality of the feedback — that is, whether it was biased or valid?**
3. **Did I utilize all the possible feedback channels or did I rely primarily on one?**
4. **Would an occasional experiment like this one improve my self-management by making me more conscious of the feedback process?**

evaluated and on which we base a decision for action has had an impact on us. Our next action is based on this comparison and decision. The process is iterative.

Assessment

Assessment is the process of comparing predictions, expectations, or desires with either predictions of results or real results. The purpose of assessment is to provide us with input that will make it possible for us to take responsibility for what happens, make decisions, and take actions which affect what happens. In order to assess we must have comparative data and a base of reference. In order to assess we must identify our viewpoint and our goals. Assessment is, therefore, the process of checking up as to whether the internal program for our lives is reflected by and fits external reality as we perceive it. Our internal reality colors our perception of external reality. It is like a filter. Assessment is also a check for congruence between our self-image and the image we project in interactions with other people. It is a comparison between our external and internal career plans. It is a check to see if the actions we contemplate can possibly create the outcomes we desire. It is both part of a planning and part of the execution processes.

As a planning process, it is similar to charting before the trip the course for a plane to fly between two points. Advanced data about weather and geographic location are paralleled by data about the nature of a career and the necessary study or skills necessary to succeed in that career. As part of the execution process it is similar to what happens in flight when the pilot makes a course correction and checks on its effect or direction by reading the compass. This activity is paralleled in our lives by trying to do something and observing the results. For example, trying to carve the head of an animal in a cake of soap is tested by whether it fits our expectations and looks like the animal. If others can also see the animal our internal and external realities seem to be in agreement. If they don't, then we try again and check further. Assessment is necessary in planning our lives and careers and also for managing them on a day-to-day basis.

What can we do to improve the effectiveness of the assessment process? One way is to sharpen our perception of inputs. To the extent we can accept feedback for what it is and feed it into the assessment process, this should contribute to positive outcomes from the process. One way is to improve our abilities to make comparisons between inputs and expected inputs, or to make comparisons between apparent achievements and desired goals. Still another refinement is to find specific feedback and assessment techniques which work best for us. And a final way is to improve the linkage between our assessments and what we do.

With this as a theoretical background the remainder of this chapter is devoted to examples intended to make assessment more understandable and improve our mastery of it. This should result in improving the conduct of our lives and improving our vitality.

What to assess

Many aspects of our being, our knowledge, our skills, our relations with others, and our satisfactions with life and work can be assessed. Since we are concentrating on vitality and growth, our discussion of assessment will emphasize those aspects of life which can affect our vitality. This does not narrow things down very much because it is hard to think of an aspect of living which cannot contribute to vitality and growth. Therefore, it is "open season" as to what we assess. In essence, we must assess all inputs and all feedback.

The way to start a study of personal assessment is to start with a problem. If your job does not seem to be going well, or your health is poor, or you are having difficulty relating to others, these types of problems can provide the grist for sharpening assessment. As an example, you might start with an assessment of how your life is working for you. This problem will provide many topics for deeper study. Do this by listing those things which you feel are standing in your way—keeping you from having the full, exciting, growth-providing life you desire. Then rank these in regard to their strength as blocks. If this provides you with some aspect of self which seems to be getting in your way, then look for ways to assess that aspect. Two assessment processes which may work for this purpose are included in the companion volume. One, in Section 3, is a career assessment. It was designed to provide you with a quick way of analyzing whether your job and career are providing satisfaction and growth right now. The other is a life and vitality assessment in Section 2. It asks you to reveal to yourself how you are doing on many aspects of your life. Try these assessments right now. They are both short and will take you less than thirty minutes each.

Career
assessment

In order to assess your career, we must agree upon what it is. For our purposes, the career consists of those things you do at your job, your major life purpose. For a job to be a career it should have been chosen by you. For your job to be a career it should relate to some basic preparation for it through study and experience. For your job to be your career it should not just be a momentary, passing thing but rather something pursued over a period of several years. Assuming you have a job that fits these broad criteria, assessing your career consists of determining the fit between you and that career from the standpoint of interests, skills, relationships, and sources of satisfaction. Assessing these things requires getting at least your own reactions to a group of questions about you and your job. A thorough assessment would also require that you get inputs from others, your coworkers, your supervisor, and your family. The reason for collecting others' opinions is to provide some check on the possibility that reality as you see it is different from reality as others see it.

Here it will be sufficient to reflect on some aspects of your relationship to your career to demonstrate the type of questioning you need to undertake as part of personal assessment. The first question should probably be a gross one: Do you like your job? This should bring out a positive, neutral, or negative response. If your response is positive, you should ask how positive, whether it is changing, and why. If it is negative, you should ask how negative, and why. Is your like or dislike of your job temporary or permanent? Does it follow from the nature of the work, the nature of associations, or the nature of work rules and controls? A second broad type of question is: What does your work provide? Does it provide income, an opportunity to grow, satisfying personal relationships, a sense of meaningfulness? Are you a fuller, more completely developed and realized person as a result of your work? Does it contribute to your vitality? What are you taking home from your work? Do these things you take home come close to meeting your expectations and needs? Follow-on questioning can and should become more detailed by dealing with task assignments and the match with your capabilities. Is there any aspect in which your initial questions show a hint of mismatch?

Such an assessment or measurement must reflect the fact that your relationship to your work is dynamic and changing, not static.

Thus career assessment must be continuing or, at a minimum, periodic. The best way to really understand whether your career is working for you may be to look at the differences and changes in your answers over time. The trend of change may reveal more than your specific answers.

In this assessment, as in any other, it is important to recognize that a 100 percent fit and score of complete satisfaction is neither desirable nor achievable. It is not desirable because differences are a source of growth motivation and because total satisfaction might lead to a special kind of irrationality. With 100 percent satisfaction we would simply get "swelled heads" and living with us would become difficult. Full matching is not achievable because of the dynamics and changes in our interaction with people and things. Yet examining the lifelines which people draw to represent their lives with both positive and negative experiences does frequently reveal that there are more positives, and that positives have a longer duration than negatives. When we find ourselves in a markedly negative life or work situation, we often do something to end it. That is, we change it if we are managing our lives and taking responsibility.

Strong vocational interest tests

If your initial, and possibly superficial, career assessment indicated potential need for a change, there are several ways of looking deeper. One is to read, study, and talk about other careers until you find one or more that have some of the characteristics you are looking for. Another way to look deeper is to see whether your values and interests seem to align with those of others pursuing the same career. Neither of these approaches tests your skills and capabilities, which is another necessary assessment. Both these approaches merely feature an interest perspective.

The *Strong* test is one of the oldest career-assessment devices available. It was constructed on the thesis that people who are successful in a given career respond to questions and choices in a way that reflects values and interests that are characteristic of people in that career. Whether these values lead people to this career, or are developed by the pursuit of the career, is not entirely clear. However, by making a series of forced choices that reflect style, outlook, and values, a pattern or profile is developed for you.

Your answers are then compared with the choices made by people in many fields. Results are reported to you in a manner which highlights your tendency to have a pattern of interests and values like, or very much like, people in specific careers. For instance, if your answers look similar to those of concert musicians, you may consider that career. The results do not predict your ability as a concert musician but suggest this is a field which you might consider. The suggestion is based on the parallelism between your values and the values of those in that field.

If you are desirous of checking up on your interests, the *Strong* test, administered at most universities and in many companies' career-counseling sections, is a good way. It is a valuable tool in assessing interests.

Personal growth and vitality inventory

In the companion workbook I have included several personal-assessment devices. The one we will discuss here is symbolic of the self-assessment process. It is the vitality inventory. The inventory is designed to help you determine how you feel about various aspects of your life as well as your relationship to your work. It should sensitize you to your desires and sources of satisfaction and help you to become more articulate about them. Thus the answering of these questions should improve your ability to take responsibility for your life. Answering searching questions can help you to face up to real feelings if you are frank with yourself. If, on the other hand, you answer them with what you feel are acceptable answers, or the answers you feel you should give to maintain some role you have assigned yourself, the questions will be of little help. In other words, your attitude and expectations can affect the usefulness of any inventory. These questions cannot reveal something about you which you do not know, but they may reveal something you have set aside, suppressed, or been fearful of expressing. The inventory should be used again and again and by noticing, by becoming conscious of, how your answers change with time, you can become aware of the most revealing aspect of the assessment. Becoming aware of your changes in values and attitudes can make a significant contribution to improving your vitality.

Some of the questions are deceptively simple. Some of the questions will normally be answered differently if you answer them quickly rather than pondering over them. Some of the questions will seem to be important to you and others will not. Not all questions are equally valuable for all users. The same question may vary in importance to you at different times. In fact, the same question will be seen in different perspectives and evoke different responses at different times. Because of this, question topics are presented first as broad general questions. If this gets you started, fine, and if not, the general question is followed by supplemental ones that may trigger responses. It is important that you understand that there are no right or wrong answers and that you're answering them for yourself. More philosophy and suggestions about how to use the inventory and analyze your answers are included as part of the inventory.

To really understand personal assessment and to gain the most from the discussion of how one can build assessment through the use of this device, we suggest you now try Personal Experiment 19, which is a sampling from the inventory. Some personal feeling about the nature of the questions is helpful in pursuing our understanding of this type of assessment. The questions provide a means of creating feedback. The inventory is a special kind of mirror designed to enhance self-understanding. If you have experienced this type of feedback, you can begin to understand the process.

Questions in the inventory are organized into broad sections covering growth, learning, interests, utilization, self-concept, vitality, satisfactions, motivation for change, and life and career direction. The section on motivation for change is the source of the examples used in Personal Experiment 19 and this discussion of self-assessment because it is different from the kinds of things previously discussed in this chapter. The first question is: What is your desire to change? What you are asked to analyze is whether you fear or look forward to change, whether you are reasonably satisfied with who you are and what you are doing, or whether you feel a strong motivation to change. The purpose is to test the price you are willing to pay to change. All changes include risk and investment of self. There is a cost to change, and deciding to change is based on your evaluation of payoff. Risks are loss of relationships you value, loss of job, and loss of satisfaction, however limited, in the search for greater satisfaction. Investments include, for example, energy for study, energy for increased awareness, and expenditure of money and time. Investments are thus both physical and psychological. Risks are both physical and psychological. Payouts, too, may be either or both.

PERSONAL EXPERIMENT 19

Assessment requires taking stock. This can be done either by analyzing what is happening or by creating a series of questions which heighten your sensitivity and stimulate analysis. Here are some questions as motivations for change. Answer these questions now.

1. What is your desire to change? Are you reasonably satisfied with yourself, your job, and your life? If not, what kind of change do you want? How badly do you want to change — what price will you pay in energy, hours, dollars, loss of position, etc.?

2. What was the last major change in your life? How did it come about? Did it happen to you or did you do something to bring it about? Was it a change for the better? Did it relate to work or did it occur outside work?

3. Are your family, friends, and management supportive of change in you? Do you feel boxed in and limited by pressures from others? How would you go about effecting improvement in their support or change in you?

The second question is: What was the last major change in your life? The purpose here is to get you to identify changes in yourself and their causes. Is your concept of self-change primarily that of response to a changing world around you, or is your concept that you bring it about? How you look at major changes in your life can be revealing. For example, you probably would classify major changes most often with respect to those aspects of life which you value highly. Thus the question also tests your values.

Managing change requires finding support for change. Managing change requires creating techniques which will lessen fear and anxieties and which will increase the probability of positive outcomes. Thus, the third question concerns whether your associates support change in you. Associates may be at work, at play, or family. Suppose you wanted to make a major change in your appearance. What would be the reaction of those close to you? How important is their reaction, and would a negative reaction rob you of some of your desire to change? How would you go about gaining their support? This type of question aids you in surfacing some of the techniques you use to manage change. You may discover that you already have techniques for making change feel more comfortable or that you do not and need to invent some.

This experience with Personal Experiment 19 should have shown you how the right questions can help you with personal assessment. These questions are not the only such devices but, rather, they exemplify this kind of self-analysis. Our discussion here may have transmitted the impression that assessment is merely asking questions. Questions are used to heighten your sensitivity and sharpen your aim as a supplementary process to living. Active and ordered analysis through questioning is not the only form of assessment, however. Much of the assessment we do goes on daily and continually in the process of living. The earlier discussion of feedback is demonstrative of those processes. Assessment can be nonverbal; therefore it can occur at the physical level as in the feel of a muscle or the feeling level in response to emotions.

Assessment through
another person

Assessment by another person or through another's view and that feedback to you is first encountered in your relationship to your parents. Later a similar process evolves with your teachers and your friends and peer groups. In the work situation such a relationship exists with your group and manager or supervisor. A similar relationship exists with your doctor or dentist. There are special characteristics of each of these relationships which make them helpful or not helpful. Since we are interested in assessment, your understanding of the way you can gain assessment through another can help you to set up future conditions for improved assessment. Learning to use the inputs from others is an important aspect of your life management.

A first principle in using someone else's input is respect. You must trust and respect the other person's view, knowledge, and capability to help you. If you don't, the input will not be valued and therefore will be of little effect. A part of trust is feeling that whatever the other person does or says, however acceptable to you or not, is sincere and intended to be helpful. If you feel that the other person has some overall interest or goal which transcends interest in you or is counter to your best interests, that feeling will interfere with your use of his or her input. It is the perception which counts rather than the reality.

A second principle has to do with privacy. It is necessary to have a feeling of safety in this relationship. That is, if you reveal something of yourself, you should feel the other person will not misuse that information.

A third principle is openness. This means the other person must share a willingness to be frank, to say things not just because they believe you want to hear them but because that is the way they see them. Openness is two-sided. You must also be willing to hear frank statements and not react as if you are being attacked and become defensive. Both parties must consciously desire to share data as each sees it without negating value judgments.

A next principle is listening and providing space for your own development. A counselor's greatest help can be in providing catalytic aid in letting you express yourself and question your own views. It is almost as if you can rise to a higher level of self-understanding and capability just because of his or her support of you. Part of their listening to you can be nonevaluative reflection. Those interested in nonevaluative, nondirective counseling should read Carl Rogers' writings, for he is the chief teacher of the power of this method.

A final principle is that the counselor should not try to make you over in his or her image, but rather be open to letting you develop as yourself. This is a very difficult aspect of the counseling process and is seldom achieved. The very process of supplying you with feedback means the other person is expressing his or her perspective and most often reflecting his or her values. Parents implant their values either negatively or positively. In the negative sense their values may become the things you or I resist to which we develop a counteraction. The same is true of teachers and supervisors. But part of what you and I are seeking is this different view from another's vantage point. In other words, assessment with another person is valuable because of his or her different viewpoint and values. In that sense, we want the counselor to express his or her views but not impose them on us. It is desirable that each of us, at least as adults, be in charge and that you and I make the choice about whether or not the values of others are imposed.

Taking in input and evaluating it

Whether the input comes from our own perceptions or represents the perceptions of others, it is of value only if it is received, integrated, and acted upon. These parts of the assessment process are internal to the individual. Our receipt of the input depends on the sensitivity of our input channels. In effect, we should be tuned to hear, and tuning affects the openness of these channels. Tuning can be thought of as setting up the conditions for listening and seeing with a purpose. If we are interested in finding out whether an aspect of our life is working for us, then tuning is becoming more sensitive to the types of inputs that reflect that aspect. For example, if we are interested in knowing how we relate to others, it might require becoming sensitive to nonverbal signals such as body language.

Openness requires eliminating blocks to the receipt of and integration of data. If we carry an image of ourselves such as making friends easily and relating well to others, we may tend to deny, or not admit, data which does not fit that picture. Typically in this situation, any evidence of failure at interpersonal relations would probably be rationalized by us to be the responsibility of the other person. Openness and unblocking are discussed in Chapter 8, Unlearning. In the context of self-assessment, unlearning is often the elimination of emotional blocks.

Evaluating requires comparing the new data with stored data and making a determination of whether or not to displace the old or add the new to the old in a new combination. Evaluation also requires the willingness to base a new action on this revision of stored data. Evaluation is therefore complete only when there is acceptance.

Summary

The process of personal assessment consists of accepting feedback for our actions, analyzing it, and basing new action on our revised position. Assessment is a normal, day-in, day-out process. It can be sharpened and intensified by asking ourselves questions, engaging in projective test processes, or seeking special counsel. Self-assessment can be enhanced by the open use of another person's input. In accepting counsel from another we must stay in control and decide whether we are going to accept their viewpoint and values.

Personal assessment is necessary in all aspects of our lives. It is particularly important in increasing job satisfaction, improving our ability to communicate to and relate to others, in choosing helpful life goals, in choosing values and purposes, and in managing our health and vitality.

Suggested readings

Brouwer, Paul J. "The Power To See Ourselves," *Harvard Business Review*, Nov.-Dec. 1964, pp. 156-163.

James, Muriel, and Jongward, Dorothy. *Born To Win — Gestalt Transactional Analysis with Gestalt Experiments*. Reading, Mass.: Addison-Wesley, 1971.

Koestenbaum, Peter. *Managing Anxiety — The Power of Knowing Who You Are*. Englewood Cliffs, N.J.: Spectrum Books, Prentice-Hall, 1974.

Miller, Donald B. *Personal Vitality Workbook — A Personal Inventory and Planning Guide*. Reading, Mass.: Addison-Wesley, 1977.

Miller, Donald B. "Privacy. A Key Issue Between Employees and Managers," *University of Michigan Business Review*. Jan. 1976, pp. 7-12.

Paulus, T. *Hope For The Flowers*. New York: Paulist Press, 1972.

Samples, Robert, and Wohlford, Robert. *Opening — A Primer For Self-Actualization*. Menlo Park, Calif.: Addison-Wesley, 1975.

> *The authors describe openness as a desirable personal attitude which can be cultivated and which when applied will improve your life. By providing some incidents and some exercises, they give you a way to analyze your openness. They review values and prejudices as the underlying causes of a closed attitude. The book is designed to move you toward growing and increasing your potential for self-actualization.*

Samuels, Mike, and Bennett, Hal. *The Well Body Book*. New York: Random House/Berkeley, Bookworks, 1973.

Putting it all together

For the individual

13

Managing change

Introduction

Some people view change as something which happens to them, something over which they have no control: kismet, or luck. I believe that you can and should influence and manage what happens. This does not mean that forces outside you can't cause changes. It does mean that you can shape the change. You can set up receptive conditions for change. Your expectations shape what happens. You can project yourself into change. You can adopt a perspective and learn techniques which make changes easier to navigate. You can reduce your feeling of risk in making changes but probably not completely eliminate your anxieties. Growth is change but all changes are not necessarily growth. Changing is necessary to maintain vitality.

Some techniques for managing change are suggested and reviewed in this chapter. They range from a simple technique, such as setting up small increments of change, arranging feedback, and learning to modify your direction based on the feedback to more complex techniques, including things you can do to manage role change and how you can find support for change. Role change, affecting your whole self, is probably the most difficult of changes. It is like being reborn.

One type of change we each must manage has to do with life purpose and work. If you can really get to know yourself—finding those things that turn you on, that satisfy, and that frustrate—then it is possible to improve your sensitivity to possible alternatives. Alternatives are almost limitless, but to recognize them requires a special kind of ability. The challenge is to recognize the alternatives, define and describe them, and then find ways of matching yourself to them. Matching is a two-sided process: first, identifying your internal agenda, finding what you need; and second, finding ways to translate the needs of the world into activities which fit you. Generally these changes are career changes.

A vocation or a career is not just a collection of jobs, but rather activities which resemble a coherent whole. These activities should do two things: serve a purpose which is perceived by those being served and provide a role for the individual. Although I will discuss ways of increasing the awareness of personal potential, this is not a chapter on self-assessment nor on career management—these topics will be used only as examples of change management.

A second type of change, representing a personal-management challenge, centers around how we relate to other people and our world. This involves changing communication patterns and changing associations in the arenas of family, organizational membership, and friendships.

A third category of changes we must manage is those we make in our environment, in the organizations of which we are part, and in activities other than work and career which we pursue. Examples would be changing the locale or type of house we live in, or learning a new hobby or skill, or learning and practicing prayer or meditation. Any of these changes could significantly affect an individual's life-style.

The chapter is, in a way, a "how-to" set of suggestions. In another sense it simply attempts to take the mystery out of change. Even a life which appears to be standing still requires adjustment and change. Change cannot be avoided—but we can make the best of it.

My approach will be to present a conceptual framework from which we can build a perspective which leads to our improved change management.

Change—what is it?

There are fundamentally two kinds of change. First, there are changes which are outside us: these may be changes in physical objects; or changes in values represented by the environment; or changes in others with whom we work, live, and communicate. If, for example, you trade in your car for a new one this is an external change, and it can be recognized because of your stored data about your old car. Driving the new car may precipitate internal change. Second, there are changes which are inside us. These result from our accepting new information and using it to alter our expectations, our perceptions, and our actions. An inside change might be represented by accepting a new value such as the desirability of unpolluted air. Changes inside are measured in changed perception and changed behavior. Inside and outside changes are related, and a change in one area often causes a change in the other.

Changes can only be recognized when there is a reference. For example, if there is a ball in space, the only way we can perceive its movement is with respect to something else. If there are two balls we can perceive change, but if that is all there are we cannot tell which ball is moving. So it is with us. If you or I change our behavior it is only discernible if we or those observing us remember how we behaved before. Many small personal changes therefore go unnoticed. The first principle in managing change is that for a change to be recognized there must be a reference—we need figure and ground, the figure being the aspect which is changing or not changing, perceived and measured with respect to the background called ground. The ground is the reference or measurement base. Managing change requires data, and the perception of difference is the raw data of change.

Change also includes the concept of exchange—that of replacing one thing with another. When we replace an old theory with a new theory on which we intend to base action, we are making this kind of change. This example will, of course, lead to other changes. If we operate on a new premise, many of our interactions with the world will be different. Accepting the concept of equal opportunity is an example of this. Eliminating discrimination leads to role changes, work changes, and life-style changes both for the minority and for the rest of us. Another type of exchange is created when we move a physical object and replace it with another. The rearrangement of furniture is a good example. Again we see that this change makes other changes more probable. Our pattern of walking, talking, and using the room is changed by the rearrangement of the furniture. The second principle of change management is that one change usually increases the probability of other changes if the initial change impacts people in a way that requires a reaction. Change begets change.

The next important aspect of change is initiation. In discussing changes which lead to improvement in the organization of work, and thence productivity, George F. Farris, in "Chickens, Eggs, and Productivity in Organizations," has written a thoughtful article about who starts improvement. As he says, we normally approach the issue with an underlying assumption, usually not made explicit, that someone else should and will make the first move. Managers feel that when the employees show some spark of interest, commitment, and energy, then the managers will respond with recognition, support, and new freedoms. Probably the employees are simultaneously thinking that when the managers demonstrate openness and willingness to reward extra effort, then they will try a little harder. The third principle in managing change is, therefore, if you want change, make the first move—take the responsibility for action.

The fourth principle of change management is that we humans have conflicting feelings, wanting and needing stability and simultaneously desiring change. Part of our feeling that things are right comes from our ability to predict what will happen. Prediction requires a relationship with the past and an ability to extend trends. Prediction requires a type of stability—the holding of some things constant while we vary something else. Part of the resistance to change comes from fear of the unknown and relates to worry about survival. Part of this resistance is a feeling of limit in our capability to monitor and relate to multiple variables. On the reverse side, total stability threatens us for we know managing the environment, managing change, has caused the human to rise above other living things. Lack of change means decline or loss. Constancy of stimuli turns us off—is boring and nonstimulating. We desire both stability or lack of change, and change and new stimuli. Achieving the right balance should be our goal in improving our management of change. We want to have enough change to provide stimulation for vitality and growth, but not so much that it creates anxiety, frustration, and bewilderment.

Change by its very nature is offensive, not defensive. When we are defensive we are defending the status quo—trying to resist change. When we are in an offensive posture we are seeking change. To manage change we must be aggressors, thrust ourselves out, try new things and experiment. This does not mean we must hurt others, although our changing may eliminate something others have counted on as an element of stability. Change in us can thus be threatening to our friends, family, and associates. In managing change we must understand this threat and do things which will prepare others and minimize the negative impact on them. So the fifth principle in managing change is that to change one must be the aggressor; with this comes a responsibility of explaining and preparing others. That others may lose by our change, however, can become an anchor which causes us to decay and lose vitality. Helping others to live with our changes does not mean we should give up change and growth!

The sixth principle in managing change is that change in ourselves is facilitated by helping others to change. This happens because our fears and anxieties diminish in the presence of those of other people. It is easier to see that fears are probably not rational in someone else. It happens too because trying to aid another forces us into an outgoing role. The activity of helping another keeps us from becoming too immersed in ourselves, too introspective, and overly depressed. Activity of this type diverts us from our defensiveness.

Introducing change
as a manager

Change is one of the first things we see in management today. In fact, rapid change may be the only constant in today's management. The post-industrial era, automation, the application of social-science research to business, the changing work ethic, the new information technology—all of these factors are causing change; they are, in fact, part of it.

The manager faces two major change-based problems. The first one concerns how to keep up to date personally: how does one learn about new developments and the impact they are having on one's business? Second, how does one apply these new ideas and changes to a particular business? How does one introduce change effectively with the smallest initial disruption, and the greatest long-term profit? At the center of the manager's job today is the *management of change*. There are in concept but not in reality two systems to be managed: the technical system, containing the work process, and the social system, containing human relationships. Introducing change in the technical system seems rational, plannable, with right ways and wrong ways. The impact and success of technical change, however, almost always depends on the human response to change. So there is a direct relationship between changes in the two systems. Change, whether it is directed at what appears to be technical or social, acts as a total process. Change in either the technical or the social system can cause change in the other system.

A society or organization seldom changes spontaneously or abruptly. Changing directions, values, and ways of doing things is extremely difficult. The contrast between changes resulting from the graduated income tax and Prohibition provide a good case in point. Both were enacted about the same time in response to growing social needs. Both called for radical change. But one was imposed gradually; the other, immediately. One evolved slowly in response to the times; the other sought a quick, simple solution to a complicated problem. One has been and continues to be the most successful social legislation of its kind in history. The other was a complete failure and had to be withdrawn.

In imposing change, the problems of the manager are not so very different from those of congresses and kings. First, the manager must gather enough information to assess, sense, and finally decide whether or not change is needed. Second, he or she must analyze and evaluate the data collected. Then, in the form of a directive or, better, through participation of the people involved, he or she must introduce some change. The specific change may be all that is desired, a small part of a series, or a major shift in direction. To the initial change there is an organizational reaction and feedback. The manager must assess, feel, sense this feedback, and decide what, if any, further action is needed. The initial action and all subsequent actions must be taken on incomplete information, and this is one of the primary risks of management. The process is iterative: small changes add together to make the larger change in direction, or approach, or method for the whole organization. Changes which are perceived as positive tend to beget more positive changes, while negative changes seem to increase the probability of negative changes.

Critical by-products of the iterative process for change are conditioning and education. The 1964 Civil Rights Bill, for example, would probably not have passed Congress in the mid-fifties. But a milder one did pass then, and it helped set the stage for its stronger successor. In short, the change process is aided and reinforced when people are educated to accept it, and an amplifying effect is possible when people are educated to encourage it and improve upon it.

There is a third ingredient in the manager's role in change. A manager is responsible not only for keeping personal knowledge up to date and making personal changes, but also for training and development of employees and improving and extending the vitality of the organization. A key to this is the very process of introducing and managing change. The ability to adapt to and use change is a criterion for vitality. In summary, *first*, we need a sound basis upon which to plan for the future and anticipate change; *second*, we need to understand the mechanics of introducing change; and *third*, we need to create an environment in which change is accepted and encouraged.

These requirements are the same whether we are managing organizational change or change in ourselves. If we take a close look at these three requirements, we see that they have one basic element in common: all require learning. For change management, we need a conscious, comprehensive, and dynamic educational process woven into the very fabric of our business and our lives. Without it, the management of change becomes at best a poor risk. At worst, it is impossible.

The precursors of individual change

In order to implement changes in the processes for which we are responsible and in order to help others with change, we must know how to handle change in ourselves. We start with the paradox shown below and previously cited. The goal for self-management of change is to make the process more comfortable and to gain some satisfaction from the process itself. We need somehow to make change normal and comfortable, and to make stability less comfortable.

The paradox: Feelings of comfort and safety result from stability. Feelings of growth and progress result from change. Where do we start? Probably the place to begin is by recognizing the conditions which set the stage for change, the preconditions which establish our readiness to undertake the process and the attendant risks. These preconditions are the basis for the rationale which we must have to make our new actions or outlook understandable and to establish support for the change. Some of these preconditions for personal change are as follows:

- Vague uneasiness
- Boredom
- Repeated disappointments
- Crises
- New information which doesn't fit
- Reflection and personal assessment
- Achieving a goal
- An environment of acceptability

Sometimes the first sign that we may need a change is simply a feeling of uneasiness. Often we cannot identify the cause for this uneasiness and cannot explain why we feel the way we do. We remember, however, that that uneasy feeling has previously been assuaged by doing something different. The uneasy feeling is in itself a change from normal. It establishes an internal climate for action.

Boredom is also a form of uneasiness. We usually ascribe boredom to a lack of new stimuli. It may result from our failure to take responsibility for what is happening to us and from our expectations that we are owed something for our previous activity; that is, a feeling that positive things should happen since we've already paid the price. Boredom is an internal state. It may actually have been caused by a change in the environment around us, or it may have been caused by cumulative internal pressures from unrealized expectations. It may also reflect personal indecision. Boredom, like uneasiness, is a useful indicator which should promote action on our part to change the condition. Reduction of boredom is often attempted through busywork. A better way is through an activity which changes some basic aspect of our lives.

Repeated disappointments or acknowledged unfulfilled expectations are somewhat stronger motivations for action than vague uneasiness or boredom. Whether true or not, what counts is that we feel we have evidence of specific negative input. A disappointment is negative input. Disappointments are, therefore, a more concentrated form of precondition for change. Disappointments are specific evidence that our life is not working. We feel we can ascribe our malaise to specific incidents and this should generate openness to change.

Crises are severe forms of disappointments. Crises are generally perceived as external incidents over which we feel we have had no control. Loss of a loved one, an accident, or loss of a job are typical life crises. These incidents force an adjustment, force acceptance of new rules for the game of life, and encourage a reassessment. Although crises are viewed as negative, the changes for which they are a percursor may well be positive. Converting crises into positive inputs for improvement requires intelligent action on our part.

New information which fails to align or fit with our previous experience may be found in a disappointment or a crisis. We have the power of choice as to whether the new data is positive or negative. Think, for example, of the process of reconciling your bank balance. When you add up the checkbook and then work back from the bank figures and get different results, you have information which doesn't fit. This requires a change, a different approach to the problem. Either answer may be correct. Which one is correct

PERSONAL EXPERIMENT 20

Identify a recent change in yourself, your work, or your relationships. List the causes or preconditions which you can now remember which may have stimulated you to take action which led to the change. What was the first happening which elicited a feeling of uneasiness, disappointment, or crisis? What was the time period from first evidence of a need for change to conviction and action? What finally tipped the scale?

Next try to identify current feelings, incidents, or conditions which may be preconditions for new changes. What are they? What change would reduce or relieve these feelings?

depends upon an analysis of your actions. Your original calculations may be wrong, your reconciliation may be wrong, or even the bank may be wrong.

Sometimes as the result of one of the other conditions, such as information which doesn't fit, we pause to reassess our lives. Sometimes this self-assessment is deliberate, and sometimes it just happens. Sometimes the first change is the seeking out of a process of self-assessment. Such an act could require sensing a feedback and discovering it is inadequate or incomplete. Such an act of reassessment could result from a sense of the passage of time during which we feel conditions have changed or from a change in our goals. Sometimes it can result from the next item on the list—achieving a goal. When we get that sense of completion, or closure, it almost automatically sets in motion the search for a new goal. This search for a new goal, whatever the cause, is another precondition for change.

Sometimes the first event of which we are conscious is simply that we find ourselves in a position or situation where we no longer have to support our mask, or "personna." Suddenly we are conscious that it is safe to say what we really feel, to release those feelings and attitudes for which there has been an inner urge but no previous safe space in which to let them escape.

Such a climate of unanticipated acceptability is sometimes found at a cocktail party or social event at which we meet a good listener whom we perceive as having no contact with our regular life. Or we sense that someone to whom we relate is relaxed, at peace within and open to listening. Another possibility is that a professional counselor, psychologist, minister, or psychiatrist sets up these conditions under which it is safe to reveal and deal with our true feelings. Still another condition which sometimes leads to this perception of acceptability is travel. Being detached from the usual constraints and routine can open for us the space of acceptability. Being detached can open the space for self-analysis and an objective view of one's normal life relationships.

The change process

To begin our understanding of the change process, it is necessary to have a concept of the relationship of the individual to the environment. In Fig. 13.1 the individual is shown oversimplified, consisting of three elements: characteristics and abilities, experiences and be-

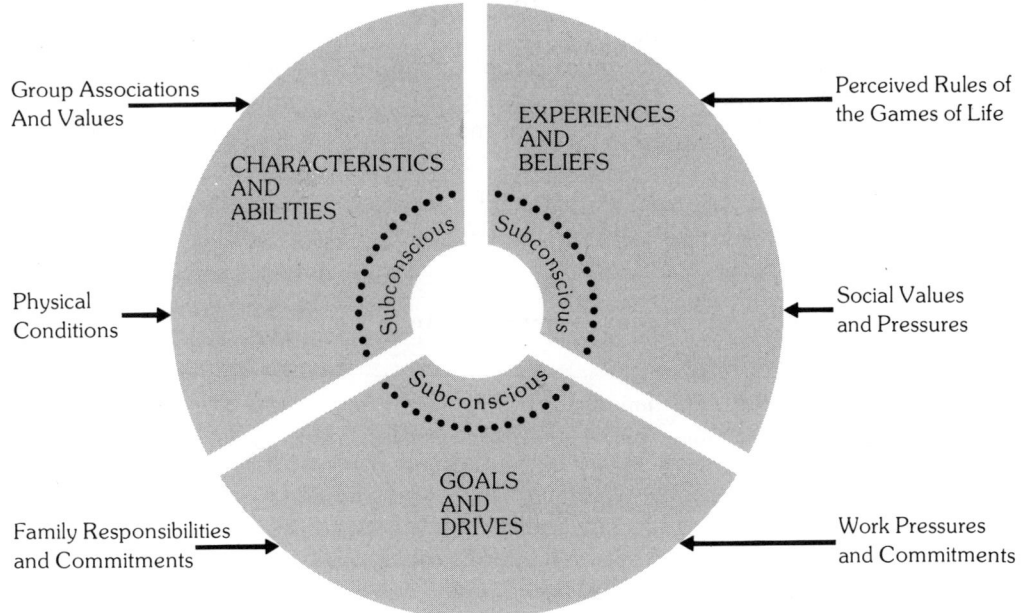

Fig. 13.1 The individual and the environment

liefs (which include knowledge and skills), and goals and drives or motivations. Each of these segments is divided into a surface, conscious representation and a central portion of subconscious elements. For example, the conscious part of a goal might be the purpose which we communicate to someone else; the subconscious part might be an increase in our feeling of self-worth. These two levels, conscious and subconscious, would be expressed in different language and perhaps in different actions. Surrounding this pictorial representation of the person are a series of arrows which portray relationships with the environment which have an impact on the individual. For example, work pressures and commitments could relate to schedule and performance aspects of our work. The picture portrays elements intrinsic to the individual and some of the inputs to the individual which come from life and work.

How does this picture help us understand the change process? First, it shows that the analysis and comparison upon which we determine change take place inside us but may or may not utilize deeper, or subconscious, information. Second, it portrays the feeling of pressure or conflict potential. Third, it can help us see what we have already discussed—that movement can start outside or inside. Acceptance of new information modifying our internal pattern is the basis for change.

The process by which people change is shown in the listing which follows as stages of sensing, preparing, and doing. These steps highlight the process to make us more conscious of our actions. Often the process seems to occur all at one time and we are not aware of these steps. In minor changes the steps merge, and in major changes of life-direction, the process is longer and the stages are more easily discerned.

The change process — people change by:

Sensing:

- Gathering information
- Becoming aware of a difference
- Analysis of what accepting new data may mean
- Seeking counsel to help understand what is wrong

Preparing:

- Giving themselves a reason
- Deciding to change
- Openness and sharing the perception of need for change

- Study and work to increase capability

Doing:
- Letting go
- Immersion in changed environment—finding acceptance
- Establishing change increments with feedback
- Modifying the direction and implementing further changes

Sensing is the process of identifying the existence of one of the preconditions discussed earlier. It occurs when we become conscious that something does not fit and change may be imminent. We are sensing when discomfort becomes sufficient to motivate us to action or at least consideration of action. Sensing happens when we perceive a difference. The difference can exist without our perception—but we will do nothing in response. It is the *perception* which initiates our action. When, for example, someone else is awarded the promotion we wanted and we recognize we may need to change—this is sensing.

If it is a major change, or if it is threatening or risky, part of the sensing operation is to gather additional data. We check the new input. We ask others if they have reacted similarly. We try another perspective to see if we get the same new data. Our analysis of the information, its impact and potential risks, may be entirely internal, or we may talk it out with someone else as an advisor or counselor.

Deciding and preparing are the next stages. Deciding is finding a rational, dependable reason, acceptable both for yourself and for telling to others. The reason is often found by concentrating on the expected outcome or benefit. Being open and talking about it is a part of the process. Sharing probably increases the commitment and the sense of safety or security. Study and work also help increase our mobility by increasing our self-confidence. Preparing requires doing something about it. Often, enrollment in a course or exposure to a book or article containing new data is necessary to give us the feeling of being ready and of increasing the probability of success. Preparing in the case of the missed promotion would be understanding what experience, characteristics, or knowledge would influence the decision in our favor.

The final stage, doing, is actually making the change. It requires taking action—not just getting ready, but incorporating the change and using the new data. First, we have to break with the past, and then thrust ourselves forward into the changed situation. This means letting go. In a way, this is like unlearning; it is an unhooking or actually springing off the diving board. Letting go is moving forward with faith in ourselves and trust that the change is good and we will succeed. Whether letting go comes before, during, or after the action step is not clear. In fact, there may be sequential steps of letting go. As we gain comfort and reward from the new, we are able to give up a bit more of the past. Failing to let go leads to divided loyalties or counter pulls from different goals. Failing to let go uses up energy—but not beneficially in pursuit of the change. Many attempts at managing change are unsuccessful because of failure to let go.

Both as a part of the action of making change and as a technique for providing support in change we should immerse ourselves in a changed environment. It is easier to break and let go when we are in an environment which is different. An unchanged environment tends to support and reinforce our old patterns. A new environment, even if it does not specifically reinforce the new patterns, at least breaks with the support of the old. It is even better if we can find an environment which supports or reinforces the new patterns or modes of behavior. The school classroom should be an example of an environment which supports change. In a good learning environment, it should be acceptable to exhibit confusion and to make mistakes. In a good learning environment, it should be expected that we will try new things, new behavior. A good teacher should be a catalyst for this process of change, providing support as we try new patterns. The same things can be said about a good work environment.

Taking small steps, gaining feedback and modifying our course where possible, helps the process. First, it helps by getting us a quick reward and payback and by contributing to feelings of success. Sometimes the specific act is an all-or-nothing situation, but there is no commitment to repeat it. For example, the first jump off the diving board commits us to immersion in the water once, but if the experience is not satisfying, it is possible to choose not to do it again. The one-time commitment to this is all-or-nothing, but there is no lifelong commitment. By contrast, accepting Christ as our teacher and leader commits us for a long time, and the initial or one-time act is probably not as shocking as the immersion on diving into the pool (instant conversions excepted). Part of doing includes the iterative process of taking small steps which we've already described. Part of it is a longer-term cycle. This requires going in one direction of change long enough so that we can take new measurements and see if we are going in the right direction. It's like tacking in sailing: if we change direction too often, we lose the race because we've used up too much time and energy in just turning and not moving toward our goal. The situation is similar in making changes in life. While we must be sensitive to feedback and open to modification, we must avoid wasting our energy just making changes and not getting anywhere. There needs, therefore, to be a deliberateness and a pacing, a commitment for long enough periods to have a chance of getting somewhere. Such a commitment maximizes the effectiveness of our changes.

Techniques for making change

There has already been some discussion of technique. Now that we have a picture of the process of change, however, it is possible to look more deeply at specific techniques. The several reviewed and discussed here are not the only ones. Without trial by you, no one can know whether they will work for you. Most techniques deal with decreasing the feeling of risk—that is, making you more comfortable with the idea and process. Some techniques provide incentives so that you can see the payout, and still others work at lowering the threshold or barriers to change. Here is a list of some of the techniques to be discussed:

Techniques for managing personal change

- Identifying personal challenge or reason
- Setting up an agreement or contract
- Finding a climate of acceptance
- Setting up incremental steps and creating a checking process
- Deliberately seeking variety in an aspect of living, such as changing dress or appearance as a process aid
- Personal assessment which may create discomfort and increase motivation
- Choosing those aspects which you won't change
- Changing your basic philosophy of life or perspective
- Changing the threshold of consciousness
- Setting up, identifying, a frequent occurrence as a reminder

We must see some benefit to be gained in order to motivate ourselves actively to pursue change. This can be seen at an elementary level in nonthreatening changes. The act of choosing a different necktie to go with a particular suit can, for example, be supported by envisioning our improved appearance. This change is probably so minor we are not usually conscious of the need for creating a reason. The decision to take a different route to work can be supported by a need to overcome boredom, or by creating an errand or a stop requiring an alternative direction. Or route change could be rationalized as a need to see new things. Preidentifying the benefit or reason can help in motivating ourselves to action.

Closely related to identifying a reason is challenging yourself. A young weight lifter creates the need to try a little harder by setting a goal of surpassing the weight lifted yesterday. The perceived payoff or benefit here is both increased prowess and satisfaction of achievement. On a deeper, or major-change level, we can identify the same processes or techniques and recognize their power. For example, the decision to take a course of study can be forwarded by preidentifying the things that may happen as a result—things such as increased pay, a new job, or enhanced self-worth. Often this process of personal challenge and preidentifying the payout is done at a subconscious level. Doing this consciously, making our preidentification of payout explicit, may help in managing change. This aspect of the process is particularly necessary in introducing change in an organization or group. Communication and acceptance of the need can overcome one of the major barriers to organizational change.

Another technique is the establishment of an agreement or contract. The contract may be with ourselves or with another person. Such an agreement, in effect, raises the penalty for not changing. If, for example, an individual decides to lose ten pounds and communicates this to a partner, this represents the type of contractual change-aid we are discussing. Both Weight Watchers and Alcoholics Anonymous use this principle of sharing commitment with others to make the resolve more binding. A similar technique in the case of weight loss would be to promise oneself a new suit or dress upon achievement. It is most powerful to couple penalty motivation with positive reinforcement.

Finding a climate of acceptance requires us to recognize that a block to change in ourselves can be those around us. Part of our relationship with them is an obligation to remain the same. A young father told me of an incident which demonstrates this. He went to the park with his children and bought them balloons. He also bought one for himself. His children reacted negatively in several ways because he had in effect broken with the implied contract to be an adult—a father. Fathers don't play with balloons. Wives, husbands, children, friends, work associates, and managers can all act in a way to make change harder. By discussing the change and getting our companions to support it, we can reinforce and support the change process. Had the father recognized the need, he could have enlisted his children's support in his need for a balloon.

This example of the father and the balloon raises an interesting supplemental idea. It has to do with the role of ritual in life and change management. Ritual has positive and negative aspects. Ritual in the positive sense provides support and consistency. By so doing it makes it possible for us to be free to change other aspects of our lives. In the negative sense ritual is a substitute for thought, a convenient way to do things without being sensitive. In the positive sense ritual allows us to direct our energies and enhances our change-management capability. Thus the ritual of the church has historically provided freedom in other parts of life. The rituals of our roles, like father, provide for simplification and sometimes efficiency in living our lives. Yet the ritual of our daily lives may literally contribute to our loss of vitality. The unanswered question is how to have enough and not too much, how to break the ritual, how to break through and make contact with what is happening in order to assure our vitality.

Perceiving the need and acting to establish a climate of acceptance with our associates can ease change. Establishing the supportive climate may merely require a preannouncement of intent which draws out and deals with the anxiety-creating aspects of the change for them. On the other hand, it may mean finding a new group that does not know of our previous patterns and so, therefore, does not feel the need to keep us in our rut. Deliberately seeking out new friends, going to a place, formal or informal, where change is expected is a technique for aiding change in ourselves. For example, leaving one organization and starting in a new one can overcome the "once a mailboy, always a mailboy" phenomenon. In the organizational sense, we do this often by changing the supervisor. Such a change frees the members of the organization from the necessity of being hampered by the expectations of the old boss.

The bigger the change, the greater the risk and the greater the amount of energy which must be committed to making the change. If we must wait a long time for the positive evidence that the change is working and is beneficial, we reduce the probability we will stick it out. Or, at a minimum, we increase the need for strong resolve or strong support. It is good, therefore, to ask: How will I know I am making progress? If you preidentify signs of progress and then see these become real, you provide some interim reward. Recovery from an illness or an accident may be a good way to visualize this process. The fact that you can sit up a short time the first day, a little longer the next, each day making a little progress, can provide this reward for and recognition of improvement. Or, as another example, think about some sport such as tennis for which you have taken lessons. Getting a higher percentage of your first serves within the lines might be an example of progress. Your ultimate transformation into a competent tennis player who wins more games may be a long way off, but seeing some small improvement can be encouraging. It means you must deliberately set intermediate or small goals. This is particularly true when things have not been going well for you. Lowering the expectation, taking smaller steps, and getting the lift from achievement can turn depression into a positive feeling. The personal sense of progress can be achieved by deliberately picking a small task and completing it. In writing a paper, for example, to find a reference or to complete a page is such an incremental achievement. You must act, and recognize these achievements, and you must reward yourself.

Sometimes we are faced with the desire to make a large change in a high-risk area such as changing employers or jobs. It is normal to be frightened. A technique which sometimes works is to identify some other change such as change of hair style or buying a new dress or suit which, when accomplished, provides encouragement for the larger change. Finding acceptance and reward for a small change or a change in a low-risk area can increase our courage in taking a larger risk and making a bigger change. This is similar to the incremental steps, but here the two changes are not directly related. The safe change helps us make the hard one.

Checking up on where we are or how we are doing can increase our awareness and perhaps make us discontent with our current status. Looking in the mirror in the morning is a simple example of this process. If we don't like what we see, it can intensify our resolve to change things. Taking a self-administered test of competence is another way. The *Reader's Digest* "Test Your Word Power" tests are like this. Another example might be the attempt to solve problems at the end of a chapter in a textbook. If you answer the questions, do the self-analysis, you become more aware of your status; and such awareness can form the basis for change of behavior or activity.

PERSONAL EXPERIMENT 21

The way to make these change-management techniques come alive and be useful is to try them. Identify some change you have been considering or would like to make. Probably you should experiment with a small change. A change in dress, hair style, morning routine, reading habits, television-viewing routine, or relations with another person would be preferable to trying to experiment with job or career change. When you have chosen an experimental change, try the following steps:

1. **Decide on a reward you can give yourself for completing the change. This may be a sequence of little rewards for incremental progress.**
2. **Share your desired change with friends, associates, or family. If possible, elicit their support for the change in you.**
3. **Embark on the change after devising ways of measuring your progress.**
4. **Test your progress and reward as appropriate.**
5. **Continue to the completion point you picked.**

Did this process help in making the change? Would you use these or other techniques discussed in making another change based on this experience?

Still another aid to managing change can be identifying those things you will not change, thus ceasing to spend energy worrying about them. You are then able to concentrate your energy on those aspects of your life you are willing to change. The vague feeling that your life or job is not working for you is a typical condition which responds well to this treatment. For example, some people who feel frustrated about their careers, after some self-analysis, learn that they want and value some aspects of their current relationship to their employer. This may lead to the positive decision to stop dreaming about leaving and to start trying to make things work where they are. This action would stop the wasting of energy and time on the "what if" game, constantly looking for greener grass. Thus freed, the individual can concentrate on identifying what parts of life are amenable to change in the current job.

It is fairly common for us to waste our energies carrying around a list of hoped for changes we can't realistically make or are not really willing to commit ourselves to make. Crossing them off the list can increase our ability to make other changes. One of my experiences might reinforce the point. For years I had a weak but recurring desire to learn to play an electric organ. Because the desire had persisted for 20 years or more, I finally bought an organ. For three months I spent an hour a day at practice. I experienced some progress and some satisfaction. I recognized that, for about that expenditure of time, I could eventually arrive at the point of enjoyment. However, I assessed the investment of time as not worth the payout. This assessment was not totally at the conscious level. I gave up my desire. This lesson was financially costly. In retrospect, it would have been better to have rented an organ. But by eliminating the waste of always feeling I might find it worth the effort and never knowing, the lesson was probably well worth the expenditure. The principle of facing yourself and coming to the decision is a cleansing, healthy, necessary part of managing change in your life.

Changing your philosophy or overall perspective toward life is itself a profound change. Sometimes, however, such a profound change is a necessary precursor to making other changes. In other words, identifying the keystone change and concentrating first on that is a technique for managing change. Changing your church and the particular interpretation of religion you use as the guiding theme for your life would be another example. Giving up the "rat race" of working for an employer and living in the wilderness like Thoreau would be another example. Changing your work from intellectual to physical is still another example. Such major changes alter the threshold for other change. Finding a better understanding of self is probably the most basic and most necessary use of this technique.

Finding self and changing the threshold of consciousness of self are probably closely related. By changing consciousness, I mean increasing one's sensitivity to self. This might result from meditation, biofeedback, encounter, or simply paying attention to one's feelings. Some of these concepts will be discussed more fully in Chapter 16, Finding Oneself, and were discussed in Chapter 12,

Personal Assessment. For our purpose here, however, increasing consciousness is like finding other keystone changes. This seems to be an enabling action which affects our ability to make and manage other change—to manage the course of life.

Tying a string around your finger is an old technique for heightening your awareness and forcing recall of a decision or commitment. It is also possible to use some regular occurrence like brushing your teeth as a reminder for your commitment to change. Think, for example, of a decision to improve your posture. What might you do to increase the number of times you consciously pay attention to posture? One technique would be to decide to check up on posture each time you clean your teeth. Another might be to place a full-length mirror at some place you frequently pass in your daily life. Still another might be to tell yourself each time you get up from your office chair that you will check up on whether or not you are standing straight. Setting up reminder techniques can help in managing change by increasing the times you are conscious of your behavior.

These are but a few of the techniques for improving the management of change. Think about the techniques which have worked for you and use them consciously. Try some of these suggestions or use them to trigger your creation of new techniques for yourself.

Summary

Managing change requires a positive perspective and an attitude of desirability. The individual must see the self as in control of life and able to influence what happens. The individual must recognize that, although there are risks associated with all change, change is a necessary part of living and vitality. Even trying to tread water requires change. The power of choice over what happens is a personal change-management technique. To manage change, individuals must recognize and understand the elements of the change process. Elements of the process were set forth for that purpose.

Managing change is based on sensing, deciding, and doing. We must first become conscious of the preconditions which raise the potential for change. Next we should do some self-analysis and seek counsel or guidance. Next we ought to make the decision to change and engage in the preparation we believe will help. Part of the decision phase includes being ourselves, recognizing and sharing our feelings and establishing openness. After these two phases, we should take specific action and sensitize ourselves to the feedback which results. Taking the necessary action requires letting go as well as accepting the new. Modification of direction is based on assessment of feedback and our personal feeling that the new condition is better than the old. It is also important to recognize the danger of getting caught up in merely changing and not making forward progress.

Increasing our ability to handle change results in part from understanding the process and in part from providing ourselves with interim satisfaction from the process, as well as assuring ultimate satisfaction from the result. We can also increase our comfort with change by seeking an environment which supports rather than impedes change. Since we are part of the environments in which we live, we can in part shape them. Change begets change. So as we learn to "hang loose" we increase both our comfort and the potential for movement. Adaptability to change, being the master of change, is an important ingredient of personal vitality.

Although little emphasis or space was given to organizational change, the same principles apply. The vital organization is one which knows how to introduce and manage change. Many of the principles discussed in individual terms also apply to the organization. One of the primary techniques of managing change is periodic measuring and recording of change. This process increases consciousness of change and the resultant payoff and satisfaction.

Suggested readings

American Friends Service Committee. *Working Loose*. Philadelphia: American Friends Service Committee, 1971.

Bennis, Warren G. *Changing Organizations*. Douglas Murray McGregor Memorial Lecture, M.I.T., Feb. 1966.

Crystal, J. C., and Bolles, R. N. *Where Do I Go From Here With My Life?* New York: Seabury Press, 1974.

Olson, Kenneth. *The Art Of Hanging Loose In An Uptight World*. Greenwich, Conn.: Fawcett, 1974.

> *Dr. Olson writes about how to manage your life for greater satisfactions, acknowledging the fact that this is a time of daily shock, hourly shock. He talks first about the negative tapes we play, the results of unsatisfactory experiences that we allow to run our lives. He argues as a tough fighter for you to take responsibility, manage your life, and think positive*

thoughts. He says "the truth of the matter is you more than anyone else in your world determine the state of your emotions." One of the negative games we play he describes as the "what if" game. This is a fear- or anxiety-oriented game. Another is described as the "it ain't fair blues" and another as the "perfectionist game." Hanging loose is his way of helping you to manage your life. He helps you to develop a positive philosophy of life as a means of guiding your life. His advice is sound and helpful.

O'Neill, N., and O'Neill, G. *Shifting Gears.* New York: M. Evans, 1974.

Tofler, Alvin. *Future Shock.* New York: Random House, 1970.

14
Redesigning your job

Introduction

Having a job which provides you with the necessary psychological satisfaction is a primary way to maintain vitality. Yóur psychological income needs change corresponding with conditions, goals, and different phases of life. Sensitizing yourself to your needs is basic to your taking the responsibility for the redesign of your job.

Many feel that leaving their current job or career and seeking another one is the only way to find job satisfaction. This chapter explores the ways you can change your job and yet remain in the same one. Ways of changing some of the aspects of your job's scope, depth, newness, and work cycle are suggested. Techniques for changing job design are discussed in the light of what is known about psychological factors affecting satisfaction, along with what is known about the relationship of satisfaction to tasks and how the structure of the job can be altered.

A standard set of design criteria is not what is offered. I don't believe standard criteria exist. Rather, you are led along a path which should result in the development of your personal job-design needs. You should not expect to achieve 100 percent of what you want or need, but rather be able to alter the way the job is balanced if the current balance is not working well for you. If your current job is meeting your needs, if it is fun and rewarding and you expect it to continue to be, you do not need this chapter now.

If, after trial, redesign of the present job does not work, then some techniques for setting the criteria for and searching out a new job can be explored. The risks and the special competencies and energy necessary for this task are suggested. Seeking and finding a better job is almost always more difficult than modifying the one you have.

The general hypotheses on which this chapter is based were presented in Chapter 10, Job and Organization Design. This is a personal "how to" chapter. It is based on the assumption that no one, even one working at the most rigid and prescribed of activities, is totally without power to change those activities. It is also based on the feeling that most of us as individuals have a capacity to redesign our jobs which we have never explored.

Everyone can change some characteristics of the job

Working on a paced assembly line is considered the epitome of a controlled and limited work environment. The pace at which one works is controlled. The individual often has to get a substitute to take a break. What the individual does has been broken down into finite task elements which make his or her performance almost as predictable as that of a machine. Admittedly, what one can do to change the job in these circumstances is limited and to a great extent external to the basic work process. What the individual can do may even be negative in the eyes of those measuring productivity or those responsible for maintenance of the system. But the individual can do something.

Since the job is repetitive, simple, and routine, the first personal problem is survival. Survival techniques usually mean looking beyond the work itself for stimulation and reward. One place to look is to the group of which the individual is part. Banter, conversation which occupies the interest and provides a reason for enduring boredom, is one form of modification of the job. Since the job does not require one's full attention, it is bent to include the social stimulus. It is also possible to add a personal activity in parallel with the work which is not occupying one's attention. Daydreaming would be an example of this. It is possible also to build mental games around routine tasks or even internal musical accompaniment. Admittedly, all these modifications seem to be compensations or coping techniques, but they serve to demonstrate the inventiveness of humans faced with a necessary, boring repetitive task.

At a level of more specific change in the work activity, it is possible to invent new ways of doing the job and attempt to convince management of the need for change. Suppose someone is putting in a couple of screws to hold two odd-shaped metal pieces together and discovers that the parts can be bonded less expensively by welding or gluing. Such eliminating or substituting changes the job activity. Of course there is a risk it may eliminate the job held by the individual. Where the supervisor is open to changes in methods it may be possible to get support from the group. Then it is the group that restructures the work and the allocation of tasks.

Most of us are in positions and assignments which provide much greater freedom than is found in the assembly-line example. The proportion of nonpaced and loosely prescribed work has grown rapidly over the last years while tightly prescribed work has shrunk. Examples include the growth of service-industry activities and the proliferation of administrative and technical jobs. This change results in part from the increase in automation and process industry. Jobs in the service sector are, by their nature, more open to individual influence and redesign. For example, appliance service persons or the attendants in a dry-cleaning store can change the order and timing of their activities. The introduction of behavioral science into the work environment, and the experiments with workplace redesign, variable work periods, participative goal setting, and a myriad of innovations have all also opened the potential for personal job redesign. Both the nature of changing work opportunities and the understanding of how to organize work give us increased potential for job redesign.

An example should point up both the potential and the problems and set the stage for further discussion. Let us suppose we work as an accountant in a large financial department. This probably means that we have responsibility not for overall accounting, but rather for a particular class of transactions. Perhaps our area is travel-expense accounting. In this role we audit for accuracy and assure that the charges go to the right accounts. While this requires skill, it is a fairly routine kind of job. What can we do to redesign the job? One expansion technique would be to analyze trends and report, for example, on the averages and the escalations in meal costs. Another might be to suggest ways to improve and simplify the form. Still another would be to work on automating handling of certain aspects so that we would have free time to develop in other accounting areas. If there are several of us doing related activities we might get with the others to discuss rotation of the most boring parts or reassignment and redesign of the activities. By analyzing the cost of various auditing and processing steps, we might be able to show they are uneconomical and should be eliminated or changed to statistical sampling approaches.

These are but a few suggestions. There are some common characteristics, however. Several involve expanding our responsibility beyond processing to analysis and improvement of the function. Several involve adding activities which provide variety and add to the interest. Several involve looking at our function from the broader perspective of the business and management. Some techniques actually eliminate some of the less desirable functions.

How to know
what you need

If you are to redesign your job to increase the psychological payouts and satisfactions, you must start by understanding what you want. Much of the thinking about work in the past and many of our own attitudes about rewards of work have been limited to pay, benefits, and good working conditions. This was compatible with the view of work as a means to an end. Work was seen as providing us with the basis for a life which was totally outside of work. With this perspective, you and I were not encouraged to think about work as providing satisfactions of a complex psychological nature.

Yet work did provide some of our satisfactions, even when we were thinking of it only in terms of pay. A couple of examples will make the point. How often have you introduced yourself by describing your work or your position title? Doing this is unconsciously recognizing that work is a way to tell others of your personal worth or value. If I can say I'm a teacher, this helps to establish my value in society. How often have you come home after work and described some accomplishment at work? In doing so you are acknowledging that part of your sense of contribution and impact comes from the work process. If I can go home at night and say I completed a report or had a successful test of my design or even got out thirty letters today—that is demonstrating satisfaction with accomplishment. If you or I have a job which results in physical, measurable, visible, countable, or weighable results, we gain this sense of satisfaction relatively easily. If, however, we deal with knowledge work, concepts, planning, and long-range activities, we probably find it harder.

Those who have studied work and what human needs work should satisfy have come up with lists representing psychological incomes. These lists contain factors like challenge, a chance to learn, a sense of impact, freedom to make decisions, meaningfulness, compatible associates, a future, and a sense of personal worth. Lists can be very detailed and reflect the growing understanding that work is a very important part of life. For most people work can provide a sense of purpose, a way of growing, and a way to gain a sense of self. For some it does not provide these important payouts because its design does not reflect these needs. Identifying psychological incomes is, therefore, an important first step in improving work. Knowing your priorities or needs requires knowing what to look for and continuing self-analysis. The process is continual because our needs change with changing personal goals, circumstances, and phases of life.

Knowing what you need, therefore, is first asking yourself, based upon your experience, what provides satisfaction and what does not. Next, it is asking yourself if you can have but one of two things you need, which is more important to you? Forced value choice is a way of finding out what is really important. The analytical devices of the *Personal Vitality Workbook* and the personal experiments of this volume are designed to help you do this. It is probable that paper-and-pencil answers to questions will not do all that is necessary for you to understand your needs. In this case, it may be necessary to find a friend or counselor who will probe and reflect your answers to help you find the real meaning. Another approach is to enroll in a workshop or class in which you are part of a group involved in asking these kinds of questions to find what each member needs. Chapter 12, Personal Assessment, also provides suggestions for this process.

Aspects of a job which can be changed

Assume that you have discovered there are some aspects of your job which are not positive and that you want to change. How can you tell if it is possible to change them? Or suppose, on the other hand, you have identified some positive aspects. How can you determine how they can be expanded? Are there some aspects of work that are modifiable and some that are not? Are some aspects of work more amenable to redesign and, therefore, more likely to be improved than other aspects?

The following list presents some aspects of a job which are amenable to change. This list is drawn from several sources and is by no means exhaustive. Rather, it is intended to be suggestive and to provide you with some clues as to the aspects of your job which you should identify as items that might be changed.

Job elements — candidates for redesign

- Scope—The breadth and depth of the activity.
- Cycle length—The time from beginning to closure of a definable part of the job.
- Feedback—Both the nature and timing of indications of results.
- Communication requirements—The amount, character, and sources of input and output data.
- Activity proportions—The percent of time spent on different types of activity.
- Interfaces—Where the job begins and where it ends, including control of quality and what is transferred at input and output.
- Technology support—How much and what aspects of the job are done by machines or supported by the technology or the process.

Definition of the scope of a job establishes its boundaries. The individual who sees a job as broad in scope and whose view is supported by the organization has more opportunity to vary tasks and activities. This chance to vary activity provides opportunity for matching work to personal capabilities and needs. It provides the opportunity to add the variety necessary to sustain interest. If, on the other hand, the scope of the job is narrow, then the individual may feel confined, or limited, and this can lead to demotivation and loss of vitality. How much breadth is right or necessary in a given job is a question of balance. Too much breadth could lead to frustration since it usually means a lack of clarity as to what is wanted, where to start, or who is responsible. Yet, not enough breadth can negatively affect self-image and self-importance, and can contribute to a feeling of inadequate challenge and opportunity to make decisions.

Scope involves not only breadth of activity but depth as well. For example, the amount of learning which results from work is affected by the specification of depth. An engineer who is told to develop a device and works only with the available hardware to create a working model is dealing with one level of depth. Another engineer given the same problem might study the technology, the materials, and the alternative embodiments or techniques, and thus deal with the problem in greater depth.

Often decisions about scope are really in our own hands but we do not perceive that we can vary the job scope. We become so influenced by schedules, budget limits, and organizational pressures that we do not push back. Often, too, we feel that the rewards for expansion of scope are not commensurate with the increased energy we must expend. The balancing of scope with our changing needs requires us to discover how scope is affecting our learning, growth, and satisfaction. Changing the job's scope may require negotiating with others to change the job's boundaries or our negotiating with management on a clearer definition of our job.

Short cycles are usually associated with simple tasks and tasks with physical output. Long task cycles are usually associated with complex and conceptual accomplishments. Short cycles tend to make it easier for us to see what happens as a result of what we did. Feedback is quick and our ability to correct, as a result of failure or the receipt of inadequate reward or satisfaction, is relatively easy. Long cycles increase the difficulty of associating what we did with what happened. Long cycles also mean we must sustain our moti-

vation without reinforcement for extended periods. Long cycles require a higher level of self-confidence and ability to direct one's own
activities. The work of professionals, knowledge workers, and
managers tends toward long cycles.

The individual's tolerance for cycle length—delay in reward or
feedback—is highly dependent on his or her feeling of security and
self-sufficiency. It is often possible, even with long-cycle activity, to
create intermediate measurements or feedback. Suppose, for
example, you are engaged in the design of a complex product
which will require several years to complete. Only at the end of a
several-year cycle will you know whether it works, whether it can
be produced at a satisfactory cost, and whether it will be bought by
customers. What can you do to shorten this cycle, or provide intermediate feedback, if you decide that this is our need? One way,
which is quite common in engineering or programming endeavors,
is to break the job into phases. Phase one might be a paper-and-
pencil test of the concept. If you pass this first test, then you gain
some confidence to push on. Another technique might be a simulation, and still another technique might be a bench test of a part of a
subassembly or a part of the device. An industrial-design concept
model, for example, can provide a way of evaluating the finished
product, or even getting potential-customer reactions, without
actually having the innards of the device.

Changing the scope can also change cycle length for a given
individual. The point is that cycle length is amenable to change and
in a long-cycle job you can break it into phases and improve your
psychological income. When you find yourself in a long-cycle job, it
is often possible too to add supplementary or parallel short-cycle
tasks for variety. A simple example of a supplementary task for a
writer would be to grab a bunch of pencils and sharpen them. Feedback from accomplishment is immediate and visible. Even this
change of pace and activity may provide stimulus for fresh insight
on the major activity—writing.

The timing and nature of feedback can have a direct effect on
your motivation to work, your sense of accomplishment, and your
satisfaction. Imagine yourself in a driving simulator with a failure of
all the feedback devices. Imagine a condition when you turn the
wheel or step on the gas and have no way of knowing what happened. Frustration is immediate and loss of incentive to continue
follows quickly. Feedback is vital and necessary. Generally the
more immediate and specific the feedback, the better job it does in

reinforcing behavior. However, the more-immediate feedback is usually simple and of less consequence than the longer-term feedback. For example, putting your coins in a vending machine supplies you with immediate feedback—the delivery of the item selected. Longer-term feedback comes from the satisfaction of using the item. In most cases the longer-term feedback is of greater value. Varying the nature and timing of feedback may be an aspect of your work you need to change. One of the best ways to find out is to try.

Some of us enjoy the process of communicating with others and gain a sense of satisfaction from it. Jobs require different amounts of interaction and interchange with others. We can change these interactive requirements. As I sit writing this chapter, I have deliberately limited my opportunities to communicate with others, limited the chance for interruptions such as phone calls and

---

PERSONAL EXPERIMENT 22

Identify some specific task inherent in your work or some project you are doing. Before engaging in the task try to identify all the various types of feedback you may get from doing it. For example, if it is a manual task, identify the muscular sensations, the visual indications, the results, and the indications of accomplishment (like comments from others). Try to identify as many types of feedback as you can. Now do the task, and each time a feedback you have identified should occur try to be extra sensitive to it. In each case try to sense its impact on you. Does it encourage you to do more? Does it give you a warm feeling of accomplishment? Does it provide discouragement? Does it push you to try another way? When you have finished ask yourself if changes in the feedback, having it come quicker or changing its nature, would have affected your performance. What could you have done to design different feedback, more frequent feedback, or more rewarding evidences of your accomplishment?

meetings. This is done to provide concentration on the objective. Yet when the flow of thought dries up, I deliberately seek interaction. Sometimes even physical activities afford a change of pace. This kind of communication or change is not dependent on the scope of the project. Scope changes, however, can also vary communication needs. For example, if I choose to write on a subject which I must research or where knowledge of the area is not yet documented but in the minds of others, I have defined a task which requires talking and listening.

The amount of physical and mental effort the task requires can be changed. Take the task of washing dishes. Do this task first without and then with the aid of the dishwasher. With the dishwasher you have changed both physical and mental effort and substituted button pushing for these activities. This example shows variation in activity type and variation in skill requirements resulting from the amount of technology or mechanical support.

No matter what we do, we are part of a system which provides us with inputs at a transfer point which has been established by defining the scope of the job. At the end of our activity is another transfer point where we hand over something to the next person in the process or send it off to the customer. What gets transferred at these interfaces and where they are set are aspects of the job which can be changed. Suppose, for example, you are going to bake a cake. As input you can choose to utilize and accept all the various ingredients and a recipe from a book or you can choose to accept a cake mix in a box, or you can choose a prepared cake which has been frozen and merely requires baking. Sometimes an organization makes these choices and defines the process for us. Even when the decision appears to have been made by someone else, however, it may be possible for you to change or influence it.

How to gain support
for your changes

Your relationships with others at work and with the system provide both limits and potential for job redesign. If you are in a position in which your work has been defined by someone else and specified in detail, then change requires communicating with that person or persons and gaining their commitment to change. For this to happen, they must see a gain for the organization and, of course, for themselves. Even if you are in a position of great freedom to define your own work, your acceptance in the organization and your continued employment depend on the management and others perceiving some value in what you do. Consequently, change which alters outputs must be shown to have value to others. In other words, doing your own thing, increasing your satisfaction, will only work in the context of the group and the organization, and the organization must continue to place equal or increased value on what you do. It must also recognize your contribution as positive with respect to the organization's goals.

Making changes in your job, therefore, requires not only identifying your needs and what to change but also selling the changes to your management and to others in the organization. This requires understanding how your changes will affect both the process and other people and, additionally, how the changes will be valued in the culture of the organization. You should be able to show them how they, the organization, and others will gain. In other words, it is not acceptable to the organization for improvements in your effectiveness and satisfaction to come at the expense of the organization's own overall effectiveness. Putting yourself in the shoes of others and understanding how they will view the benefits is essential if you are to gain support. How this is done is highly dependent on the culture of the organization. It is easier to do this in an open, adult organization where participation in planning and goal setting is encouraged. It is difficult or almost impossible to do it in an autocratic and regimented type organization. It is also easier to do if you have had previous experience with managers which have established their confidence in your capability and commitment. It is easier to do this if you can demonstrate concrete payoff for management and if you can gain its interest in trying out an experiment. In attempting to convince management, it is desirable to set up a series of descending goals such as:

1. Total agreement and decision to take action.
2. Agreement, but more facts or sampling needed before total commitment.
3. Agreement to take initial step.
4. Request for changes in scope, cost, size, etc.
5. Questions to be answered before decision is made—come back with answers.
6. Will consider further.

You should clearly understand what level of approval you have received. Operating with a level-one approval is quite different from operating at level three. It is easier to do any of these things if your immediate management feels relatively secure and free to make changes without detailed review by higher-level management. Therefore, your knowledge of the culture, the environment, and the range of acceptable deviations is a necessary part of gaining support and implementing redesign of your job.

You must gain support for changes in tasks and jobs not only from management but also from your peer group. If you work in a group where the general attitude about work is that it is a necessary evil, others will view you as both strange and perhaps not playing fair if you try to reorganize work to make it more interesting. If, on the other hand, you work in a group which shares your values and where each member wants to improve his or her work, you have potential for support or conflict. If the other members can see themselves gaining too they can help you make the changes. If the other members view it as a competitive gesture and suspect you may be trying to get the better work, it may be all-out interpersonal war. In these situations it would be possible to have management support for the change you want to implement, yet be defeated by a flank attack from your peers. Cultural knowledge both of the organization and the group and a kind of business "maze brightness" is therefore a requirement in gaining support for your changes.

How to implement redesign

Assuming you see the need to change elements of your job, you know what you want to change, and you have the support of others, how do you start? It is probably best to start with that element which is easiest to change and which you assess as having the most immediate identifiable impact. For example, a redefinition of job scope which immediately allows you to do something different, engage in some new activity tomorrow, would be a good place to start. This would assure some positive feedback and probably encourage further change. By contrast, a change in scope which means you may do something different a year from now would be less desirable as a first change. Pick a change that will give you rapid feedback and hopefully positive reinforcement for the process of change. This probably means starting with a small change.

Depending on the nature of the support by the organization, it is probably also desirable to pick a change which will show prompt and measurable payback for your manager and the organization. If your manager sees an improvement, there is a high probability of continued backing as you make more changes. If, on the other hand, your manager feels that the new freedoms or changes you have made are becoming evident to others and open to potential question, then this will usually be perceived as increased risk for the manager.

Methods for redesigning your job

When you have identified the nonrewarding or debilitating aspects of your job, when you have analyzed and identified your needs, and when you have support from management and peers, then you may consider methodology. If, for example, you have found that your job does not provide you with a sense of completion (closure or ending of an activity), how do you tackle changing this? First you might look at the question—does it ever end? That is, does the cycle reach completion in the next phase or with some other person? If it does, is there a way of trading functions so you each gain control over a complete cycle which allows measurement and sensing of completion? Or perhaps should you unilaterally give up the beginning of the cycle which you now have? These questions typify the methdology. Alone or with aid from others, you must analyze the aspects which fail to provide psychological income. This approach starts with a lack or a problem in the current job.

Another methodology is to start with a search for an activity, task, or project which if added to what you now do would provide variety and improved satisfaction. If your manager has this activity within his or her control, ask to be allowed to do it on a trial basis. If the activity is not currently being performed, ask to be allowed to try it, or propose how it might be done and identify its advantages to the group or organization. This approach, then, consists of searching for additions to your job.

A third approach is to search out and secure the opportunity for rotation of activities within the group. Are there some things each of you do which when given to someone else provide opportunity for variety and learning? This methodology is based simply on rotation or periodic change of activities to provide variety and learning.

Also consider the opposite of the first example, where you were concerned with closure, or what activities came after you. Look upstream at activities which come before you. Expansion or shifting responsibility on either end of your job provides change.

Still another methodology is to start from the perspective of asking what can be eliminated. Most of us do things which are not necessary. If we can identify these tasks and gain agreement to stop we then provide time and opening to be asked to take on something new. Business experience suggests that a job which includes preparation of reports for others is particularly amenable to this approach. Frequently we continue reports long after the need has disappeared.

With these examples of methodologies as a base, the following list which includes the examples should provide suggestions for approaches to job redesign:

- Upstream and downstream shifting of duties to provide a greater sense of wholeness of activities and closure or completion.
- Temporary shifting of duties within a group to provide variety and new learning.
- Analysis of functions to identify those which are not rewarding and consideration of elimination or transfer of those functions.
- Increase in job loading by addition of new tasks or functions without elimination of old ones.
- Identification of and trial of new activities not currently being performed.
- Elimination of function or functions as unnecessary.
- Search for equipment or facilities which would when added change the nature of the work by taking over boring or repetitive activities or enhance human capability.
- Analysis of the proportions of different activities and gaining agreement for change in proportions.
- Negotiations with management to change the goals of the group or organization in a way which will positively influence jobs.
- Negotiations with management to change the reward and punishment structure so that it more nearly matches the realities of the work and the needs of the group.

When to search
for another job

If you have tried to redesign your current job or assignment and it has proved to be unchangeable, then you can consider search for another job first within the organization where you are. The reasons the change failed are important in thinking about a new job. Did you fail because of lack of support, systemic requirements which could not be altered, or inability to indentify and change important elements? In other words, was it the environment or your own capability which blocked change? Job change outside your organization is a third choice because it involves a risk of loss of position and effectiveness and anxiety problems are greater in a new position. Also, the process of job design and matching needs to your capabilities is more difficult in an organization which is new to you and where you are not known. Nevertheless, there is a time for seeking a new job (several times in a life probably), when this kind of shock is the only way to stop your decline in interest, motivation, vitality, and growth. Forcing oneself to adapt to totally new conditions is probably the greatest stimulant for growth that is possible. Some reasons for seeking a new job may have nothing to do with your relation to the current job but rather to your prediction that the need for the job is running out. It is far better for your health and vitality to have a job in which the need for the activity is growing rather than declining. The declining situation tends to create a negative outlook which easily seeps into your outlook in all aspects of life. Having to endure just existing for an extended period in a negative environment reduces your resiliency and ability to make the necessary eventual change.

The time to search for another job is when you are still winning on the one you have. I know this is a great philosophy but that most people will not have the guts or the sensitivity to impending change to quit while winning. Most will quit only after they have been losing, and thus try to build a positive change on a negative basis. There are classic examples of this. Henry Ford, whose creative genius had built cars that sold and developed one of the three major automobile companies, failed to step down at the right time and almost killed the Ford Motor Company. Sewell Avery hung on too long at Montgomery Ward and Nicholas Murray Butler too long at Columbia University. Nevertheless, people who have gained in

moving from one organization to another have generally moved
before their decline or losses were evident.

PERSONAL EXPERIMENT 23

This exercise is designed to help you make a quick
determination of whether it may be time for a job
change. There is no special magic in the exercise —
whether it helps is dependent on your personal sensitivity and the right listing of pros and cons. For your
present job list all of the positive rewarding aspects
you can. These may include current rewards and
satisfactions as well as future expectations. A current
reward could be something like: I feel I'm useful. A
future reward might be: If I stick it out for x years
there is a good retirement income. Next list the cons,
or negatives, both current and expected. After listing
the negatives, draw a line through any you believe job
redesign could eliminate or improve. Usually the positive list outweighs the negatives. Try next to list pros
and cons for another job you might consider. This is
more difficult because you are relying on partial
information. Also we are often prone to the "grass is
always greener on the other side of the fence"
phenomenon. Compare the lists for your current job
and the possible other job. Any of the following conditions might cause you to look further at possible job
change.

- Excessive negatives on the current job.
- A failure to identify many positives on the current
  job.
- Inability to perceive job redesign as a solution to
  negatives on the current job.
- A positive list for the other job which is more than
  two times the length of the positive list on the
  current job. (You should probably set a high
  hurdle like this 2 × requirement in order to bias
  the analysis in favor of staying on the current job.)

Timing your change is a major challenge in maintaining vitality and growth. It requires schooling ourselves to change before decline becomes pervasive. This may mean choosing to change when we sense small defeats and impending increase in dissatis-factions. Change before major defeats runs counter to the normal human tendencies. When things are going well we want to hold on, to savour our success. We can see the failure to select the right timing better in others than in ourselves. The evil of hanging on to a success too long is that we destroy both our capability to change and the chance to extend vitality. Choosing the time to change thus is learning to sense the fact that improvement in current growth and current success is slowing down in its rate of change. It is learning to take a small defeat and go on to a win and time your leaving with the win. This is much like advice my grandfather, an orchardist, real-estate entrepreneur and developer, used to give. He said, "Take your first loss and get out. The first loss is usually the smallest loss."

Another aspect of sensing when to change jobs has to do with becoming sensitive to shifts in your acceptance or impact. When it becomes evident that your efficiency or effectiveness is declining, when it takes more of your energy to make a given impact—that is a signal for change. This is not easy to do for it is easy to rationalize such shifts or change. One rationalization heard often in business is that the world is becoming more complex and interdependent. While true, this may, in a given case, cloud the reason for your decline in impact. Another rationalization is that the failure was due to poor communication. Communication inadequacy is most often identified as the source for performance failure. This makes it someone else's responsibility. Sometimes, too, the source of reduced effectiveness may be your lack of technological data or just being in the wrong political camp. Sensing these often subtle changes in your effectiveness means cutting through these reasons and being able to relate your energy input to the impact you are able to make and the psychological income you can collect.

How to go about searching for a new job is a subject for a whole book. There are good books on this subject and some are listed at the end of this chapter. Many of them take the position that there are jobs to be found by the people who will work at selling themselves and work hard at the search. To be consistent with my perspective, I would rather adopt the attitude that there are needs to be identified which can be made into jobs and careers. Creativity in matching oneself to needs is at least equally important as the search techniques stressed most in job-search literature.

Summary

You, with support from management and associates, can redesign your job to improve your success and satisfaction. Matching your personal needs and capabilities with the needs of the organization and its capacity for support improves personal growth, work motivation, and productivity. Improving the match requires improved definition of both organizational and individual goals and organizational and individual understanding of your strengths and weaknesses. Successful redesign of your job must increase the good components of work and reduce the poor ones as perceived by you. Redesign of your job should enhance your psychological income.

Self-assessment is the route to the increased self-under-standing required for job redesign. Such assessment requires knowing what satisfies and what you do best from experience and experimenting with change. Once you know your strengths and weaknesses, then it is necessary to identify elements of your work to be changed and to try to change them. Making changes requires support from management and peers as well as a change in personal management techniques. Redesign is a continuing process of experiment, feedback, and modification. It is continual both because your goals and needs change and because jobs and the work environment are not static.

If attempts to redesign your job do not succeed, or if you sense that your job, even with changes, does not provide growth, then you should consider changing jobs. First consider changes within the organization where you work because your knowledge of the system is most applicable. In such a search, the design of the new job should be undertaken before you are stuck in the old and before decline and failure are prevalent. As a last resort, you may consider change of jobs outside the organization. Such changes are most difficult because you do not know the organization's goals and culture and because you are not known for your capabilities. They are also difficult because the best opportunities are not defined, not advertised in job-opening columns, but have to be designed and created.

Suggested readings

Bolles, Richard N. *What Color Is Your Parachute?* Berkeley: Ten Speed Press, 1972.

Campbell, David P. *If You Don't Know Where You Are Going, You'll Probably End Up Somewhere Else.* Niles: ARGUS, 1974.

Conarroe, Richard R. *Bravely, Bravely in Business: 32 ground rules for personal survival and success in your job—any job.* New York: AMACOM, 1972.

> *This is a good book because it treats a serious subject with a sense of humor. Conarroe says in his introduction that he feels qualified to write because his work is stimulating, he has redesigned his job, he has made money, he works hard, and his job gives him freedom to do other things he likes to do. We can all learn from someone who has been successful at turning work into rewarding fun. His 32 rules range from picking a sponsor and sticking to him to searching for seeds of victory in disaster and disaster in victory. It is an easily read book which should supplement this chapter and push you forward in your analysis of what sucess at work is for you.*

Greco, Bennedetto. *How To Get The Job That's Right For You.* Homewood, Ill.: Dow Jones-Irwin, 1975.

Haldane, B. *Career Satisfaction and Success. A Guide to Job Freedom.* New York: AMACOM, 1974.

Pearse, R. F., and Pelzer, B. P. *Self-Directed Change for The Mid-Career Manager.* New York: AMACOM, 1975.

Uris, Auren. *Thank God It's Monday.* New York: Thomas Y. Crowell, 1974.

15
Physical
and mental
health

Introduction

We are becoming more aware of the possibility of improving our personal management of our health. We are learning of its relationship to success and happiness. With the advent of periodic and thorough health screenings and the collection and storage of longitudinal information about many people, we are becoming better able to predict outcomes when we identify deviations from norms. We are beginning to release ourselves from absolute reliance on a single form of medicine. That is, we are integrating Chinese, Indian, and other forms of health care with our own. This, combined with growing psychiatric understanding, leads to preventative programs for the individual which are both more definable and more viable. Personal health-maintenance programs are easier to pursue than ever before and our interest in them is very high.

In this chapter I intend to present ideas about building a balanced, healthy life. These ideas should help you determine what it is necessary for you to do about your health and how it relates to vitality. No program should or can offer protection against all risks. I am not a doctor and I am not prescribing. This is not a medical text but rather an introduction to a broad range of alternatives. The suggestion is strongly made that a primary reason why whatever form of curative process works for you does work is your belief in that form. In addition to belief, goals and a life purpose are presented as a major input to the maintenance of a healthy, vital, vigorous life.

Health of the mind is at least as important as physical health, and body-mind integration is also presented as an important goal. Stress relief is also a significant need in the maintenance of personal health. Included too are brief excursions into the use and purpose of dreams, the role of meditation, the need for some private time, and the relationship of sharing feelings and experience with others to personal health. You, the reader, have the responsibility of designing your own program. I hope you will be both better able to do so and convinced of the need for such a program after reading this chapter.

Good health —
what is it?

Vitality is the underlying theme of this book. Being vital and alive is being healthy. Good health is indicated by our ability to turn on extra power and exert energy when it is needed. Health contributes to ability to achieve goals. Good health does not necessarily mean the total absence of illness or physical defect. Rather it means being in condition so that we recover rapidly and easily. Illness and defects need not overly sap our strength or keep us from living a generally successful and satisfying life. Good health means making the most of what we have. Good health is the feeling of having one's physical and mental health under control. Health shows in the physical radiance and psychological wholeness of the individual.

When we don't feel well it may be because we are dominated by our negative feelings, and thus we truly feel badly. On the other hand, we may merely claim we feel badly as a risk-avoidance technique. We may also say we don't feel well because we have no evidence of feeling good. When we say we feel well we may merely be avoiding a frank sharing of how we really do feel. Is it possible we can't trust what we say?

When we say we feel good, we may, however, be in touch with our feelings and really feel good, warm, comfortable, and satisfied. The point is that what we say because of the social conventions of our society may or may not reveal our true physical-mental state. We may be so out of touch with our body and our self that we are unable to reveal how we feel even to ourselves. Understanding the nature of good mental and physical health, and managing it, therefore, presupposes that we can find a way to get in touch with our real selves.

Good health may possibly be more of an attitude than a physical state. Two people exhibiting the same measurable evidence of disease (two equally red sore throats) may express different levels of discomfort, and may or may not be letting the sore throat interfere with normal activity. In other words, sickness or health may not reflect our absolute physiological state, but rather our personal interpretation of it. This interpretation takes into account past experience, what is going on at that time with us, and whether we really are looking for an interruption in our normal lives.

As readers who are willing to be frank, you can probably relate to this excuse aspect of ill health. Can you remember claiming a cold to mask an embarrassment at school over an assignment undone or a test you wished not to take? Can you remember waking up with a sore throat on a day when the work situation was threatening or at least boring? Using illness to avoid something we don't want to face, or as an acceptable excuse for a change, is an almost universal life-management technique. For the moment, I suggest you and I withhold our judgment as to whether it is right or wrong.

Ability to recover seems to vary with the individual's willingness to take responsibility for getting well and wanting to live. Dr. Carl Simonton, a radiologist treating cancer, discovered that patient recovery was varying according to something other than the treatment he used. He developed a technique for eliciting the patient's participation in the cure using mental imagery.* One might, therefore, suggest that good health implies an ability to recover, and that recovery probably results both from the patient's participation and the medication or treatment.

It is possible to examine the measurement or identification of good health from still another perspective. Industrial managers measure employee absenteeism. From statistics, they can develop norms. One who is absent more than the norm for the group is not as healthy as one who is absent less than the norm. In health screenings it is possible to develop norms for measures such as triglycerides, cholesterol, pulse rate, weight, blood pressure, blood sugar, etc. One who exceeds the norms for his or her age group on several factors can be said to be less healthy than one who measures within the norms. However, persons who recognize their deviance from the norm and take responsibility for it by modifying their lives sufficiently to correct the measure may be more nearly achieving good health than those who have not yet had to take active control. From this we are left with at least a question as to whether deviation from some statistical norm indicates poor health.

Good health, therefore, is an achievable balance which, for the individual, assumes ability to turn on energy when needed, minimizes illnesses and deteriorations, and assures that body and mind are in support of, and part of, an active, vital, satisfying life. Good health does not mean we must all jog, eat health foods, or meditate. These may or may not be activities which contribute positively to our health balance. Good health is not conforming to someone else's model. Good health is active management of a dynamic balance which fits our personal structure, goals, and life phase.

---

*   Dr. Simonton's work is described in Irving Oyle, *The Healing Mind* (New York: Pocket Books, 1975) on page 119.

Getting in touch

If good health is, as I have suggested, a difficult to define but reasonable personal balance and not something that can be described by specific criteria, then we must look inside ourselves for the recipe. Getting in touch is knowing the state of our body and of our mind. Getting in touch implies awareness, consciousness, and trying to do something with this information to make modifications.

One way of getting in touch is through arranging for some feedback. This may be as simple an act as looking in the mirror, taking your temperature, or having a professional listener or counselor feed back what you seem to be expressing. When you go to the dentist with a vague ache in the jaw and ask him to poke, he will ask you where it hurts most. You are getting in touch with the specific source of pain by using another person to assist in creating targeted feedback. Concentrating on the feeling created when someone massages your body is an example of using another person to heighten your attention. Biofeedback, which provides a mirror for specific bodily functions of a kind which you are not normally conscious of, is a high-technology way of getting in touch. With feedback we can monitor the effects of our actions to control, improve, or make corrections.

It is possible to heighten your awareness by blocking a normally overriding form of input. For example, you can get in touch with your sense of touch better with your eyes closed than open. Sight most normally overrides the sense of touch. It is also possible to concentrate your attention by building better contact between mind and body. For example, Moshe Feldenkrais in *Awareness Through Movement** teaches his students to think about the muscle which is creating the movement. This is his way of helping you to get in touch with your body in action. Just closing your eyes and asking yourself to locate a spot in your left foot can help you become aware of what is happening in your left foot. You may look at a pain locale or source of discomfort in the same way. Teaching yourself to focus your attention is part of getting in touch.

The Sufi teaching story expresses the concept of getting in touch not so much in the physical sense as in the sense of thinking and feeling. The typical Sufi parable catches the listener in assump-

---

* Moshe Feldenkrais, *Awareness Through Movement* (New York: Harper & Row, 1972).

tions or logic sequences which limit one's ability to get in touch with what is happening. The stories help the listener to understand what is happening. Unblocking is, therefore, an aspect of getting in touch. Getting in touch can, also, mean determining what it is you know or believe. This is normally accomplished by asking yourself to state it or to share your feelings or beliefs with someone else through writing or speaking. Trying to teach someone else is also a variation of getting in touch. In these cases, it is more an intellectual than a feeling sense.

Beliefs and experience can have a great effect on whether or not we become ill or recover from an illness. This is both because of the effect our minds have on our bodies and the effect our experiences can have on our expectations and thus the course of life. Examples include the belief that older people slow down, are not as quick, may not learn as well, or may be less satisfactory employees. One suspects that many of these types of beliefs are self-fulfilling prophecies. There are well-known quotations which set forth this precept, such as: "As he thinkest in his heart, so is he," from Proverbs 23:7. Getting in touch with what we think is, therefore, important in improving our health.

Emile Coue, who had hundreds repeating one hundred times a day, "Every day in every way I am growing better and better," was building positively on the relationship between belief and reality.

One starts on the route to good health, therefore, by getting in touch with feelings, by creating healthy feelings and thinking healthy thoughts. This is a cornerstone of Christian Science, founded by Mary Baker Eddy.

Causes of stress

The causes of stress in life are legion. In fact, the presence of stress-causing situations is part of keeping us alive, sharp, growing, and learning. Stress management, which will be discussed a bit later, is not total avoidance of stress but achieving the right balance of stress. Achieving vitality probably requires learning to live at a higher level of stress than just managing to stay alive. Let us discuss the causes of stress as a basis for understanding how to manage them.

A broad category of conditions creating stress is included in our relationship to our work. For example, stress is created in work

PERSONAL EXPERIMENT 24

A quick health inventory is the intent of this set of questions. It is a test-your-health checklist. Choose the most appropriate suggested answer or create your own answer.

1. When you choose a goal which requires a burst of energy—the ability to push hard—can you do it? (Yes, surely) (Yes, sometimes) (Haven't tested it) (Probably not) (No, definitely)

2. Do you have a positive outlook and expectations with respect to your health? (Yes) (Most of the time) (Except when really sick) (No)

3. Have you set useful goals for your life, including physical and mental capability goals? (No, none) (A few) (Yes, some) (Don't see the need or applicability)

4. Do you have a program of physical exercise which is appropriate for your life needs, phase of life, and personal goals? (Yes, and I pursue it regularly) (Yes, and I do it most of the time) (Yes, but I forget most of the time) (No)

5. Do you have a program of mental exercise appropriate for your needs? (No) (Some activities most often missed) (Some activities occasionally pursued) (Activities regularly pursued)

6. Have you found a personal eating pattern or program which seems to keep you feeling fit? (Yes) (I'm still searching) (I'm not searching) (No)

7. How do you handle stress which is negative in your life? (I handle it well with techniques appropriate for me) (Most of the time I can handle it) (I don't know) (No, generally I don't do too well)

8. Have you learned to take responsibility and participate in your cure when you have an illness? (No) (I don't think so; that is, not consciously) (Yes, sometimes) (Yes, generally)

These questions may help you arrive at a conclusion about how you are doing at your own health maintenance. They may suggest other questions appropriate to ask in your case. If so, ask them of yourself.

when the organization, through its demands, puts pressure on us to perform. So long as we are in a position to turn this pressure into action which leads to performance, this stress is most normally not bad. If, however, we are in a stress-causing situation and there is nothing we can do to relieve it, this will lead to anxiety and a generally negative situation. Conflict in the work situation also causes stress. Whether it is a difference with our supervisor over how to do something or a difference between what is expected and the reality as we see it matters not. The stress is there. Again, if we can find a way to turn it into action or relieve the pressure it need not be a bad situation.

Lack of personal recognition can cause stress at work or in life in general. Lack of a sense of impact or a feeling of accomplishment or completion can also cause stress. Just as pressure at work can cause stress, so, too, can the lack of pressure cause stress. One of the most stressful work conditions is the lack of something to do. Causes of stress at work, therefore, fall into the following categories:

- Unresolvable differences between pressures applied and our ability to use or relieve them.
- Unchanging differences between expectations and what happens.
- Poor match between capabilities and requirements.
- Too much or too little to do for extended periods of time.
- Failure to achieve feedback and payout.

In the home and family situation stress is caused by similar conditions when what we feel should happen and what actually does happen are different. Family stress is most often caused by failure at interpersonal relations as opposed to the activity-related failures discussed under work. This does not mean a total absence of the other types of stress, but rather a predominance of the kind caused by crossed relationships between people.

Transactional analysis, with its Parent, Adult, and Child classifications of communication between people, provides a basis for understanding these causes. When transactions are crossed—when one behaves as a Parent and is received as a Child—stress is usually the result. Another type of family-induced stress has to do with physical proximity in restricted space and with resulting potential conflict of desires and needs. Still another aspect of family stress has to do with the sense of responsibility inherent in the parental role and the resistance to authority inherent in the role of the maturing child. There is no scarcity of potential for stress in this aspect of life.

Without going further, it is evident that we can find causes of stress wherever we look. Stress, which is a problem, needs our management attention. It can negatively affect our health, and negative results seem to occur when we are unable to do something to eliminate the causes of stress.

Stress management

We normally think of stress as bad. One reads articles which talk of executive stress as a special kind of malaise. Actually, stress is normal and an important part of life. It can result from good conditions as well as bad conditions. It is bad for us, causing physiological deterioration or change, only when sustained and not relieved. Stress is a part of each learning experience. Zero stress is no stimulation and eventually death. Learning to manage stress, to keep it in the right range and thus avoid wasteful use of energy and physiological deterioration, is a part of maintaining good health.

Stress, in its basic form, is evidenced by secretion of adrenalin and preparing the body to respond to danger. Without it humans would have succumbed to the stronger and more vicious animals. Without it athletes would not perform ever-increasing feats of prowess. This kind of biological reaction is necessary and useful. It becomes a problem only when we do not use the shot of adrenalin to run faster or when there is no way to translate anxiety into physical action. In our modern life we often have no place to use the shot of energy because the time or circumstance is inappropriate, and so we bottle it up. Bottling it up leads to health problems.

A couple of examples may help. Think of the youngster on a birthday surrounded by gifts and friends. There is stress, excitement, and anticipation in this event. Probably the heart is beating faster, speech is faster, and things would not be described as calm. The time comes to open the packages and energy is expended furiously tearing off wrappings, trying each toy, running and exclaiming. This was a positive situation and a reasonable release of stress. If that child were to demonstrate, in our judgment, overexcitement with tears, fighting, or a temper tantrum, we would feel that the child was not handling stress well.

One time in my early working career I worked for an industrial designer. I was at a drawing table all day long with the assignment to *create*. There was a high order of work-induced stress. My own desire to be productive added to it. I became tense and irritable, yet I was enjoying the experience. One technique I used to relieve some of the stress was to pace the floor. Physical activity is stress reducing.

Managing stress first requires becoming sensitive to the evidences of it in your actions and/or your body. Feeling the tightening and tensing of muscles in your neck or lower back is an example. Another is increased sensitivity to changes in pitch, rate, or form of speech. Change in speech is usually most evident when we become involved in an argument, one about which we feel deeply. Stress may also show up as a change in our threshold for emotional response. Stress can show up in inability to concentrate or seeming inability to relax, just the thing we need most to do. In fact, usually at that time, the harder we work at relaxing, the more tense we become.

After becoming sensitive to the evidence of stress, we must develop stress-relief techniques. One stress-relief technique relates to the body's biological changes and it suggests using up energy. Thus a game of tennis, or some other form of hard physical exertion, is necessary for relief of stress. Quite the opposite technique is to plan some quiet time, or to develop a set of simple relaxing exercises, or to practice meditation. Another form of stress relief is diversion. Reading a mystery story, international intrigue, or science fiction often provides this type of release. Note, however, that if the basic cause is not dealt with all these activities are merely temporary relief. With the exception of exercise which uses up energy, these techniques tend to be diversions and do not deal directly with the cause of the stress. Even exercise does not get at the cause but it probably mitigates the bodily damage. Suppressing the symptoms is not achieving a cure.

Managing stress, then, in the longitudinal or whole-life sense, is more than becoming sensitive and developing short-term relief techniques. Managing stress in life is *putting your act together*. The secret is in congruence between your inner and outer lives. The closer you come to living your inner life, the closer you may come to a stress balance. If you can work to bring the real life and the imaginary life of your psyche together, you are eliminating a prime source of conflict or stress. In a way this whole book, which contains suggestions for managing vitality, is dealing with achieving balanced stress through this congruence.

Hans Selye, who has made a life work of the study of stress, adds another dimension. He suggests that since our life balance depends upon our ability to have positive relationships with other people, the way we act with respect to them is important. His prescription is rephrasing the biblical "Thou Shalt Love Thy Neighbor as Thyself" to conduct your life so as to "Earn Thy Neighbor's Love"* Our attitude and outlook are interpreted by others through our actions. If they see us as acting positively toward them this can help us avoid stress.

A theory of illness

Until recently, most people assumed illness was physical in origin. That is, the development of modern Western medicine was based primarily on the germ or virus theory involving an invader or the malfunction of an element of the internal system. This is an oversimplification; however, it contrasts with the Christian Science belief that illness is in the mind. The cause of mental illness was thought to be entirely mental until recently when we found some chemical causitives. We are now moving toward a multifactor theory of illness which states that several factors may be involved simultaneously. This multifactor theory suggests that illness or human-system malfunction is often the result of an internal cause such as a mental depression or fear which sets up the conditions where the external cause or invader can survive and multiply. In other words, for reasons of which we may or may not be conscious, we have need of our illnesses, malfunctions, or diseases. Cure, therefore, may well be related to admitting, understanding, and managing that need in a way which does not require the illness.

Sometimes allowing the disease to take over provides a needed opportunity to stop some unwanted activity, to rest and recover. Sometimes a disease provides us with needed attention and sympathy. Sometimes a disease provides an excuse for impending failure. In a sense, disease or breakdown is a symptom of the human system defending its existence when the circuits are

---

*   From *Stress Without Distress* by Hans Selye, p. 118 and 112. Copyright © 1974 by Hans Selye, M. D. Reprinted by permission of J. B. Lippincott Company.

overloaded and there seems to be no other way to cope with the problem. The condition of overload and the resulting disease, however, may be in apparently unrelated aspects of our being. An example, used earlier, would be if we avoided a negative situation at work by creating a sore throat. While hard to condone on the surface, it may in a specific case be a legitimate stress-management technique, although not the best nor most healthy.

The process
of cure

If we accept a multifactor theory of illness, there should be a multifactor process of cure. Steps or elements of a multifactor curative process might include acceptance, understanding the causes, strengthening one's will to live and purpose for life, taking responsibility for recovery, medication or medical assistance, belief, rest, and moderation of diet and exercise. We may not consciously go through all these steps. For example, to talk of strengthening the will to live when we have a simple cut on the finger may seem unnecessary. In another sense, taking responsibility for cure of a case of athlete's foot may not seem all that necessary. Nevertheless, these are set forth as the elements of the curative process. Let's talk briefly of the function of each of these steps or elements.

Acceptance requires recognition of our state and getting in touch with it. Have you noticed the curative power of finally admitting you need help and going to the doctor? How often my symptoms disappear in the doctor's office! Acceptance stops your cover-up activity—your failure to face reality. Acceptance is a key in the Alcoholics Anonymous recovery system. The individual starts by accepting the fact of alcoholism. Acceptance is also an important first step in the cure of mental illness. Telling someone to see a psychiatrist will not effect a cure. He or she must admit the need and take the action. The function of acceptance of our illness can be seen, therefore, as opening the possibility for cure.

Taking responsibility for cure carries on from acceptance. This step implements the individual's commitment to work on the problem. Taking responsibility means you have accepted a stake in the outcome and you are willing to accept responsibility for failure as well as success. Taking responsibility may mean active participation on both a mental and a physical level. On a mental level, it may be levelling with yourself about the conditions which caused the disease and changing your expectations. On a physical level, it may, for example, mean going through some curative activity such as physiotherapy, bed rest, or restricted diet. Taking responsibility means committing yourself to work on your cure. It may be work you do alone, or with the doctor, or with some other outside intervenor.

Understanding the causes requires analysis of many possible factors. It may just mean self-analysis; for example, finding the cause of something internal like stress or the sharp object which caused an external wound like a scratch. It may mean subjecting yourself to extensive medical diagnosis. It may mean extensive psychological probing, either self-directed or externally directed. The extent and depth of the search should be in balance with the severity of the problem. Understanding the causes may be a basic requirement for designing the specifically applicable cures. By contrast, in some serious problems protecting yourself from the total immensity of the problem may be necessary for your cure. This is the factor that leads the medical profession into debate about the wisdom of telling the patient the disease is incurable.

Strengthening the will to live and the purpose for life is necessary to provide a goal worth fighting for. The purpose, or goal, is key to mustering our energies. There are instances in which merely deciding to stay around to see a particular event, or to finish something, has extended life. On the other side, deciding all is finished can end life. There are some who believe that in this sense all deaths are suicides. Choosing a goal or purpose for recovering is a primary element of cure. Obviously this step is far more important in a serious illness than in a minor one and in a prolonged illness than in a short one.

Medication or medical assistance can range from specific physical and biochemical intervention to simply providing comfort and support. Comforting is a form of medical assistance. The mother's kiss on the child's injured knee is part of this realm. External help is necessary when the body's defenses and energies need encouragement to rise to the level of combat.

Belief is specific to any curative process. If you do not believe you will recover, it will require much personal convincing to create a cure. If you do not believe the doctor's medication will help, or if you are convinced you are dying, you will impede the cure. The power of expectation is almost supreme. The mother's kiss on the knee works in part because the child believes. Cures which are

PERSONAL EXPERIMENT 25

The next time you have a minor ache, a pain, a minor injury, a sore throat, or a cold, try active participation in the cure. First use whatever method you normally use and in which you believe. If this means seeking medical help, do so. In addition, find a quiet place where you will not be disturbed. Assume a meditative, relaxed but alert, state. Use whatever technique works for you to attain this state. If you don't have one try this: find a comfortable position, close your eyes, tell yourself you will be successful in relaxing, begin repeatedly counting 1, 2, 3, 4 slowly. When you are in a relaxed state picture your medical problem; try to locate the site of the irritation or pain. Next visualize your body fixing it. Don't try for a particular picture, don't struggle; take what comes. After a few moments of this tell yourself you are getting better and that you feel better, open your eyes, and resume normal activity. Follow this procedure two or three times a day for several days or until the irritation has passed. When the symptoms are gone ask yourself about your participation in the cure. How did it feel? Was recovery easier? Will you try it again?

Note: For much more complete understanding of these techniques see *The Healing Mind* and the *Well Body Book,* referenced at the end of this chapter.

labeled miracle cures, those things which happen at the famous curative centers, seem to be primarily based on belief. Expecting and believing are necessary elements of any curative process.

Rest, moderation of diet, and exercise are processes which allow the body to concentrate its forces on the disease. If we stay awake long hours, stress our system with overeating or drinking, or over-stress with exercise, we are diverting too much energy from the curative process. These reductions in activity are required to give the body the best chance. Left alone the control systems of the body attempt to restore normalcy.

Prevention

Prevention relates to cure. Prevention requires establishing a positive outlook and a healthy balance between inside reality and outside reality. Prevention requires a balance of good food, moderate exercise, and body maintenance, as well as periodic medical examination. Examination does not necessarily mean extensive x-rays and testing—the trend is away from this. Rather, it means discussion and review with someone skilled in listening and health management. It also requires a basic set of personal routines to establish and maintain a healthy mental balance. These routines should include mental exercise and mental rest to ensure a proper feeding of the mind. Prevention also requires both long- and short-range stress-relief and stress-management techniques.

There are as many prescriptions for prevention as there are theorists. We have all read the comments of 100-plus-year-olds who ascribe long life equally to use or abstinence of a particular food or pursuit of a specific exercise. There is probably no one right prescription. There is, however, a generally right course for you. You find it by getting in touch with what is happening in your mind and body. Basing your life plan on the knowledge of what causes your stress and then learning to manage these aspects, good food, exercise for body and mind, and stress management are good places to start your prevention program.

Elements or techniques of health maintenance

Some of the elements of a health-maintenance program have already been suggested. In this section, however, they are set forth in a more organized fashion. It is important, however, to recognize that this is not a standard program but, rather, a set of elements from which you and I may build our own program.

What is important is the achievement of a balance that matches our goals, our outlook and interests, and our stage of life. For example, no one should jump into a strenuous exercise regimen without knowing the state of his or her physical health and then building up to the desired level of activity progressively and slowly. It is equally important not to step into a vigorous mental exercise program without preparation and a matching effort with goals.

Elements of health maintenance

1. Positive outlook toward living
2. Useful goals and purposes
3. Balanced physical exercise which matches needs
4. Balanced mental exercise which matches needs
5. Proper eating for life-style
6. A stress-management program
7. Personal responsibility and participation in cures for malfunctions and invaders

Expectations set the stage for what happens. A positive set of expectations for our life and for our relationships with others is, therefore, a basic prerequisite for good health. Good health and good life are necessary for each other. A positive outlook requires a set of beliefs and principles. This set may be a very personal religion or may mean being part of an accepted formalized religion. Closely related to a positive outlook is a life purpose or set of purposes and goals. Moving toward something which is of importance to us, a goal, provides a rationale against which to measure the value of the actions and relationships we are choosing. Measurement is a neces- sary element in managing change. A set of goals also provides motivation for growth and learning which can, of course, be pur- poses in themselves. Growth and learning goals are a necessary constituent of a program to maintain vitality and health.

What is balanced physical exercise? In my terms, it is that set of activities which keeps our muscles in tone and operating at a level to support our activities. In that sense, it is not right to train for box- ing if we are not going to box. On the other hand, neither is it right to train for inactivity. Without some effort at maintenance, normal wear and tear and deterioration will slowly limit our abilities. If our work requires sitting at a desk, then our exercise program should require mild activity to offset the negative aspects of desk-bound life. If our work requires physical output, then our training must build us up to the requirements of the output.

What exercises you should use can be determined by experi- ment and counsel with someone who is trained to match an exer- cise routine with your needs. This book and this author are not the source for such advice.

Mental exercise, like physical exercise, must balance and complement our other activities. If our work requires primarily physical activity, then our planned exercise of the mind most probably must take place outside of work. If our work requires analytical mental effort, then some other type of mental exercise should be planned. As with physical-exercise programs, our planned exercise should probably develop some specific aspect such as memory, concentration, or fantasy life. As with physical exercise, we should build slowly. Regularity of practice is important. Exercise programs are probably necessary parts of stress management.

Whether to eat organic or traditional foods—that is the question! There are eating fads, there are theories of cholesterol input, and there are pros and cons on vitamins. How do we choose an appropriate nutritional program? Frankly, I do not know. There are, however, some general concepts. Medical practitioners know, for example, that many people can control excess or inadequate blood-sugar levels by limiting sugar intake. So if we have a specific diagnosed problem which is amenable to dietary control as recommended by our doctor, we should follow it. If in all specific measures we are normal, then balance and moderation, eating less than most of us do, monitoring weight changes and managing them, are probably good general precepts.

Stress management requires techniques for both relaxation and mental control. This means we each need methods for "cooling it" when experiencing a severely stressful incident. We also need programs for dealing with longer-term stress which probably results from some major imbalance in our lives. Physical activity, autogenic training, and meditation are typical examples of techniques for "cooling it." Longer-term techniques require getting our inner reality and our outer reality together. For example, career management by bringing our job and our goals together may well be a significant part of managing a source of long-term stress.

Health management for each of us is a careful, thoughtful, and ever-changing blend of these elements. We must take personal responsibility for health maintenance as well as for participating in a cure when we are not well. Even the best of prevention programs cannot protect us from all illness.

Summary

Good physical and mental health are essential to vitality, growth, and success in life. Good health does not mean matching the strength of an Olympic gold medal winner, but rather finding and achieving your own right balance. Good mental health similarly does not mean never being disappointed, or negative, or under stress, but managing life so the general tone is positive. There are many applicable concepts and health-management techniques. Central to the health-management approach of this chapter is the absolute necessity for each of us to take personal responsibility. Our outlook and our expectations go a long way toward determining what happens. It was suggested that illness probably results from a combination of factors. For example, in our subconscious we deliberately set up conditions for and sometimes use illness. Since we participate in creating the illness, we can be the cause of the cure of our illness if we participate in the cure.

The prevention perspective was based on a balanced life with a positive outlook and useful goals. Prevention also requires personal stress-management techniques. This does not mean elimination of stress but, rather, managing it in the range which is self-correctable. Stress is required for growth and living. Sustained, unrelieved stress can be deleterious. Long-run stress relief requires achieving a life balance. Short-run stress relief requires diversion and relaxation techniques. Health maintenance also requires programs for balanced mental and physical exercise. Balance means programs which fit the needs and the goals of the individual. Balance is required to establish appropriate life tone and to complement the energy requirements of the individual's main activities.

Suggested readings

Benson, Herbert. *The Relaxation Response*. New York: Avon, 1976.

Friedman, M. *Type A Behavior and Your Heart*. New York: Knopf, 1974.

Hutschnecker, Arnold A. *The Will To Live*. Englewood Cliffs, N.J.: Prentice-Hall, 1958.

Jongeward, Dorothy, and James, Muriel. *Born To Win—Gestalt Transactional Analysis with Gestalt Experiments*. Reading, Mass.: Addison-Wesley, 1971.

Jourard, S.M. *Healthy Personality*. New York: McMillan, 1974.

McKain, Robert J. *Realize Your Potential*. New York: AMACOM, 1975.

Newman, Mildred, and Berkowitz, Bernard. *How To Be Your Own Best Friend*. New York: Ballantine, 1971.

Oyle, Irving. *The Healing Mind*. New York: Pocket Books, 1976.

> *Dr. Oyle has written a very readable book which makes a convincing statement about the power of the mind in healing. Through patient examples and practical suggestions he shows you how you can participate in curing yourself; in fact, in keeping yourself healthy. This book brings you to the forefront of the merging of Western medicine with the older practices and some new discoveries. If you want a healthier life and are willing to take personal responsibility for your health, this book is for you, right now.*

Rogers, Carl. *On Becoming A Person*. Boston: Houghton Mifflin, 1961.

Samuels, Mike, and Bennett, Hal. *The Well Body Book*. New York: Random House/Bookworks, 1971.

Selye, Hans. *Stress Without Distress*. Philadelphia: J.B. Lippincott, 1974.

16

Finding oneself

Introduction

"I looked in the mirror, and there I was!" Central to your identity, growth, vitality, and continued development is your concept of self. Feeling at home, being yourself, provides an important part of the security necessary to take the risks of growth and change. How do you find yourself? Some techniques for doing so as well as an outlook on the challenge are the topics in this chapter.

Finding oneself is putting together a set of philosophies and techniques of viewing the world and oneself which make sense—a complete and harmonious whole. Finding oneself can be approached from the point of view of life planning or career planning. Here an understanding of one's strengths and weaknesses, likes and dislikes, values, and activities that provide satisfaction are the building blocks. Finding oneself can also be approached from the viewpoints of humanistic psychology. In this case, it is becoming aware of feeling and the body through experience so that one can learn to relate to others and achieve self-actualization. In addition, finding oneself can be approached from the viewpoint of psychotherapy, where getting in touch with one's inner feelings through analysis and learning to be at home with self is the process. Finding oneself can be approached from the techniques developed in the East. Such finding of oneself comes from long, hard training at contemplation or meditation to learn how to face and understand the inner self. Finally, Western religious philosophy would suggest that finding self is finding God. All of these views are rational views, and each has worked for different people at one time or another. All these approaches can be helpful.

Since all of these approaches have validity, what works for you is right for you. Knowing oneself is necessary for growth and vitality. Therefore, it is necessary for you to search for and find the special perspective, philosophy, or way that works for you. The right approach is probably not a constant but, rather, something which changes with phases of life and with life goals. In fact, the key to finding oneself may well be in "hanging loose" and not becoming wedded to any one approach.

Yet, it is necessary to take an approach and invest enough time and energy to give it a chance to work for you. Too frequent a change of mode probably makes the actual finding of self more difficult. So here, as in other aspects of managing your vitality, both an openness to exploration and experimentation and commitment to a particular approach are important. The balance between the two is ever changing.

The process

The process of finding oneself is sequential and never ending. First, there are many selves; and we change and grow. Second, there is no one right path for all. There are some experiences which speed the process or allow us to make longer jumps toward the truth. There are other experiences that seem to take us backward or slow our discovery.

As an analogy, consider that life is spent in some massive interconnecting series of subway systems—or, as an alternative, a massive interconnecting bus system. Let's say life is going along normally. We are traveling on a local train and we come to a station at which it is possible to change trains and board an express. Something causes us to get out on the platform. It can be a vague uneasiness, the comment of a friend, a decision to go somewhere specific, a momentary disorientation—any of a number of things. We see the express, a train we have never taken before, pull into the station. There is some risk, for we may pass by some interesting places; the higher speed may be less comfortable because we lose some freedom to change; and all sorts of anxieties or fears may fill us—just the fear of the unknown is enough to make us anxious. But we get up the courage and step on to the express. Perhaps it is only partly a conscious decision, for we may be pushed a bit by the crowd. The express can be likened to some new experience which brings us closer to self. It could be a revealing session with a close friend or counselor, a religious experience, a momentary flash of insight, an emergency for which we find new strength, a revealing meditation, a compatible new friendship, or a chance to study.

Some of us become enchanted with the thrill of the new experience and become temporary prisoners of the express train. Others take the express for a short distance and get off. Having accomplished this, they now have the power of choice, the experience of what the new train can do, and an enhanced set of capabilities for taking new strides toward self.

As we grow in our capability, experience, and relationships with others, we realize that the subway system we started on is not the only one. We find that there are interconnections and extensions. As we understand ourselves better, we become capable of taking advantage of the whole range of possibilities for activity, for learning, for growth, and for extending vitality and aliveness. Or, in terms of the subway, we learn to play the system, to use it to amplify ourselves and reach new destinations and new experiences. Our vitality or aliveness is a measure of our ability to play the subway system. Our sense of self is related to our willingness to risk the new because we feel at home with who we are. Again, in terms of the subway system, after we have regularly used several lines and trains with various designations, our fear of trying a new line is reduced—we become self-sufficient and confident subway riders.

From this analogy, we see that finding oneself has at least two identifiable dimensions: first, the experience with the system of life and the ways in which it can be used to enrich our experiences; second, the self-assurance, sense of worth and feeling of being at home which come from having had successful experiences in using the system.

There is a third aspect which complements our confidence in ourselves, and that is confidence in others. Just as we gain an ability to ride the subway system of life, we must also gain in ability to relate to others. This includes taking them as they are and being able to have a useful, satisfying relationship. This should be a relationship which is of value to both parties. Self-confidence needs to be complemented or we live a very lonely life and often one filled with unnecessary conflicts which arise from not being able to live in harmony with others. Part of finding self is finding our ability to be with, live with, and work with others.

The experiential way

Probably the easiest way to find oneself is just to live one's life. That is, finding oneself is a main part of what life is all about. If this is so, then why a chapter on finding oneself? The primary reason is that the experiences of our lives tend to trap us, to direct us, and to limit us if we fail to take charge. Experiences tend to trap us by being so all-encompassing that we begin to feel that the experience is all there is to life. Such an experience in its most pure form is one in which we are so absorbed we want it to go on forever, and we literally lose contact with the world. Total absorption in a job where we lose touch with time, total immersion in a good book or a movie, some absorbing physical activity, or some thrill such as the roller coaster are examples of total absorption. This trap has several aspects. First, the activity is so encompassing that it takes our total attention, and we lose touch with other activity. If it could be extended, we would literally be like Rip Van Winkle and come back at its end to a strange world. Another aspect of this trap is that it diverts us from our other activities and we lose our balance of stimuli. A third aspect is that the experience becomes a standard of reference. If it was seen as really fun and rewarding we might use the memory of it to judge a future experience. But such judgment tends to limit our ability to get full value from our next experience. Our goal if we are stuck becomes the reproducing of that same feeling which we had before.

Reproduction of a feeling we had before is a diversion from the learning, growth, and vitality goals of life. Such a goal tends to cause us to get stuck, literally to derail and devote energy to going backward or to standing still. This may not be dangerous, or too deleterious, if it happens in but one aspect of our lives. The danger is that it will become one of our standard reaction patterns and that we will get stuck the same way in many aspects of our lives. This is a pattern destined to reduce vitality. It leads to a standard of negatives for comparison with our future life experiences.

Limiting comes about as the result of our experiences, helping us to build blocks to new learning. An example may help. If we try some activity such as building a table and discover that we are unable to cut all four legs the same length, we learn that this is difficult and/or that we cannot do it. We tend to eliminate that and related activities so that we will not again be faced with failure. Even though the technology may change to provide adjusting feet or a process for assuring controlled length, or even provide pre-machined length-controlled legs, our earlier experience will tend to keep us from trying again. A positive experience can also build blocks. Let us suppose that in the same example we were successful in getting all four legs the same length by a process of cut and try. This continuous approximation approach was inefficient and consumed extra wood; however, it worked. We learned that to be successful we needed to start with an extra two inches of length and to allow for trial and error. Such an experience will lead us to believe we know "the way" to such an extent that we will probably also resist new technology. Not getting stuck requires maintaining a bit of dissatisfaction with the tried, and openness to new ways.

Those who have studied and tried to improve the learning and growth aspects of experience suggest several ways to avoid or limit the negative effects of the traps. Six broad categories of techniques will be discussed for enhancing the prospects of furthering the goal of finding oneself. The techniques are:

- wanting to find self,
- concentrating on the long-range goal,
- increasing consciousness of experience,
- sharing experiences,
- using a guide, teacher, or counselor, and
- supplementing with special experiences designed to enhance our capability of managing life.

Wanting to find oneself hardly sounds like a technique. Yet none of the other techniques will be very successful if we do not start with desire. It is like wanting to grow, to learn, to be vital, or to be healthy. The establishment of a goal in itself starts a process of applying oneself in that direction. This should not be taken as an indication the process is best or always a conscious one. We all must work out for ourselves the way we relate to our entire environment, including our own bodies and our minds. The secret seems to lie in making that relationship as harmonious as possible without serious surprises that threaten one's whole life. This is not simply cognitive knowledge about self. If it were, doctors, knowing more about bodily functions, would always be more healthy. Yet this is not so. It is rather a goal of becoming a natural person in harmony with nature.

One of the traps of experience is loss of contact with other things going on around us and the subversion of the long-range goals. Improving our concentration on the long-range goal is, therefore, a way to offset this negative. The first and most obvious way of doing this is to write down, rethink, and update long-range goals. Knowing where we want to go, what we want to achieve, and then reminding ourselves of the value and desirability of these goals is a process we can build into our lives. Although New Year's resolutions come in for a lot of jokes, properly done as an annual plan they can be a help. Such plans probably should be supplemented, however, with five-or ten-year goals. Although goals beyond that in time may be of some use, long-range plans must be kept close enough that they can be real and we can do things to prepare for them, not just dream about them.

Establishing useful long-range goals and having some regular annual or semiannual review, supplemented by review when major incidents or crossroads in our lives may change them, is a first step. Examples of major changes which might alter our goals would include loss of a job, starting a new job, change in family status, change in health status, or completing some new training or education. The next step is to build in a reminder process and a technique for commitment. The reminder process could be as simple as typing

---

PERSONAL EXPERIMENT 26

What are your long-range personal goals? That is, what are your goals for the next five to ten years? Think about them and pick three that are most important. For one month, try the following process and assess your feeling at the end of the month about your progress. Take the following steps:

1. Discuss these goals with some other person who is close to you. In the process of telling that person, make a commitment to get back at the end of the month's trial and report progress.

2. Set up some personal reminder technique like putting notes on a card on your mirror, or on top of your desk, or setting aside a specific time every day when you will review them.

3. Find some incremental step in the direction of one or more of the goals which can be accomplished in a month. Decide how you will identify that accomplishment.

At the end of the month review your progress and share it with your friend. Rather than concentrating your total review on goal progress, however, check up on your answer to the question: "What have I learned about myself?" As a minimum, write down the things you have learned. If you feel comfortable doing so, share some of these discoveries with your friend.

the goals on a card and affixing this to our mirror so that each morning we see them and read them. Repeating these goals at the end
of a contemplative or meditative session would be another way.
Establishing appointments with others for the purpose of reviewing
and discussing them is still another. We should suit our reminder
technique to our life and style.

Commitment is closely related to reminding oneself. For
example, part of commitment is having meetings with others to discuss goals and to talk about them, thus increasing the probability of
achievement. What we tell others we are going to do takes on a
higher priority because we work to maintain our positive image.
Another technique for commitment is to list the actions one can
take and set time goals for meeting them. Or one can strengthen
commitment by promising oneself rewards in the short run for
reaching milestones toward long-range goals. Making a pact with a
friend to meet at a future time to be able to report having
accomplished something is another technique. This could be an
agreement with the boss for him to include certain accomplishments
in one's performance rating. Let us commit ourselves to being
ingenious at designing our own commitment process.

The second broad category of techniques includes ways of
becoming more conscious of what is happening to us. *Be Here
Now,* the title of a book by Ram Dass and one of the themes for the
growth movement, is one aspect of this. If we can learn to be
conscious of what is going on in us right now, then it is possible to
become sensitive to when we are being trapped or entranced. One
method is to cultivate the habit of periodically asking oneself the
question: "What am I feeling right now?" Such a process might help
us know what activities are associated with a sense of growth and
forward movement of new strengths and capabilities. Knowing this
should help to increase these experiences. Another technique is to
form the habit of taking a time at the end of the day to review what
happened. "What did one accomplish?" "How did one affect
others?" "What did one learn?" These are typical questions to ask in
such a review. Learning to meditate may be another way. Because
most forms of meditation teach one to learn to concentrate, the
process of meditation should increase one's effectiveness and
awareness of what is going on.

The third general technique for enhancing the growth value of
experience is sharing. Sharing simply means setting up conditions
under which we let some other individual know what happened to

us and what we feel. Sharing is when we let another person experience something with us and then talk together about our reactions to it. Sharing has the advantage of reinforcing the knowledge that, although we each experience a given event differently, we have all had or are still having similar feelings. Sharing breaks down the feeling of aloneness. Being able to share is a demonstration of confidence in others. Sharing also has the advantage of keeping us from locking up experiences in a way that can form obstructions. Similarly, sharing an experience which built an obstruction may be a process for unblocking or unlearning. When we share, we do not have to tie up energy maintaining the memory of the experience. Sharing, therefore, frees energy for new activities, new learning, and new growth. Thus, sharing enhances vitality. There is a danger that the process of sharing can itself become a hangup. Such may be true of the individual who dominates the conversation with his or her experiences, often repeated, and never allows anyone else to share. That form of sharing is playing the game but does not unblock.

Using a guide, teacher, or counselor is related to sharing. A guide has a function, however, of intensifying the learning by questioning and by causing us to look at aspects of experience that might slip by with little notice but which are important, not to be missed, events. A teacher who is really in contact with us can also help us to sense when we are ready to move on to some new experience or when a reassessment of goals or techniques is in order. A guide or counselor serves as a highly selective, tuned feedback device that helps us to differentiate signal from noise. Each of us somewhere, sometime, should have had such help. It happens when we are not conscious of what the other person did or of whether we did something. Then all of a sudden we achieve clarity, insight, and understanding. When this happens more frequently in the presence of one specific person, that person is at that time performing the role of guide and teacher. There is a danger. If the counselor-teacher allows us to place too much responsibility on him or her, then we have a crutch, and the value of the guide is diminished. It may also become comfortable just to be with and take guidance from the counselor. This can interfere with growth. Both teacher and student must be ready to face the time when the student must move on.

Supplementing regular life experiences with especially designed experiences for learning and growth is the basis for educational institutions of all kinds. Most recently, and in the context in which we have been talking, the institutions of the growth movement have been in the forefront. These are the institutions which have been stressing "experiential" as opposed to "cognitive" learning. In the business world simulations or business games which highlight and concentrate certain experiences have represented this element. Team building or organization-development processes in which groups identify problems of communication, work relationships, and work organization are another example. When effectively run, such sessions can contribute to learning about learning and to helping work groups learn to use their potentials for problem solving.

In personal development, the growth movement has provided an ever-expanding array of processes, each with its pros and cons designed to enhance openness, unblock and increase the potential for the finding of self. Broadly, these processes divide into several categories. Many deal with the body. The thesis is if one is in touch with one's body, one step in finding oneself is under way. Being at home with one's body opens one to other experiences. These techniques range from massage to Rolfing to Tai Chi, to nude baths, and to group activities including body contact. A second group of activities deals primarily with interpersonal relations. These are designed to enhance interchange and feedback on a verbal level. Here activities range from encounter groups to transactional analysis. A third category of activities is designed to help the individual get in touch with inner life. In this category we would include Gestalt dream analysis, biofeedback, certain extrasensory perception processes and experiments, and altered states of consciousness. Learning to maximize the growth aspects of experience and to use these experiences to assist in finding self, is a course of action followed by many. Provided that one does not become too entranced with the novelty of the experiential process, these activities should prove valuable.

The contemplative
way

The essence of the contemplative approach is learning to listen to the inner self by quieting the ongoing input from the world and from the repetitive unceasing talking to ourselves. Those who recommend this approach believe that it increases the individual's ability to find the route of life by teaching self-control. Understanding of what happens in and through meditation has not been investigated in depth until recently. The advent of large-scale marketing and the practice of meditative approaches such as transcendental meditation have begun to change this. Both Bloomfield and Le Shan, referenced in suggested readings, provide studies of the changes resulting from meditation. There are many ways of achieving a meditative or contemplative state, and a brief review will give us some hint as to how the process may relate to finding oneself.

One of the most difficult ways of meditating and one which requires precise control of consciousness is to make the conscious thought a blank. This is difficult, and because of this most of the ways provide some busywork which takes the mind's thoughts off itself. Certainly if you can tell yourself to quell the ongoing thoughts and internal activity and make your thought process blank, you must be able to understand or at least control what causes the activity.

Closely related to this process is another one of focusing attention on an object. Care must be used here that one does not just create a hypnotic spell. This must be a conscious looking, but only looking, at the object. Again, if you can learn how to handle distractions and how to keep this from becoming hard work and consuming a lot of effort, you should learn about yourself in the process. *The right meditative process is one which you can achieve without extensive effort.* Contemplation should not be work in the sense of energy expenditure. Not only should the achievement provide enlightment but, once achieved, it is then possible to contemplate an aspect of self. Such use of contemplative power is to think of a question such as, "Who am I?"—but only that one question.

Concentrating effortlessly on a rhythmic bodily function such as breathing is a way which creates the meditative state easily for many—simply count breaths to four and then repeat. Concentration on this process limits thought and creates a synchronism of body and mind. Biofeedback techniques may create similar situations by extending the kinds of functions to which we can be sensitive—biofeedback makes it possible to concentrate on a bodily function of which we are not usually conscious. A buzzer or a needle on a meter become the point of attention. Repetition of a nonsense phrase or word called a mantra is another way. Here again the technique involves limiting the activity of conscious thought and concentrating on one activity. When you do this, there will be other thoughts which you should just let float by without trying to understand or analyze.

Another technique often associated with relaxation is to go through a sequence of activities which are guiding the mind to a less active state. A typical sequence might be: find a spot in your left ankle, etc., going through the parts of the body. This process provides a sort of mental busywork which focuses on the body and shuts out many of the regular repetitive thoughts.

Finally, it is possible to attain a meditative state through repetitive physical activity. The dervish dance is a spectacular example. A form of this has frequently been suggested as a technique for falling asleep, but the difference is that to fall asleep one tells oneself to tense a muscle and then relax it. It is important to understand that meditating is not falling asleep. It is, rather, creating a condition of single-mindedness and relaxed attention. In meditation one's consciousness of self probably becomes more acute. Regular achievement of a meditative state seems to help the individual to improve life management and often results in an improved ability to avoid or resist overreaction to the incidents of life. By reducing the energy the individual has to use in maintaining stability, there is an increase in energy and vitality for useful-positive purposes.

Meditation is, therefore, a possible prescription for vitality, a way of training oneself to be more effective. Through the process of training, one becomes more conscious of self and improves one's ability to manage thought and deed. The data that is currently being collected demonstrated that those who have attained this control are more effective and more vital. *

Other
ways

As examples of ways to find self, we have discussed experience and meditation. But the ways to self-knowledge are myriad. For example, psychotherapy is a process through which people are aided in finding themselves. Psychotherapy provides an opportunity and support for a process of recall of experience and thought by bringing the past into conscious thought where it can be dealt with. Repressing a negative past experience probably uses energy in a nega-

---

*   See H.H. Bloomfield, *Transcendental Meditation* (New York: Delacorte Press, 1975).

tive sense. Therefore, release of the necessity to repress releases that energy to be used in other ways. In a way one can think of this as a cost for not having completed and closed a life-transaction or not having faced self and the consequences of our choices.

Another route to self is to deal with feelings. These may, of course, be surfaced in psychotherapy, in communication with others, in meditative activities, in any technique which increases one's consciousness of one's feelings. Carl Rogers in *On Becoming A Person* discusses this as follows:

> *I would like to say something more about this experiencing of feeling. It is really the discovery of unknown elements of self. The phenomenon I am trying to describe is something which I think is quite difficult to get across in any meaningful way. In our daily lives there are a thousand and one reasons for not letting ourselves experience our attitudes fully, reasons from our past and from the present, reasons that reside within the social situation. It seems too dangerous, too potentially damaging, to experience them freely and fully. But in the safety and freedom of the therapeutic relationship, they can be experienced fully, clear to the limit of what they are. They can be and are experienced in a fashion that I like to think of as pure culture so that for the moment the person is his fear, or he is his anger, or he is his tenderness, or whatever.* *

So any process, here suggested by Rogers as psychotherapy, which puts one in touch with feelings, lets one be his or her feelings, is a route to finding self.

Religious experience and training is another route to self. Whether the religion be Zen with meditation and yoga or Western Christianity with the study of the Bible and prayer is not the issue. The important point is that the study of a philosophy and the understanding of a body of thought added to a search for contact with a supreme being is a way to learn more about self.

Tai Chi, which has already been mentioned, is an active way of finding oneself and of improving the balance between self and nature. Tai Chi, which consists of from 37 positions (short version) to 108 positions (classic version), is a way of exercise which emphasizes the synchronism of mind and body. The desired end is a healthy body, increased energy, centering, improved effective-

---

* Carl R. Rogers, *On Becoming A Person* (Boston: Houghton Mifflin, 1961), p. 111. Reprinted with permission.

ness through working *with* nature and improved understanding of self. Tai Chi can be thought of as active meditation or meditation through motion.

Sufism, as a teaching system, is a way of finding self in its own right—that is, it is a process and it is also a religion or part of some religions. For the moment, let us examine the process. Teaching in Sufism has as a central feature parables or stories designed to catch the listener and make the listener conscious of his or her thinking. By providing a vehicle for revelation of an aspect of self, it provides a way to find self. A typical Sufi story will illustrate this. The central character is Mullah, a fictional dervish who took the vows of poverty and wandered, teaching others. Often by appearing stupid or making himself the butt of his stories, he provides enlighten-ment. In life we often identify things by describing them as similar to another or as different from another. This process of trying to type events and people becomes so much a part of us it can even show up in our dreams.

"What's in a name?" One night Mullah had a dream. In the dream he was hearing a business proposal. All seemed to be going well and he was about to buy, for he was convinced. Suddenly he learned the name of the man making the proposal. The man's name was "Brand X." Mullah knew then, regardless of the merit of the proposition, that it was not to be believed.

In our contemporary culture "Brand X" has become the less acceptable in a comparison advertisement. The story illustrates how we carry over from one experience to another and apply judgments which may not be applicable. The individual's name has nothing to do with the quality of the proposal. The listener should, as a result of listening to the story, be open to learning something of self. How often do you judge by a cover or a name?

The ways
to self

Engaging in creative arts is another route to finding self. When one tries painting, one can learn to express balance or line and color as one sees them. It is as if in painting one takes something which is internal and puts it out where one can see and judge it.

The ways to self are limitless. Just living life is part of the process. However, by trying things which increase consciousness and cause one to focus on and develop one's feelings and thoughts in the manner one develops one's muscles through exercise, we can enhance the process.

Designing your own way

In the final analysis, this is what each of us does. We find our own way. Even though we may follow some recognized teacher or approach, our way is uniquely ours. For some people, the process of design is conscious and evident. For some the process of design is never separately identified and is not conscious. In one sense, there is no known way to tell others how to design their own growth process. But in another sense, that is what this whole book is about.

If by exposing yourself to the processes used by others you are encouraged to try something that you have not tried before, you are working at building your own design. Experimentation is the key to discovery. At this point, an appropriate approach seems to be for me to rewrite and paraphrase Polonius' guidance to his son, Laertes, in *Hamlet* (Act I, Scene III):

"Vitality-Oriented" HAMLET

And these few precepts in thy memory
Look thou at character. Give thy thoughts no tongue,
Nor any unproportioned thought his act.
Learn by doing. Listen to thy teachers,
But recognize you must leave them behind.
Be religious, but be not caught up by it.
Be thou familiar, but by no means vulgar,
Yet, in sharing, learn something of thyself.
Those friends thou hast, and their adoption tried,
Grapple them unto thy soul with hoops of steel,
But do not dull thy palm with entertainment
Of each new-hatched, unfledged comrade. Beware
Of entrance to quarrel, but being in,
Bear't that th'opposed may beware of thee.
Give every man thy ear, yet take only
That which works for you. Give few thy voice,
But when thou doest, speak solely from thine heart.
Take each man's censure, but reserve thy judgment.
Costly thy habit as thy purse can buy,
But not expressed in fancy; yet experiment,
For clothes can lead to new discovery,
As the apparel oft proclaims the man,

And oft opens doors to new experience.
Neither a borrower nor a lender be,
But give wisely of thyself, for tis through
Service to others that one oft discovers self.
Seek experiences, but do not allow
Thyself to get stuck in them. Be conscious
Of thyself, learning to quiet the din
Of life and yet also to turn on thy power.
Do what you do with full vigor, but be
Mindful of thy effect on others.
This above all, to thine own self be true
And it must follow, as the night the day,
That thou wilst find thyself, for this is the
Highest achievement in any man's life.
Farewell; my blessing season this in thee!

Summary

Guiding oneself through life in the search for self and meaning in life is an important part of maintaining vitality and extending one's growth. "Doing what comes naturally," the phrase from the musical *Annie Get Your Gun*, goes a long way toward achieving a discovery of self. Some life experiences, however, teach us to be unnatural in life and tend to block or inhibit growth from new experience. The individual can do something about this. What is required is finding a way to enhance openness and take charge of one's growth process.

After presenting an analogy of the subway to describe the process, this chapter explored ways of enhancing learning about self. One broad category of techniques covered enhancing experiences. Ways of intensifying the consciousness of experience and supplementing normal experiences of life were discussed. These included concentrating on a long-range goal, sharing, using a guide, and dipping into the packaged programs of the growth movement.

Next, the contemplative approach was reviewed. Various techniques of meditating were discussed. Meditative states were described as being achieved by creating a blankness of mind, repetition of a mantra, concentrating on a bodily function, focusing on an object, guided or sequential steps of busywork for the mind, and physical inducement such as a dervish dance.

The objective is for each individual to find the sequence of ways that makes sense in his or her life. It was pointed out that no one way will suffice if growth is to take place. The great range of ways was illustrated by briefly mentioning religious approaches, teaching methods, and self-devised techniques. The range of literature, schools, and teachers for these processes is growing at a phenomenal rate. Modern communication and the thrust of our times have assured us of exposure to ways from all over the world.

Suggested readings

Bloomfield, H.H.; Cain, P.C.; and Jaffee, D.T. *Transcendental Meditation — Discovering Inner Energy and Overcoming Stress.* New York: Delacorte Press, 1975.

Feldenkrais, Moshe. *Awareness Through Movement.* New York: Harper & Row, 1972.

Hamachek, D.E. *Encounters with The Self.* New York: Holt, 1971.

James, Muriel, and Jongeward, Dorothy. *Born To Win — Gestalt Transactional Analysis with Gestalt Experiments.* Reading, Mass.: Addison-Wesley, 1971.

Mahoney, M. *Self-Control: Power To The Person.* Belmont, Calif.: Brooks/Cole, 1972.

Ornstein, R. *Psychology of Consciousness.* New York: Viking, 1973.

Rogers, Carl R. *On Becoming A Person.* Boston: Houghton Mifflin, 1961.

Samples, Bob. *The Metaphoric Mind: A Celebration of Creative Consciousness.* Reading, Mass.: Addison-Wesley, 1976.

Schutz, W. *Joy.* New York: Ballantine, 1973.

> Will Schutz writes this book from his extensive experiences in the growth movement and from a position of sharing the real joy of his own life. His joy is similar to our vitality in that he believes in openness as a cornerstone and the childlike interest in exploration as a desirable state. The book surveys the various approaches he has used and he has seen contribute to this reopening experience. He covers ways of getting in touch with your body, understanding yourself, your interpersonal relations, and ways to gain the most from group and organizational relations.

Tart, Charles. *Transpersonal Psychologies.* New York: Harper & Row, 1975.

Watson, D. E. *Self-Modification for Personal Adjustment.* Belmont, Calif.: Brooks/Cole, 1973.

Watts, Alan. *Nature, Man And Woman.* New York: Vintage, Random House, 1970.

Watts, Alan. *Meaning Of Happiness.* New York: Harper & Row, 1970.

For the business

17 Vitality: an organizational strategy

17

Vitality: an organizational strategy

Introduction

If up to this point the book has helped to convince you that vitality is important, what can a business organization do about it? Can a business contribute to personal vitality? What is the relationship between organizational and personal vitality? Our purpose here is to suggest ways an organization can put a higher value on vitality. Strategies and actions are discussed which change the relative value of vitality vis a vis other desired goals. The business or organizational need for vitality is equated to the need for productivity. The business need for vital people is based on the thesis that a vital organization is built with vital people.

I believe that a work ethic is a belief system which sets values and expectations and which guides activities. Some ideas about how a work ethic comes into being and what the organization can do about it are discussed. The thesis is that changed values expressed in the work environment change behavior and lead to new expectations and goals for both the organization and the individual.

Productivity is measured as the ratio of output to input. A productive process has outputs of greater value than the material, energy, and human effort that are put in. Improvement in productivity implies an increase in capability of the organization. Productivity is improved when the output increases with fixed or reduced input, or when outputs of higher value are created. The challenge of productivity is both in how one measures it and how one changes it. For many years we were satisfied with dollar measures but these now seem inadequate. Measurement approaches shape activity and set priorities. Productivity measures tend to be determined by consumers and the society—others than those responsible for the process. In these times of changing values when we are setting new priorities, such as protection of the environment, describing and evaluating the outputs is both crucial and volatile.

Although inputs, the materials and ideas which are the raw material for our organizations, are generally better defined and more measurable, we have tended to think only of certain kinds of inputs. We have measured the input of energy, raw materials, time, and capital in those processes which produce the output we count.

We have failed to measure or understand such inputs as personal motivation, goal credibility, love, support from coworkers, and other less tangible inputs. We have also tended to exclude from consideration all inputs to processes not part of the gross national product. For example, the love and care a mother gives to her children are not counted in a national productivity measure based on GNP. The enhancement of human assets through education is not counted, although the ultimate application of improved capability should enhance productivity and the quality of life.

I want to explore how vitality relates to productivity. Improvements in vitality should be contributions to tomorrow's productive capability. A definition of the productive enterprise is proposed. This hypothesis includes some of the previously unmeasured components. Personal productivity is presented as the result of a series of factors or elements. The evaluation of these elements and their relative power in affecting output is an open issue. The power of the concepts expressed will be most evident if they can bring you and me together to a point where we can do a better job of talking about the issues, managing improvement, and recognizing the importance of vitality in our lives.

A work ethic

A work ethic is a generally accepted and believed reason for work. Work ethics reflect the culture and the needs of the times. Because of the new values emerging in our society, the time has come for a work ethic which reflects the value of growth and learning through work. Such a belief will support increased emphasis on the conservation and enhancement of human resources and will balance our increased attention to natural resources. Such a belief will guide us in taking advantage of the fact we have arrived at the time when work is not as necessary for physical survival as it was in the past. But it will give meaning to our understanding that work is necessary for psychological survival.

How does a work ethic come into being? First, it comes to be believed because it reflects and gives meaning to the way we act; the statement of the ethic explains the general behavior. If management does things which demonstrate support of a particular concept, then the concept will tend to be believed. Action based on a stated principle supports the building of an ethic.

Second, an ethic or belief will come into being if we want it to. For vitality and growth to be reflected in work, we, as people and employees, must demand that it be so reflected. Management must decide it is important. Government leaders must decide it is important. If as a group we demonstrate more concern about salary than quality of work and psychological payout, then our actions do not support this new work ethic. Rather, they support a historical perspective that work supports life, which is something other than work. Seeking vitality may mean we sacrifice some pay for vitality.

Third, for personal vitality and growth to become a new work ethic, they must meet real human needs. If management and employees pay lip service to the concept, nothing will really change. To a certain extent, we can make them important merely by saying they are important; but this alone is not enough. Our need to gain psychological payout from work must be real. If it is not, this will, of course, never become the new work ethic.

What can management do?

In his McKinsey lectures at Columbia University, which are published in the book *Vitality In a Business Enterprise*, Frederick Kappel of AT & T set forth his answer to this question. The elements of a vital business are shown in the opening chapter in his book. All are applicable and necessary criteria, but for our purposes here, I am setting forth four concepts or steps.

This book and this chapter build on the thesis that increased productivity improvement and improved quality of working life are positively correlated. Improving the quality of working life increases the probability of improved productivity. The perspective, therefore, is that managements can and should take actions which increase productivity and life quality through improving the quality of working life. Improving the contribution to human vitality is seen as improved work/life quality. These concepts should be usable in many organizations. Here are four concepts for such improvement.

1. A first step in improving the quality of working life is *to raise the value and priority of human satisfaction, continued learning, growth, and personal vitality* in the work environment. This means that getting the product or service out with the right performance, at the right price, and on schedule must be weighed against the human cost of not providing human satisfaction and growth. It means that management must demonstrate, both in actions and in words, its commitment to providing the individual with opportunities for sustained growth and personal development. It

means all decisions must be checked against the question: How will this affect human vitality and personal growth?

2. A second step is to find out what will cause employees to grow throughout life and *to provide a better growth environment* through redesign of work for improved psychological payout and the establishment of continued growth as an expected output of business. This probably means redesign of organizations, change in styles of management, redefinition of tasks, and changes in measurement and reward systems. It also means building learning into business life, including the provision of courses and other educational activities.

3. A third step is *to define productivity* from the perspective of both the organization and the individual. After describing the elements, it then is possible for managers to talk about it and manage it. The definition and descriptions must be understandable by both the employee and the manager—and the descriptions must be usable, not just abstract theory. The organization's productivity concepts must help in decision making.

4. A fourth step is *to encourage employees to increase self-understanding* so that each individual can work to maximize personal contribution to the organization's goals and simultaneously improve personal satisfactions from work. To accomplish this, the organization through its management must become more adept at setting and communicating useful organizational goals. Both manager and employee need to understand life as a series of careers and learn to identify changing personal needs, ways of making personal change and of improving personal goal setting. The employee and manager must both become more competent in negotiating at the interface between the organization and the individual to improve the congruence of personal and company goals and the matching of capabilities with needs.

Embarking on this improvement strategy requires both corporate and individual commitment. If the corporation alone does it, the employee cannot but become more dependent. If management's sincerity is not credible, employees may react to these programs as just one more strategy for management to get more for less. An individual alone cannot change a working environment in which the complexity of the tasks requires the facilities and support of the company. Yet each side must desire improvement and commit energy to the process. The employee must take prime responsibility for managing his or her working career. The corporation must support improvement through appropriate understanding and the management of both the social and the technical systems of the business.

Some examples of actions supporting each of these four concepts should clarify them.

Raising the value of personal growth

Actions and programs which demonstrate management's belief in the value and need for personal growth have become increasingly important. These may be programs to provide more opportunities for learning and growth, programs which shift emphasis from the technical to the human aspects of the business, or unique activities which make environmental statements designed to change values. (An environmental statement is a management action which is more significant for the value it expresses than the cost or effort it requires.)

An approach to implementing this concept might be to set up a series of committees to study productivity and vitality in the organization and to recommend action programs. The first purpose of these committees would be to gain broad understanding and involvement in the problem. Since the need for vitality is many-faceted, such committees could start by assessing strengths and weaknesses of the organization. One committee might, for example, concentrate on the technical knowledge of the employees and the changing needs for skills and knowledge. They might try to answer such questions as: Does the organization provide sufficient educational opportunities? Does the organization utilize the skills it now has? Is personal growth of capability seen as valuable? And what can we do to improve learning in our work environment?

Another way to change the perceived value of personal growth and vitality in the organization is to establish new policy. It might take the form of a support for education such as tuition refund, or the improvement of tuition refund to pay for courses which prepare for new careers, or the acceptance of course enrollments during working hours. It might take the form of a policy which supports individual variation in the work day to pursue personal growth activities. It might be as simple a change as giving publicity to people on bulletin boards and in company papers for changes which represent personal growth, thus reinforcing and endorsing these changes. Such bulletin-board posting would, for example, meet our definition of an environment statement. The actions that represent changed values in a particular organization depend highly on the culture of that organization.

Redesigning the environment

The difference between the first step, changing values, and the second step, redesigning the environment, is subtle. There is overlap. The best way to differentiate between the two is to think of step 1 as actions which primarily affect values and attitudes and step 2 as consisting primarily of substantive changes in what is done and how it is done. (These changes can also affect values.) The changes necessary for this step are more likely to occur in an environment which places a high value on personal growth and vitality.

We grow by adding interests, knowledge, and skills. These we translate into accomplishments which, in turn, provide payout and satisfaction that lead to more growth. The process is circular and self-reinforcing in both positive and negative directions. If we try newly acquired skills and we fail to gain new and positive payoffs, we lose motivation to learn further new concepts. This is the negative cycle. A most common example in the industrial environment has been management-development education. Many managers comment that the world of the classroom is special, since upon return they find an unchanged environment, unreceptive to their new ideas. Positive reinforcement for learning and growth must be built into the work environment if we mean to foster human growth as an important output of the business enterprise.

How do we improve the capability of the environment to provide and support learning and growth opportunities? One way, for example, in a stable organization is the establishment of techniques for job rotation. Another is to increase the educational offerings that are responsive to this need for growth. Still another way would be to improve the personal satisfaction or payout from work, thus increasing work motivation and personal effectiveness. Examples of this type of redesign would include attempts to improve the alignment of rewards with organizational objectives and with human needs for recognition. Here an example might be including requirements for evaluating the growth and development of people in the appraisal of a manager. This would offset the tendency to see results as exclusively technical and/or numerically measurable.

In a dynamic and growing organization, change of assignments and new responsibilities result from this dynamism. But in a stable organization changes in job assignments for broadening and for growth must be managed. In a declining organization increased responsibilities often take on a negative connotation. The reason is that often such an increase in responsibility is being asked to do something which had been perceived as someone else's function. Change of assignments or rotation is not always an automatic improvement. Change of assignments which enhances human capabilities is more than just forcing additional responsibilities and more than just movement. Yet change of assignments contributes to individual learning, growth, and vitality. What can the nongrowing organization do to respond to this concept?

An example of such responsiveness would be the design of new techniques to enhance the opportunities for job change in the organization. One such technique has been tried by some organizations—job posting. This technique makes opportunities visible and allows the employee to bid for them. A limitation of this technique is that a downturn in the company's business is made obvious by a reduction in openings. Another limitation is that jobs tend to be described in their historical context; that is, the design of jobs to fit individuals is much less evident than the matching of individuals with jobs. A third negative may be the necessity of constantly explaining why someone does not get a job he or she desires. With all its faults, however, it does open the environment for job change. This is an area for further experimentation and organizational innovation.

A second example of environmental redesign might be greater emphasis on human-resource enhancement and management in the appraisal of managers. A greater emphasis on this subject in performance evaluations would transmit changed values. Items to be rated would provide guidance for managers. What we measure and pay attention to becomes important. The appraisal emphasis change should require comment by the manager's manager on: employee development, including appraisal and counseling, recognition, equal opportunity, career development, and vitality; communications; delegation; work redesign and experimentation; sensitivity to employee goals; and other areas. The appraising manager should probably declare what percent of the total performance rating of the appraised manager is represented by his or her management of people. If it is a small percentage of the total appraisal, an explanation should be required. Such a change should reinforce the value of people management. Again, whether such an action is appropriate requires an understanding of the culture of a particular organization.

Defining productivity

Productivity improvement is important for the improvement of our institutions, for effectively combating inflation, and for gaining greater personal freedom of choice. The concept of productivity is complex, and it is becoming more complex as we include new values.

Productivity is, in the broadest sense, the margin of output over input. As output is increased in relationship to input, productivity increases. For many activities, however, the value placed on the output is a variable over which those engaged in producing it do not have control. In our era of changing values and multiple perspectives, we are facing real dilemmas about what should be included in inputs as costs and what should be included in our measures of outputs. Is air quality an output for example?

Even the costs, or inputs, are not absolute. The social costs of the operations—which include the impact on vitality; the motivations, interests, work habits, and commitment of the employees— are much more difficult to measure. A change of operations which, for example, increases the anxieties of the employees, could have a high cost. This cost might well show up as a decrease in employee health. Or it might show up as other costs which are normally unseen and usually unmeasured, including loss of commitment, loss of management credibility, and inefficiencies of operation. Even though these costs might well outweigh the improvement in output expected from improved operations per se, they are seldom even discussed when considering investment in improved equipment or working space. Many historical approaches to improving productivity have emphasized equipment and process improvement and have given insufficient or no attention to the social system.

These are but a few of the complexities, and they can easily discourage attempts to measure productivity and manage improvement. Yet, both employees and managers need a reference point for improvement, need a sense of progress, and need to create profitable and successful activities. All of these depend upon a measurable concept of productivity. Productivity is just as important for personal health as it is for organizational health. There are fundamentally two ways to improve productivity: either change what is done or change how it is done. Either way, it is necessary to understand the things which affect productivity. These fall into two classes: those which are part of the technical system, and those which are part of the social system. The technical system includes factors like capital investment, task-organization improvements, and process improvements. The social system includes factors like improvements in employee satisfaction from work, increased education and training, better decisions about how work is to be shared, improved goal statements, and the development of techniques for participation in goal setting.

One of the most complex types of productivity is that of the knowledge worker—usually a professional like an engineer, a scientist, an accountant, or a programmer. The reasons for this increased complexity are many, but here are two examples. First, the output is not measurable in the physical sense that one can count the number of assemblies turned out by a production worker. Second, the value of the output is determinable only after a long period of time. For example, the value of a development engineer's idea is not measurable in the marketplace until many years after its creation. The lack of immediate and tangible measures and the resultant feedback delay create challenges to management that aren't often met.

Human-relations theory and organizational psychology would suggest that improvement starts when management makes changes. Reorganization of the work to increase satisfactions and thus positively influence the individual's motivation has been seen as a proper place to start. This would be consistent with Douglas McGregor's "Theory Y," Rensis Likert's studies, and the sociotechnical systems approaches growing out of work at the Tavistock Institute, London, the Work Research Institute, Norway, and with the emerging Quality of Working Life centers in the U.S. George F. Farris in an article "Chickens, Eggs and Productivity in Organizations" in *Organizational Dynamics*, Spring 1975, raises the important question of which comes first, changes by management or changes in the employee's performance. He suggests that actually improved output on the part of the employee may lead management to give him or her more responsibility, freedom, and authority and thus reinforce increased productivity. It seems just as reasonable to say that organizational characteristics cause productivity as it is to say that productivity causes organizational characteristics. The important lesson seems to be that there are feedback loops and that positive reinforcement on either side can lead to improvement in the other. Negative moves by managers or employees are also reinforcing, and they tend to set up deterioration in productivity.

As an example of what is meant by redefining productivity, the following list of elements of personal productivity has been developed. This conceptual framework should be helpful in communication about the productivity of the individual, and especially the knowledge worker or professional. The understanding of its various components is a necessary part of the understanding of costs. It is also important to understand the feedback loops in order to learn how the modification of one element may affect productivity and/or another element.

Elements of personal productivity

Element	*Primarily a part of the social or technical system*
Personal Motivation	Social
Abilities	Social/technical
Time (schedules)	Technical
Information	Technical/social
Expectations	Social
Mission Incentive	Social
Facilities and Support	Technical
Trust	Social
Experience and Self-Confidence	Social

1. Personal Motivation—This factor represents the innate desire of the individual to perform well. This motivation is affected by personal goals, values, the reward system, and perceived satisfaction from work. Congruence between personal goals and company goals can increase personal motivation. Motivation is enhanced by increased personal satisfaction from work, and it deteriorates with frustrations, lack of perceived impact, and lack of perceived recognition. The openness of relationships with the manager and the manager's leadership characteristics can be an important part of this factor. Personal motivation affects all other elements since if it goes to zero there is little or no productivity.

2. Abilities—This element is a combination of knowledge and skills. They can be improved by increased education and job training. They deteriorate with nonuse and with changes in technology. One of the most important ways to motivate growth in abilities is to require that job performance lead to new capability. Programs designed to improve vitality and personal growth should also be designed to enhance this factor.

3. Time—We need time to perform functions. Within some limit, more time can lead to better outcomes because we can explore various approaches to find the best one. This contributes to learning and growth. Too much time, however, can eliminate the necessary time pressure which motivates completion and which provides part of the sense of achievement. Time, therefore, can work for or against productivity.

4. Information—There are two types of information that the individual needs to do work. The first is the information which represents input to the activity (i.e., for the engineer, cost estimates) in relation to desired outcome or process. The second is information about the organization: goals, objectives, and beliefs as well as the specific role assignment of the individual. Organizational understanding can be enhanced by open communication, and it deteriorates with restrictions of information flow.

5. Expectations—This element covers both personally expressed and culturally transmitted expectations. If the organization sets high standards of excellence, this can have a positive effect. If the individual sets high standards for personal performance, this can have a similar effect. This phenomenon of expectations is one of the most important elements of the value system which influences organization performance. If the meeting of schedules or of product specifications is important, the organization modifies its operational effectiveness by establishing these as prime values. Low expectations, either personal or organizational, can, of course, negatively affect productivity.

6. Mission Incentive—This factor covers the motivation which stems from the nature of the goals of the organization. For example, if the group feels its goal is important to human life, a high-incentive value is present. How the organization expresses and communicates its goals can also affect how the employees accept and gain motivation from the mission. A mission which is perceived as having negative values for society can negatively affect the productivity of the group.

7. Facilities and Support—Investments in facilities, equipment, and support personnel which enhance the output of the individual can improve productivity. For the programmer, enhanced computer power, or for the engineer, a new measuring device can amplify the professional's energies. A model-maker's skills can increase an engineer's output, as can a secretary's assistance or a technician's help. Merely having such support in the

organization is not enough, however. It must be easily available to the individual and it must be perceived by all parties as a positive aid.

8. Trust—Trust in the system or the credibility or noncredibility of management has a strong effect on personal productivity. In today's world this factor has become increasingly important because of the growing distrust in our institutions and in "the establishment." Trust is built slowly but torn down quickly. Trust must be two way with management trusting the employee and the employee trusting management. Frequent changes of company plans without explanation can destroy employee trust. Failing to listen to the employee can demonstrate a lack of management trust.

9. Experience and Self-Confidence—This factor represents what has happened before and the individual's resultant self-concept and personal confidence. If previous hard work has paid off in the eyes of the individual, then his or her other past experience has been positive and contributes to improved productivity. Early job experience has been demonstrated as critical in establishing a positive or negative performance pattern. One who believes in his or her own personal capability has the strength to push for productivity against greater odds than one who has low self-confidence. Self-confidence thus contributes positively to productivity of individuals except when it is so strong that it severely interferes with the pursuit of organizationally determined goals. In this case it causes friction and waste.

This list probably does not include all the elements that affect the productivity of the individual. It does provide, nevertheless, a base for conceptual thinking about managing improvement. Many of the factors are both positive and negative in their possible effects on productivity—the right amount is positive, but a little too much can create a negative impact. Or some factors can be either negative or positive depending upon the method used to implement them or the interpretation placed upon them. For example, for one person management attention may represent evidence of the importance of his or her work. For another person, the same attention may be perceived as lack of trust in his or her capability and may negatively influence productivity.

This discussion of productivity has been included as an example of a management action. By producing a set of statements about productivity and by using these as a basis for discussion, management and employee attention can be centered on the need for new action. For example, actions which increase vitality directly affect the elements of productivity in the categories of abilities, information, expectations, experience, and self-confidence.

Increasing
self-understanding

The fourth step, increasing self-understanding, is best exemplified by this book itself. If managers use this book and its supplement for training programs or even make it available to others, such an action would be responsive to the book's concept.

The employee/organization
interface

The organization and the individual meet at an interface to which each brings needs and capabilities. Increased self-understanding makes it possible for individuals to represent themselves more effectively at this interface and to negotiate for improved congruence between themselves and the organization. Making it possible for the individual to achieve personal goals in the context of the company's goals increases goal congruence, and this leads to greater motivation and enhanced productivity. Gaining this congruence requires an understanding of oneself. Gaining this congruence also requires that management define the organization's goals, needs, and capabilities, and prepare its managers to communicate and negotiate with workers at the interface.

Figure 17.1 shows this employee/organizational interface and some of the influences which affect congruence. It also provides examples of employee and organization needs and capabilities. In the illustration, the arrows representing company and employee goals indicate needs brought to the interface by the organization and the individual. Effective goal setting and clear communications are required to negotiate and modify for congruence. Modification is the adjustment of goals on either side to improve the match. The organization states its needs for skills and knowledge. The individual presents capabilities. Increased congruence requires the modifying of the skill need either by increasing capital investment to change the need or increasing employee capability through education and experience. The organization brings a capability to provide rewards and recognition which must be matched with a need for rewards and recognition on the part of the individual. This interface exists in an environment which is also affected by the outside world through laws, social pressures, and economic cycles. The internal

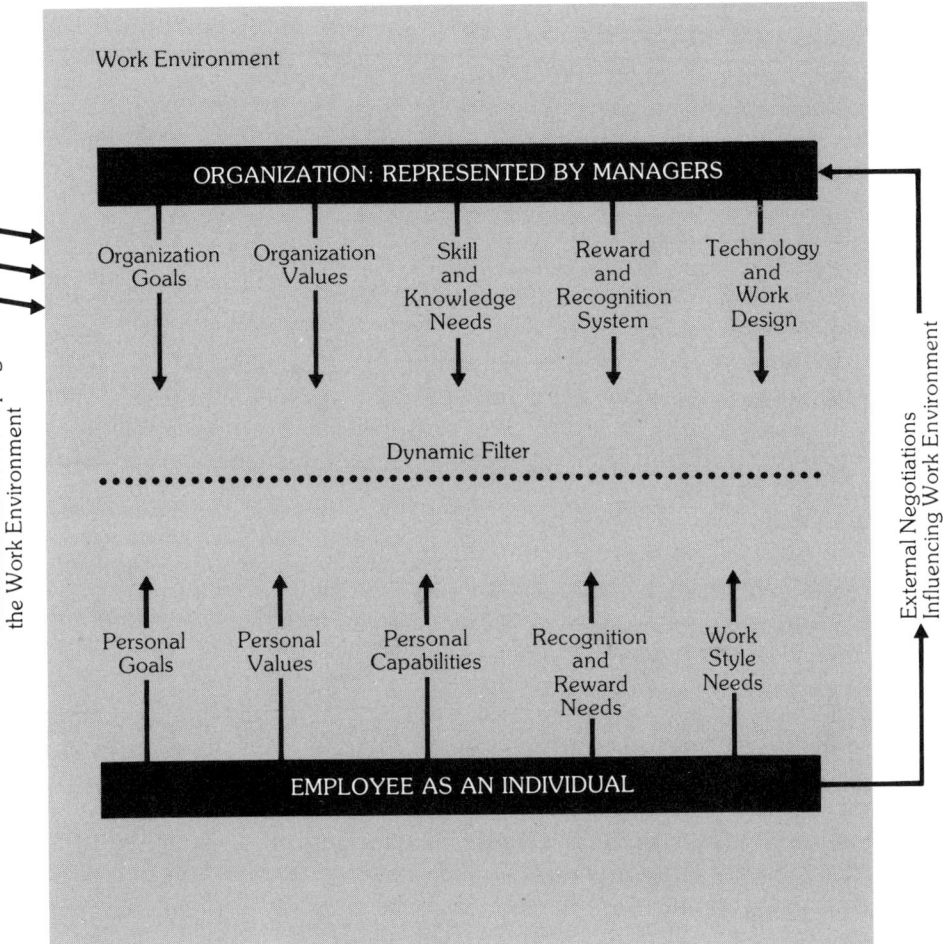

Fig. 17.1   The employee/organization interface

environment is set by policies, management style, and the mission of the organization. External negotiation can be the result of an employee influencing laws by writing a legislator or by resort to the courts or seeking of public support. The dynamic filter simply represents the fact that in most organizations there is a culture, or a structure, which can impede or enhance negotiation at the interface. In government the culture of the civil service is such a filter.

What can the organization do to improve congruence at the interface? It can set up a climate which supports and encourages open communication and negotiation there. It can provide policies which support adjustment at the interface, such as investment in tools to support the employee or investment in educational programs to increase the skills and knowledge of the individuals. By so doing it can improve the match of individual skills with skill requirements. It can support the individual in education and experience which increases his or her self-understanding and knowledge of career planning and management, or it can increase the individual's satisfaction through techniques for redesign of work. It can train managers to understand this matching process and their role in it. The employee's view of his or her career potential and personal understanding of how to take responsibility for managing it is important to this matching process. Career education is, therefore, a good example of management-initiated activity to improve matching.

Several approaches have been devised to aid in career management by sensitizing individuals to their changing interests, psychological needs, and special skills as adults. These are different from the career counseling aimed at the high-school or college student. Although programs may have different titles, such as life-script planning, career-interest review, or career-management seminars, all have in common a set of searching questions and contain some exercises designed to cause the individual to find out more about self. Most approaches help the individual to identify interests, peak experiences, negative experiences, skills, and goals. Management support of employee growth in career and personal life-management techniques is essential to survival of our organizations.

Internal (company-created) education and services are ways to meet this need. One example of a supportive program could be a one-, two-, or three-day seminar on career management. Employees given the opportunity to volunteer for this session could make the choice about exploring such personal subjects in a class with fellow employees. The seminar would probably be best as a small-group activity so that each person can participate. It might be run with six to twelve people and one facilitator. The educational process should engage the members as individuals and as a group in exercises and discussions which will identify personal capabilities, likes, dislikes, and interests. Typical exercises might include writing an autobiography, plotting a life line with positive and negative experiences, analyzing high and low value priorities for psychological payouts from work, setting up a career path, and establishing a plan. In addition to these exercises, it would be appropriate to discuss how careers develop and the needs and future direction of the organization. The results of these sessions ought to be increased capability of the participants to modify their current jobs to increase their personal congruence with the organization or to change jobs to increase their congruence elsewhere. Such an activity could be regarded as either a counseling service or an educational program.

Another approach would be for management to train managers in career counseling. Such a process could be supported, in part, by self-analysis devices such as those just discussed. The danger in any management-directed program, however, is that the approach may appear to abridge individual freedoms or to create greater dependency. The training of managers might be construed as setting up conditions where it would appear that the manager rather than the individual is responsible for careers. In many organizations that is the way it is already. This is much less healthy than creating the freedom and support for the employee to manage his or her own career. Yet, convincing managers they should not *control* other careers is very difficult.

Summary

Improvement in productivity is vitally important to the survival of the organization. It is also important to the individual employee, who we know needs work both psychologically and economically. Improvement should increase the payout for both. Management is responsible and able to make changes to improve the quality of working life and to stimulate organizational and individual vitality. Central to the approaches reviewed in this chapter is the acceptance of personal growth and vitality as legitimate outputs of the organization. Emergence of these outputs with values equivalent to other desired results such as profit and service can result from increased management effectiveness and increased emphasis on human-resource development.

Four steps for management were proposed. The first was raising the value within the organization of continued learning, growth, and personal vitality. The second was the provision of a better growth environment. This was interpreted as resulting both from better work—which in turn contributes to personal growth—and from the improvement of industrial educational facilities. The third step was creating and documenting a concept of productivity which can be used as a guide for managers and employees. It was suggested that each organization needs to learn how to talk about its own productivity. The fourth step was setting up programs and experiences for employees through which they can gain increased self-understanding. This book itself is indicative of this approach. All of these actions can lead to improved congruence between the needs and the capabilities of the individual and those of the organization. A diagram for understanding the matching of organization and employee at an interface was presented. Improved congruence between the individual and the organization results in improved productivity and vitality. This kind of improvement requires that both the organization and the individual learn improved ways of expressing their needs and their capabilities to each other. It requires the acceptance of a strategy which puts a high priority on employee development and vitality and the creation of a management style which supports this strategy.

Suggested readings

Benge, E. J. *How To Manage For Tomorrow*. Homewood, Ill.: Dow Jones-Irwin, 1975.

Boulding, K.E. *The Image*. Ann Arbor: University of Michigan Press, 1956.

D'Aprix, Roger M. *In Search Of A Corporate Soul*. New York: AMACOM, 1976.

Drucker, P.F. *The Age of Discontinuity*. New York: Harper & Row, 1968.

Drucker, P.F. *Management: Tasks, Responsibilities and Practices*. New York: Harper & Row, 1973.

Gellerman, S. W. *Motivation and Productivity*. New York: AMACOM, 1963.

Kappel, F. R. *Vitality In A Business Enterprise*. New York: McGraw-Hill, 1960.

Likert, R. *New Patterns of Management*. New York: McGraw-Hill, 1961.

Morris, William T. *Work and Your Future: Living Poorer, Working Harder*. Reston, Va.: Reston Publishing, 1975.

> *This book comes closer than any other I know to providing a basis for understanding productivity. The thesis Morris presents is that experi-*

*mentation with new ways and new organizations is the clue to
productivity improvement.*

This, L. E. *A Guide To Effective Management: Practical Applications From
Behavioral Science.* Reading, Mass.: Addison-Wesley, 1974.

For the nation

18   Vitality: a national strategy

18
Vitality:
a national
strategy

Introduction

"The stuff of the world is mind-stuff," said Sir Arthur Stanley Eddington, noted British astronomer and physicist.* We set direction and move to new frontiers with ideas, concepts, theories, and plans. For some time the nations and the peoples of the world have been pursuing a policy, either explicit or implicit, which has emphasized growth and improvement of the material aspects of human life. The stuff of progress and change is "mind-stuff"—our goals and expectations shape the events of our lives. It is time to change.

This chapter suggests that the theme of this book, personal growth and vitality, should replace unlimited numerical growth as a prime national goal. Vitality can be defined in meaningful terms and is an attractive rallying theme. If generally accepted, this theme could have a beneficial impact on what happens to the country and the world. If the vitality and growth themes do not become part of government and management thinking, a national conflict with the individual will undoubtedly grow.

Some initial thinking and some actions are proposed here in the hopes that at the very least some readers will be motivated to help translate the vitality theme into action on a national or even a world-wide level.

National vitality

Because of limited natural resources, growing population densities, and evidence that humanity is fouling its own nest, we are questioning the goals of sheer numerical growth and material improvement and attempting to redefine the meaning of "quality of life." We are attempting, for example, to decide whether the freedom of individual car ownership is more or less important to us than clean air. And we're struggling to choose between clean water and the use of waterways and oceans for the commerce of the world. But questioning alone is not enough. We need to find new goals to guide us. How we make these difficult value decisions is affected by our ultimate goal. All choices are made in reference to goals. If a goal is material wealth or numerical superiority, the actions taken are different than if human vitality is the ultimate goal.

---

*   Arthur Koestler, *Roots of Coincidence: An Excursion into Parapsychology* (New York: Random House, Vintage Books, 1973), p. 126.

Historically, nations which have made numerical supremacy and power their transcendent goals have ultimately reached a pinnacle and then declined. It is not certain that these goals were the prime cause of their decline, but we suspect that they may have been a major factor. The values of goals may be determined by the ultimate change in human condition which will result from achieving the goals. Thus a goal of eliminating war would be a goal of high value because its achievement would result in the conservation of human life and the opportunity to expend material energies in more positive directions. The question being raised here is whether choosing a goal of greater value, in this case the goal of human vitality, will extend or modify the life cycle of a country. I suspect that it will. I suspect a goal of human growth and vitality will build renewal into a nation's way of life.

Vital people are alive, growing in capability, productive, and gaining from the process of living. Vital people make vital organizations. Vital people and vital organizations can lead to national vitality. A vital nation is one that can achieve life of improved quality for its citizens, one that is functioning at its potential, and one that is contributing to the quality and character of life for all nations. Vitality in a nation can encourage vitality in the nation's institutions, organizations, and people. In other words, the influence for vitality flows from the nation to its people and from its people to the nation. Vitality begets vitality. By contrast, decay, decline, and dissatisfaction tend to beget further decline. Similarly, lack of national vitality does not encourage vitality in other nations.

We start with the thesis that national vitality and improved quality of life are synonymous. Managing vitality then becomes the art that we need to learn. It must be learned at all levels from personal to national. Are there better ways than we are now employing to manage a nation? Are there techniques which contribute more to vitality? Does vitality suggest a different form of government or different laws? Where does one start if one accepts national vitality as a new goal? A quote from Peter Drucker in *The Age of Discontinuity* sets the stage for further discussion:

> *To make our society function requires that we know how to manage, i.e., how to obtain organizational performance through the work of the individual. To make our society free will also require that the individual learn how to manage organization—how to make organization and his job in it serve his ends, his values, his desire to achieve.*

A society needs to be able to allow the individual to opt out and lead a "private life." But this is not freedom. This is indifference. In a free society, the citizen takes responsibility, above all, for his society and its institutions. In the society of organizations, the pluralist society of our time, this is a different task from that of the eighteenth century. Indeed the political tradition of the eighteenth century, the tradition of Locke, is clearly at its end. But the society of organizations may offer greater opportunities for meaningful, effective, responsible freedom than earlier society. Whether they will be realized depends on what we do rather than on what "they," the institutions, do.

We face a period of hard new thinking on the political structure of society and on the position and role of the individual in it. What we have so far is a new pluralism, a new society of organizations. What we need is a new individualism, a new responsibility. *

What Peter Drucker is suggesting is that we need new ways for the individual to relate to organizations and institutions and that we need new relationships between institutions. The management, even the design of relationships, is, he suggests, at the core of our need for reaching our potential. If we can but figure out how to make the organization respond to our needs and, in the sense of this chapter, the need for vitality, then perhaps we can create institutions which contribute to national vitality. Drucker suggests that if we find the secrets of personal vitality, we have a basis for increasing institutional vitality. It is more important what "we" do than what "they" do. A new individualism is at the center of what we must do.

In this sense, this whole book leads to a national strategy. The book exhorts people to do what they can to improve their vitality. Nevertheless, a few enabling concepts or ideas need to be discussed here. These are ideas which, if they took root on a national level, could create an improved climate for individual vitality and thus contribute to improved national vitality and continuity.

Continued education as an example

One way in which vitality could be worked into a national strategy is by improving the government's effectiveness in stimulating educa-

---

*   Peter Drucker, *The Age of Discontinuity* (New York: Harper & Row, 1968), p. 260. Reprinted with permission.

tion and the increase in the capability of its people. Engineers are but one group of people for whom improved education is critical and from whom there can be broad positive influence on others. As this is written, there is some interest in the Senate in a bill which would, through scholarships and fellowships, support continued education of engineers. Direct financial support to the individual is probably not the right way, but the fact that some bill is being considered in Congress is an acknowledgment of the importance of the issue.

If we could find ways of building continued learning and skill development into the fabric of our lives and work, it would probably be of more lasting value than scholarships. The French government, for example, requires industry jointly with government to support the retraining and extension of skills and capabilities of employed personnel. Although their law has not resulted in more continuing education than now exists in many sectors of the U.S., it is a more basic approach than the creation of more scholarships and fellowships. The law in France deals primarily with financial implementation and responsibility. Recognizing that the individual can't do it alone and that industry and government must provide the facilities and support is important to the establishment of the appropriate balance of shared responsibility. Support, evidenced in released time for continuing study and in restructuring work, may be far more important in facilitating changes in career patterns than financial aid.

If possible, a still stronger approach would be to integrate continued learning into the goals of all organizations. If tax incentives and government-contract accounting could be redesigned to support human-asset accounting or human-capital accounting this might deeply influence and popularize the worth of enhancing human capability. The ultimate aim of legislation and government action should be to encourage reinvestment in the skills of humans, the inclusion of human capability in the balance sheet, and representation of human growth as a profit. This is, of course, much easier to talk about than to do. A way to move in this direction would be for the government to set itself as an exemplar in how it operates with its own personnel. For the government to lead by example rather than control by largesse would be a major change.

In *The Quality of Working Life*, Phillip G. Herbst titles his epilogue with a provocative statement, "The product of work is people."* Building a learning- and growth-oriented world *where all activities are judged by how they contribute to enhancing people* is an embodiment of this idea. Productivity has, heretofore, only been measured by units produced and dollars returned. Now is the time to rebalance the scale, to factor in our most important asset—people.

Changed educational emphasis

Closely related to continued learning, but much earlier in the human life cycle, is the early education of the child. Here is another aspect of life where it is possible for government action to have a beneficial effect upon the personal growth and vitality of the citizenry. Government is involved in education both in the collection of taxes to support it and in the establishing of direction through research and study of the process. It is in this latter activity that it should be possible to give emphasis to the strategy. For example, educational methods can affect the interest, motivation, and vitality of the student. The educational process can build or not build the individual's ability to take responsibility and manage life and his or her career. Education for youth can be presented as preparation for life as it has been in the past, or it can be conducted in a way which transmits the understanding that learning is life and that it is not confined to the classroom.

Education is a powerful way to gain the support and understanding of the citizenry for this new life strategy for increased vitality. It is also possible that we can learn to teach ways of detecting the effects of various activities on personal vitality. In this sense, the first collection of ideas and techniques concentrating on vitality that have been presented in this book might be integrated into and expanded within the educational system of the country.

In talking about government action, it is important to say a word about the kind of action which is appropriate. What we are suggesting is not more government intervention and management of our lives and our educations but, rather, the establishment of educational goals and standards that are in accord with personal life

---

* Philip G. Herbst, Epilogue to *The Quality of Working Life*, Vol. 1. Edited by Louis E. Davis and Albert B. Cherns (New York: Free Press, 1975). Reprinted with permission.

ideals. The most effective kind of government activity is described and promulgated by Richard Cornuelle in *Demanaging America*. He states the point I have just made as follows: "But federal legislation can be written in a way that invites and encourages non federal organizations to respond. Such legislation needs, principally, to define 'adequacy' with some precision—to set a standard of performance."*

Applied to our quest for vitality, this would mean setting standards for organizational activity which contribute to human growth. With these standards and goals, we could then set up proper rewards.

Career change and utilization

I have pointed out that one of the characteristics of our time is an increase in the number of opportunities to change careers during one's life in order to increase satisfaction, respond to changing goals, and maintain vitality and interest. One of the problems with this thesis is that, while it is conceptually true, and practically true for some, there are more people than jobs. We have underemployment—people employed at less than their capability—and unemployment. Yet, we know that having a central purpose, being needed and gaining a feeling of accomplishment, are necessary components for vitality and growth. Here then is another area where enlighted government interest could contribute to work for these people and thus to the vitality of the nation.

So far government action has dealt only with unemployment and only sporadically with retraining for career and job change. The primary motivation has been economic. Therefore, the solutions have been aimed at providing income, rather than contributing to psychological rewards and human worth. No one can deny the necessity of this action, but how different it would be if a primary goal was national vitality. For a brief time in the Depression through the use of the Civilian Conservation Corps the primary emphasis was on meaningful activity. We still benefit today from creative public improvements and from creative artistic endeavors which date from that time. While some similar approach might be helpful with

---

* Richard Cornuelle, *Demanaging America: The Final Revolution* (New York: Random House, 1975), p. 131. Reprinted with permission.

certain groups, senior citizens for example, providing an incentive for private enterprise to open up new activities which might not be justified by purely economic considerations would probably create many times the present job opportunities. By establishing national goals of providing stretching, challenging, growth-oriented activity, we might find a better yardstick for making difficult value choices about where to invest tax dollars and where to improve the quality of life. The goal of job creation should emphasize the utilization and growth of human resources first, and economic support second.

Quality of life

In seeking improvement in education and creating a learning environment, we are contributing to the quality of life. In seeking to provide greater opportunity for career change and for human utilization, we are also contributing to the quality of life. Perhaps there is a way on a national level to set up standards for lives of quality and thus stimulate improvement. Improvement is desirable at all levels of activity from the individual to the organization to the government.

A first step has already been taken by the Executive Branch of the U.S. Government in setting up a National Center for Productivity and the Quality of Working Life. If this center meets its charter, it will review government actions and laws in terms of their contribution toward goals of improved productivity and improved work quality. To review actions, it must establish standards. Let us hope the impact of this initial action will be successful. Let us hope that if it is successful the quality theme will be pushed beyond the work and business environment.

There are some existing activities of national, state, and local governments which also represent attempts at influencing the quality of life. Perhaps some of these represent ways of approaching the issue of vitality. Examples include the F.D.A., the control of water and air pollution, and the establishment of zoning laws. In each they attempt to start with a standard and then measure performance against that standard. In the case of vitality this will be harder to do because there are presently no accepted measures of life quality. Therefore, one of the potential functions of government would be to set up research to determine standards.

Measures

In our world what we measure is important, and we set values by the resultant measures. Thus one way for government to increase its emphasis on vitality and to influence the human and humane goals is to establish ways of measuring the degree of vitality of individuals, of government units, and of organizations.

In our discussion of continuing education the concept of human accounting was mentioned. This is one way of approaching this issue. If we could establish accounting methods for human values, and if these methods are based on the quality of interacting skills, capabilities, and knowledge, we would be moving toward the desired goals. To the extent that someone with higher knowledge and skills is offered a higher starting salary, we are already reflecting a part of this concept. However, this condition is present just at entry into a job. We have no technique to account for the loss in value of knowledge and skills through time nor the cost of under-utilizing trained and educated people. Nor do we have a technique for rewarding addition to one's value through continued learning. All these aspects would have to be reflected in the assessment of human resources. Such an assessment would have to avoid over-reliance on course completions and credentials—measuring the act of adding value is not the same as added certified but unproved value. In our society up to now, we have often allowed the credential to take on a value of its own. The most encouraging development in making value part of the work culture has been some experimental pay systems in which pay is directly based on the skill required by the jobs the individual performs.

One of the ways of measuring vitality is to have a group of experts assess an operation's vitality. Recognizing the subjective aspects of such an assessment, a possible course for government would be to encourage the establishment of visiting task groups who by traveling and assessing would act as catalysts for increased attention to these issues. In other words, the value would result more from the process of evaluation than from an absolute measure. For example, such a group in reviewing an organization might examine the number of layers of management. Generally, flat organizations provide more freedom and openness and thus offer greater opportunity for decision making, vitality, and personal growth. Another example might be that of examining the level and character of innovation, or the rate of infusion of new talent, or the number of job changes of the employee groups. A visiting group's attention to the dynamics of the organization could improve the day-in, day-out emphasis on human resources. Such an oversight operation carrying with it a set of values is, therefore, an effective way to improve attention to vitality.

Closely associated with assessment and measure is the need for reward and recognition. If government could reward with matching monies or new freedoms evidences of vitality in local governments or local organizations, this would ensure increased attention. If government could tie certain privileges and freedoms to the addition of vitality to the nation, this would provide incentives for innovation and action which foster rather than stifle vitality. What is being suggested is a set of actions and laws which run counter to the past attempts to control and limit.

Summary

Although the capability of the individual to increase vitality, growth, and satisfaction is almost boundless, it can be enhanced by a supportive environment. The potential for increasing the vitality of organizations is also almost boundless. It, too, can be enhanced by a supportive environment. Accepting vitality as a national goal and conducting government in support of this goal is a way of building the necessary positive and supportive environment.

Building such an environment requires changes in government. But we, as individuals acting together, also are able to bring about some of these changes and thus create a positive spiral contributing to improved quality of life. The changes for which we should work are:

1. To gain the acceptance of vitality and personal growth as important, high-priority goals.
2. To support actively only those government representatives and actions which are contributing to improved vitality at all governmental levels.
3. To support government initiative which rewards innovation and vitality, and not to support those actions which reduce motivations for utilization of capability and personal growth.

There are several major areas in which government can take an effective step. First, in education, it can encourage new values for human growth and worth. Second, it can support programs and activities which encourage life-long learning as an integral part of life. Third, it can support research into the things which enhance vitality and the development of ways to measure changes in vitality.

Suggested readings

Cornuelle, Richard. *Demanaging America: The Final Revolution*. New York: Random House, 1975.

Gardner, John. *Self-Renewal*. New York: Harper & Row, 1964.

Wirtz, Willard. *Boundless Resource*. New York: New Republic Book Co., E.P. Dutton Distributor, 1975.

Epilogue

By Richard W. Schmelzer

The theme of this book has been that growth is life; stagnation is death. But growth and vitality are not something that external forces bestow upon an individual. He or she must make the effort, must make the struggle to grow and be vital.

Similarly, for an organization or a government growth is life; stagnation is death. But both organizations and governments are composed of individuals. It is their growth and their vitality that the organization or government depends upon for its own growth. Without the growth of the people who compose it, an organization or a government stagnates and begins to die. Thus it is an act of self-preservation for them to make certain that their individuals have the opportunity to grow. Rome collapsed because of the decay of the capabilities of its people. So did all of the empires from Sumer to tsarist Russia. The lessons of history are abundantly clear. We have but to pay attention to them.

The fostering of the growth of the individual is not an act of corporate or governmental do-goodism. It is an act of long-term wisdom. The most valuable asset that a corporation or governmental agency possesses appears on no balance sheet, is not measured in dollars. In fact, it has never been realistically measured because it has just lately been acknowledged as an asset. That asset is the human resources of the organization.

It stands to reason, then, that a wise leadership will seek to preserve and enhance that asset, will seek ways to measure its growth and value, will seek to add to it from the outside, as the occasion demands. Wise management will conserve and enhance its human resources and raise more resources just as it conserves its capital and on occasion raises more capital.

The wise and far-sighted individual will gravitate toward those organizations which recognize the value of individual growth and vitality, which have programs to promote and measure human growth. As both individuals and organizations grow together, added values will accrue to our nation and to the world. These added values will result in more satisfying and fuller lives, fewer frustrations and reprisals, and greater cooperation toward a vital healthy world.

Index